JOURNAL *of* CONTEMPORARY HISTORY

Contents

Volume 18 Number 4   October 1983

MILITARY HISTORY
Edited by Martin van Creveld

Notes on Contributors follow each paper

Historical Journal of Film, Radio and Television is a interdisciplinary journal concerned with the evidence provided by the mass media for historians and social scientists, and with the impact of mass communications on the political and social history of the 20th century.

The needs of those engaged in research and teaching are served by scholarly articles, book reviews and by archival reports concerned with the preservation and availability of records. The journal also reviews films, television and radio programmes of historical or educational importance. In addition, it aims to provide a survey of developments in the teaching of history and social science courses which involve the use of film and broadcast materials.

Additional information may be obtained by writing to The Editor, Historical Journal of Film, Radio and Television, Westminster College, Oxford OX2 9AT, United Kingdom.

This journal is published twice a year, in March and October, making one volume. ISSN 0143-9685.

Personal subscriptions – £11 ($16); Institutions – £36 ($54). Subscriptions available from IAMHIST, Westminster College, Oxford, OX2 9AT, United Kingdom.

Published by Carfax Publishing Company, Oxford, in association with the International Association for Audio-Visual Media in Historical Research and Education.

Historical Journal of

FILM RADIO AND TELEVISION

Walter Laqueur

The Question of Judgment:
Intelligence and Medicine

For a long time, military and foreign political intelligence have
tried to become scientific, or at the very least more scientific.
Science and technology have played a decisive role in the collection
of intelligence since the 1950s. But inasmuch as assessment is
concerned, the outcome of the search for a scientific theory
improving the predictive capacity of intelligence has been quite
disappointing. The discussions on the subject have produced many
learned papers, but no palpable improvement in the quality of
intelligence. Some observers have argued in retrospect that it might
have been a mistake to look to the exact sciences for inspiration, or
those trends in the social sciences which fashioned themselves after
the exact sciences, copying or adapting their methods. Perhaps one
should have looked for a model to the less exact sciences whose
predictive powers are not very well developed, such as seismology.
It is, of course, well known that certain parts of the globe are more
prone to earthquakes than others, and while there now exist
sophisticated warning systems to register tremors, the predictive
powers of seismology are too vague to be of practical application.
This has been explained with references to 'weak theory' on the one
hand and the relative infrequency of earthquakes on the other.
Whether the reference to 'weak theory' is correct cannot be proved
and the absence of earthquakes seems, on balance, preferable to
the emergence of a strong theory.

Meteorology seemed more promising. The philosopher Hans
Reichenbach was one of the first, shortly after the second world
war, to stress that the statistical laws constructed by and for social
scientists could be used for the prediction of individual sociological
phenomena in the same way that the laws of meteorology are used

Journal of Contemporary History (SAGE, London, Beverly Hills and New Delhi),
Vol. 18 (1983), 533-548

for weather forecasting. The argument was flawed, but it was picked up by the quantifiers. Their aim was to develop the skill to show in 'what direction the wind was blowing', how variables combined into testable hypotheses, how eventually they would fit into patterns — not unlike the variables in meteorology.[1] Perhaps it was no accident that Lewis Richardson (1881-1953), the author of an early and very influential mathematical study on the causes and origins of war, was a meteorologist by profession. It was Richardson's misfortune that his ideas about mutually stimulating arms races were first published in the late 1930s. If events preceding the first world war lent some plausibility to his model, the situation in the late 1930s was altogether different. There was no action-reaction spiral, Hitler was not afraid of Britain and France, he wanted to dominate Europe, the 'deadly quarrel' (which is how Richardson regarded wars) was a rather one-sided affair, for in Paris and London there was an almost unlimited willingness not to be drawn into any quarrel. Hitler, in brief, spoiled what had seemed a promising model. Richardson was, however, rediscovered after the second world war by a new generation of social scientists which tried to apply his concept to the cold war.

Great advances have been made in meteorology during the last two decades. Numerical prediction has largely replaced the synoptic method, and there has been a general refinement of methods. True, meteorologists cannot even now say with any assurance whether there will be a long dry spell in summer and whether the winter will be severe or not. They do not even know the causes of general circulation. But they can make more or less reliable short-term predictions; in the not too distant future they may even be able to 'make' the weather on more than a strictly limited local basis. Students of human affairs will not, however, be able to draw much encouragement if a decisive breakthrough in meteorology should occur, for their discipline does not deal with inanimate objects.

There is a more promising analogy for the student of intelligence, the one between political and clinical judgment. It has been noted on occasion by a few students of intelligence, just as similarities between detection and criminal justice were observed.[2] It is the belief of the present writer that the student of intelligence will profit more from contemplating the principles of medical diagnosis than immersing himself in any other field.[3] The doctor and the analyst have to collect and evaluate the evidence about phenomena frequently not amenable to direct observation. This is done on the basis of indications, signs and symptoms. As the sixteenth-century pathologist Jean Fernel wrote: diseases hidden in the innermost crevices of the body, that cannot be distinguished or perceived through the senses, are understood by signs. With these as evidence, the mind is led by sound reasoning to penetrate into what is hidden. But what are these signs? According to a seventeenth-century physician, they are 'all things that indicate something else (*rem aliquam significant*), or all evidence that discloses something unknown and hidden' (Daniel Sennert). Or, as an eighteenth-century doctor put it, 'anything which, when known, leads to further knowledge of something else that was unknown' (Antoine Deidier). The same approach applies to intelligence.[4]

Medicine has made enormous progress since the seventeenth century and diseases once hidden can now be observed owing to such marvels as CAT scanning (Computed Axial Tomography). Yet precisely because of such progress the similarity in concept between medicine and intelligence, or as a leading scientist put it 'between space observation and medical scanning' has become even more obvious.[5] It was probably no coincidence that the pioneer of CAT, Godfrey Hounsfield, who won the Nobel prize in 1979, was educated and later lectured in the Radar schools of the Royal Air Force. The intelligence chiefs and the military commanders use sensors in the same way as the medical expert invokes X-ray scanning, and the electronic systems have in both cases most functional principles in common. The similarities extend to both collection and analysis, or in the case of medicine, diagnosis. References to medicine have become more and more frequent in intelligence literature. Thus J. Bamford compares NSA operations to 'a physician listening to a heart through a SIGINT stethoscope, hoping to detect the first sign of an irregular beat . . .'[6]

There is at least one important difference: the patient usually cooperates with the medical expert, he has no incentive to hide and to mislead. The assignment of the observation satellite on the other hand is more complicated. In this case, the 'patient' will make every possible effort not to reveal what he does not want to become known. Frequently this may be impossible but at other times he may successfully mislead the observer. Sir William Osler said about medicine many years ago that it was a science of uncertainties and an art of probability. It is *a fortiori* true with regard to intelligence. The problem facing the doctor (again to quote Osler) is that in the same way that no two faces are the same, no two bodies are alike. Of course, it can be argued that even though every patient is unique, it does not follow that all patients are incomparable. But it also means that no two individuals react alike and behave alike under the abnormal conditions which are known as disease and that this is the fundamental difficulty in the education of the physician.[7] Again it could be argued that these are counsels of perfection, of no great importance in practice. For with all these differences, most human beings react *grosso modo* in similar ways and this is all that counts. Perhaps so, but it is also true that with all the enormous progress in medicine, the life expectancy of a sixty-year-old has hardly changed since biblical days when it was said to be three score and ten, even if lives are saved with antibiotics or surgery, or life is prolonged by a year or two with good care.[8] In short, recent medical advances have to be seen in proper perspective.

The debate on medicine as craft or science dates back to the very beginnings. Hippocrates made the excellent observation that if medicine were not an art, all practitioners (*demiurgoi*) would be equally good or equally bad, a point that seems also to apply to political analysts of today.[9] From Hippocrates to Cabanis, who lived in the second half of the eighteenth century and was the author of an interesting study on the degree of certainties in medicine, physicians agreed that while there were no certainties in medicine, there were probabilities and approximations. Experience was transmitted through human sensations. As far as the doctor was concerned, everything depended on his gift of observation (*coup d'oeil*) and a lucky instinct.[10] The nineteenth century was more optimistic in this respect as the result of the stormy development of the natural sciences. Medicine too received a major uplift and began to gravitate more and more towards a purely scientific orientation. By the turn of the century much thought had already been given to specific questions of medical logic, to hypotheses in medicine and to other theoretical issues.[11]

Yet, as so often in the history of science, great progress would only trigger off new questions, and a leading physician (and philosopher of medicine) drew attention in a little study published during the first world war to the basic difference between pure science dealing with infinite questions and medicine which deals with the 'here and now'. Medicine was a craft (*Techne* in the Greek tradition). Clinicians were dealing with a subject that was incalculable and boundless — unlike engineers and technologists.

In this connection, Richard Koch was one of the first to draw an interesting parallel between medicine and politics.[12] As he saw it, there was a scientific doctrine of politics and of war as there was in medicine. No-one in a leading position in politics or in the armed services could afford to ignore the body of up-to-date scientific knowledge that had been assembled. But this did not mean that professors teaching at war academies would necessarily make the best military leaders, or that professors of economics would succeed as ministers of finance. Which tended to show that 'scientific' competence, while an essential prerequisite, was not the only quality needed, perhaps not even the most important one. The physician, like the statesman, had frequently to take decisions with reference to mathematical formulas, his action grew out of experience, possibilities and probabilities. But what was experience? Not statistical empiricism but rather a talent, such as drawing or music, which could be developed by teaching and exercise. But in some people it could be developed only to a modest degree, while others would make astonishing progress.

This approach was not universally accepted; many thought it too sceptical about scientific progress. Koch seemed to put too much emphasis on human judgment in medical diagnosis and it took almost six decades for his views to gain recognition. A recent textbook on medical diagnosis (1979) states, 'we are beginning to reflect too much Bayes and not enough Osler', whose views in this respect were rather like Koch's. Medicine has, of course, made infinitely more progress than political science during the last sixty years. But it is also true that even in the heyday of scientific optimism the issue of experience and judgment in medicine, where it came from and how it could be taught, continued to preoccupy and bother the leading physicians of the age.

Towards the end of a long and distinguished career as a clinician, Sir James Mackenzie pondered the curious fact that no blood count, no bacteriological examination, no instrumental method could tell as much as a glance at the face and the feel of the pulse:

A thing that strikes anyone who gives attention to the matter, is the curious knowledge which some physicians and general practitioners acquire after many years practice. It enables them in an unconscious manner to estimate the patient's state with remarkable precision. The knowledge is undefinable and they are unable to express the reasons in language sufficiently clear for the uninitiated to understand. The real source of this knowledge is the familiarity, derived from experience, of the appearance of the patient when stricken with an insidious disease, a subtle alteration in the expression of the face or a slight wasting, or a faint contraction of some of the muscles of expression, a faint change in colour, coupled, it may be, with an alteration in the patient's temper, ideas or voice. [13]

Mackenzie concluded that the physician had to train his senses and this could be done only by a long process of education.

Sir Humphrey Rollestone, another leading doctor of the generation which came after Osler, wrote in a similar vein:

The valuable property of 'clinical instinct' which, although sometimes ridiculed as the assumed armour and decoration of the ignoramus or the quack, has a certain resemblance to the poetic faculty and moreover is a real asset in practice. Clinical instinct is the power of arriving without a conscious logical process at a definite conclusion and is often possessed in a high degree by old nurses who know, but cannot give their reasons, whether a patient is going to recover or die and by practitioners of long experience who similarly cannot explain the steps by which they reach diagnosis and prognosis. It may be assumed that they unwittingly draw on buried experience which without their conscious remembrance, recognises in the patient signs presented by one in the long past. In diagnosis, therefore, there are two processes, the consciously logical and the rarer, but not necessarily less correct, unconscious. [14]

Lastly, the evidence of Wilfred Trotter, yet another great doctor of the inter-war period:

The truth appears to be that what the user of a practical art needs is less the strict and limited instrument of scientific method than what may be called a soundly cultivated judgment. This requirement is more difficult to specify and much more difficult to secure. Apart from inborn capacity, it seems to depend on familiarity with the material of the art, otherwise experience and on a broad and sound general culture which including a proper awareness of science, is by no means limited to it. [15]

Similar observations were made by other clinicians when reflecting on the experience of their professional life. Science was essential but there was no shortcut to the 'wisdom process'. Experience and judgment were all-important — even though they were difficult to define and to convey to others.

The diagnostician of 1930 already had a formidable scientific arsenal at his disposal such as the sphygmomanometer, an electro-cardiograph of sorts, many bacteriological and chemical tests and X-rays. The present-day doctor has, of course, an even greater instrumentarium and the problem frequently facing him is which course of action to take out of the many which exist in pursuing his investigation. Many phenomena remain as yet unknown but this does not prevent the physician from coping with them — many medical triumphs were achieved without knowledge of cause or even without diagnosis. Yet with all this, the role of judgment in diagnosis has in no way lessened, even though some researchers may consider the label of 'art' scientifically shameful; a few envisage that in fifty years doctors will be obsolete and replaced by computers.[16] A leading bio-statistician has noted in this context that good mathematicians quite often regard themselves as artists, setting up rules which have nothing to do with reality.[17]

It is well beyond the scope of this study to dwell on the process of reasoning by means of which the physician will arrive at certain conclusions concerning the disease or lack of it in his patient. But even enumerating the main stages shows the resemblance to the reasoning of the intelligence analysts, as well as the pitfalls that exist. The moment the clinician meets the patient for the first time, a certain image emerges; how the patient looks will be registered, as will his handshake, the way he moves and speaks and so on. This diagnosis made with a glance, the *Gestalt* can provide important, even decisive clues. But by itself, it can also be very misleading.

The clinician will then question his patient about his complaint. Sex, age, occupation, general habits are always of importance. If it appears that a male patient suffering from hoarseness is an auctioneer by occupation, or that a young lady who has lost weight has engaged in a crash diet, it will not usually be necessary to look much further for an explanation. Usually, however, the most frequent complaints such as, for instance, headache or indigestion or dyspnea can be caused by a great many conditions; the clinician has to focus on one or two clues while trying to elicit more information. The doctor will then submit the patient to a physical examination and the result of the clues which have emerged so far will decide the subsequent course of action.[18] He will take the most likely symptom as his starting-point and then try to find additional clues until a more or less conclusive diagnosis emerges. This can be achieved by way of the 'branching technique' — diagnosis being compared to tracing one of many pathways through the branches of a tree, or by pattern-building (when little information is available), by suppression of information (when there is too much), by pattern recognition, by 'hunches' which have been described as more than a stab in the dark, but rather an educated deduction made almost subconsciously on the basis of a simple, perhaps seemingly unimportant observation.[19]

The physician may then go on to use the various mathematical aids and computer-assisted diagnosis. To mention but two obvious uses of the computer: storage of statistical data and its ability to retrieve them. Few doctors will recall the statistical incidence of gastric ulcers among women aged forty, yet the figure may be of considerable importance in reaching a diagnosis. Electro-cardiograms, to give another example, are very frequently not available when needed for comparison, unless they have been computer stored.[20] It has been said that the difference between a talented doctor and one who is not, is that the former will quite frequently arrive at his diagnosis by way of a shortcut. One of the most obvious reasons for taking a wrong turn in reasoning could be that the clinician is simply not a very good observer or that his training has been insufficient. Francis Galton noted the curious fact that experienced sailors could see a moving buoy at great distance whereas land-lubbers with better eye-sight failed to recognize them.[21] The reason was that the landsman, too, had in fact seen the buoy, but the fact had not registered at the cortical level, it was perceived but not recognized. The story is quoted by Richard Asher referring to the medical student who missed an aortic diastolic murmur: the student almost certainly had better hearing than his professor, but he lacked the ability unconsciously to select and reject sensory stimuli. This he would acquire to a greater or lesser degree as the result of his training and subsequent experience. Some observers had de-emphasized the importance of brilliant insight or creativity, pointing to the undoubted fact that most clinical problems can be routinely identified and resolved.[22] This, of course, is perfectly correct, but it is also true that it is precisely in critical situations in which there are elements of ambiguity that the dramatic insight comes back into its own, and this seems to apply to both clinical medicine and intelligence.

The faculty to observe is a curious thing. Ancient and medieval physicians were excellent observers and their texts contain classical and most minute descriptions. Yet on the other hand, some very obvious signs escaped them. Even an untrained observer can distinguish without difficulty the rash which appears in measles, scarlet fever and chicken-pox, yet medical science was by and large unaware of these differences until well into the nineteenth century. Observation also implies the gift of combination. For example, measles is a disease which has been known and observed since time immemorial and is always accompanied by certain spots in the mucous membranes of the mouth which appear even before the rash. Yet it was only towards the end of the nineteenth century that an American physician, Koplik, put two and two together and it has since become an elementary part of diagnosis.

God, as Konrad Adenauer once noted, has created the universe most unfairly — there is usually only one way to do things right and an unlimited number of ways in which to err. Obvious errors of observation apart, there are many other sources of mistakes:

An inexperienced doctor may forget one of the basic tenets of medicine — that common diseases occur commonly — and searches for far-fetched and exotic explanations where a simple one will do. His logic may be faulty, he may assume cause and effect where there is none. Baldness and athlete's foot often occur together, yet there is no known common cause. He may be misled by the presence of non-fitting or confused by the absence of commonly occurring clues. He may miss the wood for the trees, having looked for too long at individual symptoms and not at the overall pattern. The background noise may be strong and the pertinent signals weak and the clinician may miss them.[23] He may have early on decided in his mind on a diagnosis and may be unwilling to change his views in view of subsequent evidence.

He may focus on the less important condition of a patient and overlook the more serious disease.

He may be biased — in favour of certain diseases which he finds of particular interest, against certain patients whom he finds objectionable.

He may be tired, or under pressure — his waiting-room may still be full at a late hour, his concentration may be flagging. Suffering from a serious disease, he may assess the prospects of some of his patients too negatively. Zimmermann mentions the case of a famous contemporary doctor who suffered from 'obstruction of the liver' (gallstones?) and as a result discovered the same symptoms in many of his patients. He may be misled by symptoms which come and go — not only in psychosomatic disease.

To the student of foreign affairs and intelligence many of these sources of error will sound familiar.

If so much can go wrong, the case for making clinical medicine more scientific becomes even stronger. But how to do it? A computer programme can certainly be constructed for the diagnostic process, but mathematical approaches cannot deal with unique situations.[24] Or, to quote another leading observer: 'Desk computers will never do the job'.[25] Certain well-defined areas can be covered by algorithms, but the more distinctly human the phenomenon, the more necessary a human observer. 'Whatever can be distinguished only by human speech, sight, smell, touch, hearing, taste, movement and cerebration cannot be discerned by inanimate devices which lack the perception and the ingenuity of the human brain.'[26]

The programming of computers will no doubt make great progress in the years to come. But, as has been noted a thousand times, computer-based decisions cannot be more reliable than the information that was provided. Blood pressure, blood sugar content, ECGT waves which are considered normal in one hospital, may be thought to be abnormal elsewhere. 'Observer variations' may be substantial; experts were found to disagree about the interpretation of one in four X-rays of tuberculosis patients. Computer analysis of electro-cardiography is unsatisfactory so far in describing any but elementary abnormalities.[27] The fascination with digital data exuding objectivity has increasingly been under scrutiny in recent years and the question has been asked, for instance: how hard are the hard data in clinical chemistry?[28] To differentiate between the normal and the pathological a borderline has to be drawn and this causes a great many new problems. For the more diagnostically sensitive the test is made, the more healthy people are included in the definition together with those that are ill. There is a very substantial grey zone of uncertainty; unless this is accepted, mathematical perfectionism will result in the definition of new diseases interesting in theory but non-existent in the real world. Some experts predicted already in the 1960s that the new abundance of data, quotients and correlations was bound to lead to an information crisis which would make practical application difficult or even misleading. While the data are important, they are no more than a tool equivalent to a symptom; there is the danger of a blind belief in figures, and the binary yes/no decision which the physician or surgeon has to take cannot be taken over by binary answers from laboratory or computer.[29]

Nor is it true that modern technologies, in contrast to the judgment of the individual, are free of bias and distortion and therefore more reliable:

Human ingenuity, anxiety and fantasy can transform technologies which are supposed to operate according to unvarying automative procedures and to produce uniformly trustworthy evidence. The numbers generated by the thermometer, the graphs drawn by the ECG, the pictures of the X-ray machine, the images captured by the microscope, the diagnostic judgment made by the computer — all are generally assumed to be free of the flaws and biases that admittedly distort facts gathered by human beings through natural senses. Such evidence, it is further assumed, is therefore the most valuable in diagnosing and treating disease. Neither belief is true. The evidence produced by such instruments though valuable, is inevitably influenced by the human hand that operates them and the human mind that evaluates the results. Furthermore, the machines are denied complete access to a whole range of non-measurable facts about a human being that a physician can obtain through his own senses — questioning, observing, making judgments. [30]

On the other side of the ledger is the price which has to be paid for making clinical medicine more scientific. The modern clinician, writes Feinstein, may become worse than his ancestors in his bedside observation techniques, because his attention is so often diverted to data observed in the laboratory. Many young clinicians have lost, or have never acquired, large parts of the old skills. [31] Instead, a new type of PhD engineer has appeared on the medical scene who may be a connoisseur of statistics or computers but not of clinical observation, a connoisseur of numbers but not of medical data, capable of designing intellectual clinical strategies 'that may be mathematically splendid, computationally effective and statistically impressive, but clinically absurd'. [32] For the inclination of the engineer will always be to avoid numerically unsatisfactory data of symptoms and signs and instead to base his computer programme on demographic and laboratory data — which miss the point; he will devise strategies based on Bayes theorem, an excellent concept when applied to appropriate situations, which, unfortunately, occur infrequently in clinical medicine, because they require assumptions about nature incompatible with realistic clinical activities. [33]

There is also, given limited resources, the danger of over-diagnosis. Exaggerated emphasis on the engineering element in clinical medicine (as in intelligence) leads towards a perfectionism which is not just unnecessary but could be dangerous. The problem at hand may not be solved (or not be answered in time) and the 'wider questions' to which this perfectionism leads may never be answered. The physician engages in diagnosis for therapeutic purposes, not to find some objective truth; the intelligence analyst is expected to reply to some specific question, not to propound some theory of social change. Frequently the physician will quickly discover what he needs to know, but the attempt at making the diagnosis more scientific (which is to say to resemble the 'typical' cases described in the textbook) may only cause confusion. Diagnosis, again like much intelligence work, has to be timely and cost-effective. In real life a physician cannot tell a patient suffering from a dangerous disease to come again in fifty years when knowledge about his condition will certainly be more extensive.[34] Diagnosis, like an intelligence assessment, cannot go on forever, sometimes delays in providing an answer may be inevitable, sometimes they may even be desirable. But far more often the information will be needed for action here and now.

The clinician has to be prepared for the unexpected, the apparently inexplicable and incongruous. Habituation ('routine') in this field as in others, is the enemy of acumen. Like the intelligence analyst, the clinician faces the problem of detecting signals. A weak signal may be drowned in background noise.[35] Perhaps the most frequent of such situations facing him occurs when taking the case history of a loquacious patient: 'He hardly hears the many irrelevancies and reminiscences: his suppressive mechanism turns a deaf ear to them and they are unconsciously dismissed as are the meaningless squiggles in the pictures'.[36] But equally there is the danger of selective deafness and blindness, resulting in the suppression of some relevant information. The syndrome of ignoring some glaring fact is well-known from the most banal experiences in daily life to historical turning-points in the history of science — Spalanzani not realising the implications of his discoveries about the spermatozoa, Poincaré and Lorentz just missing the theory of relativity, Linus Pauling stopping just short of the double helix. In each case, a post mortem shows that all the necessary information was available but it did not register, sometimes because of an abundance of clues, sometimes because of a temporary eclipse in observation or critical acumen.

Reviewing the progress and the achievements of contemporary medicine, a recent writer noted that it was all impressive — the hospitals filled with apparatus that awes the layman and often the physician; libraries where journals and texts enshrine past scholarship and present advances, research institutes where new knowledge is created and so on. Yet the material aspects of modern medicine reminded him of the passage in the Bible where the prophet Elijah was seeking the Lord: 'And behold, the Lord passed by, and a great and strong wind rent the mountains, and brake in pieces the rock before the Lord.' But the Lord, as readers of the Bible know, was not in the wind, nor in the earthquake which came after, nor in the fire which followed it, but in the small voice which was heard after the fire:

> So, too, with scientific medicines. It lies not in formidable apparatus nor the myriads of available tests, nor in overflowing libraries, but in the small voice that I call critical judgment. This voice asks the important questions: "Do you see a pattern clearly? How good is your evidence? How sound is your reasoning? Can you support your inferences with the means at your disposal? What are the alternatives? What hangs on your decision?" [37]

The student of contemporary intelligence can do little but answer 'amen'. For the truth ('scientific intelligence') is not in the impressive apparatus, the ingenious photographic equipment and the amazing electronic contraptions, it is certainly not in the pseudo-scientific early warning indicators of some students of international relations, but in the small voice of critical judgment, not easy to describe, more difficult to acquire, yet absolutely essential in reaching a correct decision.

The comparison between medicine and intelligence is instructive; obviously, it cannot be carried beyond a certain point; the doctor engages not only in diagnosis but also in curing the patient. The position of the intelligence operator is more complicated; in theory, he is not usually supposed to prescribe a certain action (or actions), in practice he very often does. But at this juncture the analogy between him and the physician tends to become weak unless, of course, one establishes an analogy between medical treatment and 'active measures'. They do, however, face common dilemmas. Science alone will not solve their daily problems nor will subjective judgment and intuition, only a combination of the two. Some problems will be mainly for the scientist (or technologist) to solve, at other times instinct or intuition will have to make the decisive contribution. Many cases are routine in character, yet those dealing with them must be prepared for surprises at all times. This makes the task of the doctor and of the analyst interesting, difficult and also potentially very risky. As an unknown poet-meteorologist sadly noted:

> And in the dying embers,
> These are my last regrets:
> My hits no one remembers
> My misses no one forgets.[38]

The same applies *a fortiori* to intelligence analysts; doctors are in a more fortunate position.

Notes

1. Hans Reichenbach, 'Probability Models in Social Sciences' in D. Lerner and H. D. Lasswell, *The Policy Sciences* (Stanford 1951), 128; McClelland in James N. Rosenau, *International Politics and Foreign Policy* (New York 1969).

2. Another interesting parallel is with the art historian trying to attribute the painting or sculpture of an unknown master. Bernard Berenson's work, the location and identification of every Italian renaissance master, involved, as a biographer put it, not only scholarship but also intuition and great retentive powers; each judgment was a piece of condensed criticism. With all this, Berenson did, of course, make mistakes and was reluctant to admit them.

3. Medicine is a wide field and this observation applies to some of its branches more than others. In at least one section of the US Public Health Service — epidemiology — there are intelligence officers.

4. Jean Fernel, *Pathologiae libri VII;* Daniel Sennert, *De Symptomatibus,* Book II; Antoine Deidier, *Institutiones medicinae theoricae.* I owe these references to Lester S. King, *Medical Thinking. A historical preface* (Princeton 1982), 79.

5. Jens Arnbak, 'Observations in Space', Nato's Fifteen Nations (April-May 1982). See also *Proceedings of the Institute of Electrical and Electronics Engineers. Special Issue on Image Processing* (New York, May 1981).

6. James Bamford, *The Puzzle Palace* (Boston 1982), 190.

7. W. Osler, *Aequanimitas and other Addresses* (Philadelphia 1930), 331.

8. Paul Cutler, *Problem Solving in Clinical Medicine. From Data to Diagnosis* (Baltimore 1979), 37.

9. *About Old (Primitive) Medicine,* ed. Littré, vol. I (Paris 1839), 570.

10. Cabanis, *Du Degré des Certitudes de la Médecine,* vol. I (Paris 1956), 91.

11. A good review in W. Bieganski, *Medizinische Logik* (Würzburg 1909).

12. R. Koch, *Die Aerztliche Diagnose. Beitrag zur Kenntnis des Aerztlichen Denkens,* 2nd ed. (Wiesbaden 1920), 65 et seq. This book, written by my late father-in-law, was not known to me until I began to work on this article. Another physician who made the comparison even earlier was the Swiss eighteenth-century physician Zimmermann who practised in London; his references to politicians were, however, entirely uncomplimentary. Invoking the authority of Socrates and Bolingbroke, he said that politics was the only human endeavour in which men could be active without the slightest knowledge and competence. Zimmermann's book was an all-out polemic against empiricism in medicine, but he hated hypotheses even more. *Erfahrung in der Arzneykunst* (Zürich 1763), 7.

13. Sir James Mackenzie, *The Future of Medicine* (London 1919), 186.

14. Sir Humphrey Rolleston, *Aspects of Age, Life and Disease* (London 1938), 245.

15. Wilfred Trotter, *Collected Papers* (Oxford 1941), 159.

16. Jerrold S. Maxmen, *The Post-Physician Era* (New York 1976), passim.

17. Alvan R. Feinstein, *Clinical Judgment* (Baltimore 1976), 293.

18. Among recent elementary descriptions of the process are H. J. Wright and D. B. Macadam, *Clinical Theory and Practice* (Edinburgh 1979) and David Ginsburg, *Clinical Reasoning in Patient Care* (New York 1980).

19. W. B. Cannon, *The Way of an Investigator* (New York 1945); Cutler, loc. cit., 41.

20. Maijler, Robles de Medina, Helder: 'Future of Computerized Electrocardio-graph' in *British Heart Journal,* 1980, 44, 1-4. There is a great and growing literature on the subject; some of it is listed in Wayne W. Daniel, mentioned supra.

21. A similar story is told about Galileo who showed to the Ptolemaist Church Fathers (who denied their existence) the moons of Jupiter through a telescope. The Church Fathers saw the moons but did not see them. Frederick Suppe (ed.), *The Structure of Scientific Theories* (Urbana 1974), 212.

22. Arthur S. Elstein, *Medical Problem Solving* (Cambridge, Mass. 1978), 302.

23. Wulff gives an example concerning the rise of serum transaminase (SGOT) in a patient after myocardical infarction. The doctor may not know the patient's previous SGOT level and will find it difficult to decide whether the rise is significant or not.

24. L. B. Lusted, *Instruction to Medical Decision Making* (Springfield 1968), passim.

25. Henrik R. Wulff, *Rational Diagnosis and Treatment* (London 1976), 72.

26. Feinstein, loc. cit., 297; see also C. A. Caceres in *American Journal of Cardiology,* 1976, 38, p. 362 and Bourdilon et al. in *European Journal of Cardiology,* 1978, 8, p. 395.

27. Bruce and Yarnall, 'Computer-Aided Diagnosis of Cardiovascular Disorders' in *Journal of Chronic Disease,* 1966, p. 473 et seq.

28. Prof. D. Vonderschmitt, *Klinische Chemie: Wie hart sind harte Daten?* Inaugural dissertation Zürich University, *Neue Zuercher Zeitung,* 12 May 1982.

29. Ibid. The great Swedish economist Gustav Cassel, who began his career as a teacher of mathematics, once noted that almost any factual development could be expressed in a mathematical formula, but that it was an elementary mistake to assume that such a formula had any predictive formula.

30. St. J. Reiser, *Medicine and the reign of technology* (Cambridge 1978), 229.

31. Feinstein, loc. cit., 297.

32. Ibid. 367. How much does laboratory work add to diagnosis? Less apparently than widely believed. According to one series of general out-patients in a British clinic, 82 per cent were diagnosed correctly on the basis of history alone. Examination raised the success rate to 91 per cent, while investigations only added about one more per cent. J.R. Hampton and others, 'Relative contributions of history-taking, physical examination and laboratory investigation to diagnosis and management of medical out-patients', *British Medical Journal,* 1975, vol. II, 486.

33. Ibid. 370.

34. Edmund A. Murphy, *The Logic of Medicine* (Baltimore 1976), 151.

35. Wulff, op. cit., 99.

36. Sir Francis Avery Jones, *Richard Asher Talking Sense,* 3.

37. Lester S. King, *Medical Thinking. A Historical Preface* (Princeton 1982), 309.

38. Quoted in John A. Day and G.L. Sternes, *Climate and Weather* (Reading, Mass. 1970).

Martin van Creveld

Thoughts on Military History

A hundred years have now passed since Heinrich von Treitschke
reputedly told a hall crowded with German officers that the periods
of peace constitute the empty pages of the history books, and much
has changed since then. Not only has military history been brought
down from the lofty pedestal it once occupied to the point where it
is now often considered only barely respectable academically (in the
entire western world there is but one academic periodical being
published devoted solely to military history as such), but it has also
lost much of the hold it once held upon the training and education
of serving officers. It is the purpose of the present essay to discuss
some of the reasons behind this decline; and to suggest a few of the
directions towards which, in the author's opinion, military history
should move if it is to regain anything like its former respectability
and influence.

Looking back, military history has as strong a claim as any to be
regarded as the oldest form of history. The obelisks on which the
Egyptian Pharaoh's used to record their exploits, monotonously
consisting of the slaughter of thousands upon thousands of
enemies, for all posterity to remember; the *Illiad,* whose
supposedly earliest parts consist of precisely the same kind of thing,
explaining in great detail who killed whom and by what means;
Herodotus, 'the father of history', whose explicit purpose it was
to narrate the story of the wars which the Greeks fought against the
Persians; these (not to mention Thucydides, Xenophon, Polybius,
Livy and Caesar, all of them among the greatest historians of the
classical world if not of all times) bear witness to the central place
commanded by military history from the earliest periods on.

Likewise medieval historiography, to the extent that it can be
said to have existed at all, very often consisted of records of battles
real or staged; as Froissart bears witness upon dozens of pages
(most of them so tedious to the modern reader that they have been
omitted from the Penguin Classics edition), even the most minute

Journal of Contemporary History (SAGE, London, Beverly Hills and New Delhi),
Vol. 18 (1983), 549-566

details of a tournament, the unexpected movement of a horse or the accidental breaking of a lance, appeared worthy of being recorded. Nor is it surprising that, during an age when 'society' consisted largely of those to whom fighting was their lives' *raison d'être,* men capable of writing should allocate war a central place. Far from waning when feudalism went into decline, this interest in military history actually increased during the renaissance; by the end of the sixteenth century printed editions, translations of, and commentaries on the works of Xenophon, Polybius, Onasander, Aelianus, Polyaenus, Caesar, Livy, Frontinus, Vegetius, Leo VI of Byzantium, and other ancient military writers were available and widely read by the intellectual and military élites of the time from Maurice of Nassau downward.[1] Voltaire's fulminations against the barbarity of war notwithstanding (he himself wrote much military history whose central theme would appear to be the influence which great but slightly mad men can bring to bear on the course of events), interest in military history, often in the form of commentaries upon works handed down from the classical world, remained lively right down to the French Revolution and beyond. When Droysen helped 'found the modern discipline of' history around 1830, he chose Alexander the Great as one of the first topics which to apply the newly formulated principles. To continue this list of proofs concerning the central importance which military history once held in the minds of both authors and readers would be easy; to do so, however, would amount to a punishment which not even the reader interested in such matters deserves.

The eternal desire of kings and princes to record their deeds of valour for posterity to remember; the feeling of men from the earliest of times that wars and battles constituted 'great events' worthy, if anything was, of being recorded; and the ever present hope of learning something from the history of conflicts past — all these combined to keep interest in military history alive throughout the ages under discussion. Furthermore, military history from the earliest times has been intimately involved with that of society in general. With the possible exception of some very celestial groups, usually as short lived as they were saintly, virtually every society that history records has been based on the ultimate sanction of force — with the result that the way in which that force was organized and used played a crucial role in giving those societies their shape. As an examination of their titles will often show — one has only to think of 'earl', 'duke', 'dictator' and 'Emperor' —

rulers from the earliest times were normally military leaders first and foremost, whose authority later came to be extended into other spheres also. The role of military power in the foundation of new societies and in the downfall of old ones has always been conspicuous, to say the least, nor has there been a lack of attempts (when all else failed) to legitimize government in terms of 'the right of conquest'. For much of history, in other words, to study the organized deeds of society was to study its military deeds — both internal and external — as is also shown by the fact that, as late as the third quarter of the eighteenth century, not merely the Prussian but the British government spent about two thirds of its annual revenue for military and naval purposes.

Having said this much about the reasons why military history was preeminent for so long, the reasons for its subsequent decline will become apparent almost of themselves. Beginning with the French Revolution and later extended by Marxist ideas concerning the dominant importance of social and economic processes in shaping the history of man,[2] the contents of many history books underwent a gradual change. The long peace that followed after 1815, the decline of the military aristocracy and the rise of the industrial and commercial middle classes, all helped shift interest away from the deeds of kings and princes to those of the 'common man' and society in general. Against the background of the rapid and momentous changes brought about by the industrial revolution, military affairs in general and wars in particular for the first time no longer appeared as important as they had traditionally been. This fact in turn was reflected by military budgets which underwent a relative decline even as those for social services rose. Needless to say, this shift of interests was gradual and did not occur in all places at once. Already in the eighteenth century the ideas of the Enlightenment caused interest in military affairs to decline in some countries, notably among the intellectual élites of England and France. On the other hand, the central role which war played in the belated unification of Germany helps explain the persistence there of the view attributed to Treitschke in the first sentence of this essay. Even during a period as relatively peaceful as the nineteenth century, every war was naturally followed by an outburst of publications describing its events; nor was there a lack of times and places, notably just before 1914, when the supposed *ennui* of peace caused something akin to a longing for war and a revival of interest in its history, real or imaginary. Nevertheless, over the period as a whole the trend is clear. The rise of history as an academic discipline was accompanied by a gradual disappearance of wars and battles from the history books, their place being taken by constitutional and diplomatic, and increasingly also economic and social, history.

Passing now to the twentieth century, the move away from military history may have been accelerated by the revulsion against war which gripped most of the western world after 1918 and forced a fundamental change of attitude that persists to this day. Where war had at one time been regarded as the crowning form of human activity — one needs only to recall Moltke's dictum that 'eternal peace is a dream, and not even a beautiful dream' — such views now became increasingly unfashionable, especially among society's best educated circles. Nor was military history aided by the rise of one of the most powerful twentieth century schools of historical writing, that of the *Annales*. Carrying the Marxist paradigm concerning the dominant influence exercised on man by his environment to its logical conclusion, Braudel and many of his followers have claimed that human history cannot be understood except against the background of the often excruciatingly slow changes in climate, geography and technique. Taking the argument a step further, some members of the school have come to regard these changes as constituting almost the sole worthy subject of historical study; the result being so called 'eventless history' in which the stage rather than the play, much less a few principal actors, becomes the centre of attention.

While this representation of the views of the *Annales* school is no doubt much too brief to do it justice, its relevance to the decline of military history is obvious. Confronted with the demand for eventless history, the historian is at once reminded of the fact that wars are *par excellence* the most spectacular events in history and have for long been regarded as its most important ones too. Asked to write history without 'great men' and deeds, he has only to look at the statues of Nelson and Marlborough gazing down from their respective columns, or take in hand a street map of Paris, to realize that for much of history it was precisely military men whose deeds were regarded as the greatest of all. Furthermore, a school of thought which regards long-term changes in the patterns of life as the most important way in which human society develops may all too easily come to regard war as akin in importance to the waves which periodically ruffle the surface of a bottomless ocean. Such a view is at once true and false. To an observer coming from outer space and desirous of studying the physical properties of the earth the enormous masses of water comprising the oceans may appear infinitely more important than the ultimately repetitive, though endlessly changing, patterns created by the waves on the surface. To somebody adrift in a little boat in the midst of those waves, however, the opposite might well be the case.

In our attempt to understand the causes behind the relative unimportance of military history as an academic discipline in the present-day world, the role played by the trend towards quantification must not be overlooked. Spreading outward from management science, operations research and systems analysis, the quest for more and more 'hard' data which could be manipulated by these means has lapped at Clio's robe since 1945 and for some years threatened to drown her. No longer content simply to narrate or 'understand' history, historians armed themselves with computers and set out to measure it, the result being Cliometrics and an outpouring of writings in which the old imprecision was all too often replaced by a new incomprehensibility. Now it so happens that, as compared to the facts of economic and social history, those of military history — and especially those of campaigns and battles waged on land — are far more difficult to quantify.[3] Whereas a few simple tables and graphs may shed much light upon social and economic conditions at any one time and place, the modelling of military operations, involving as they do the interaction of at least two independent minds, is far more complex and requires mathematical tools which, even at their most elementary level (the Lanchester Equations) are too difficult for many historians to follow.[4] In other words, the intellectual climate of the last three decades during which the prestige of an academic discipline was often directly proportional to the number of figures it could muster has not been conducive to the writing of military history in its traditional sense. Instead, the trend towards quantification may have aided the move towards the study of the economic basis, social structure, and administrative organization of war — this being a problem to which we shall return in a moment.

Finally, it must be admitted that the practitioners of military history themselves have not been altogether blameless for the relative decline of their profession as an academic field. For reasons too obvious to require explanation, probably no other historical discipline except biography has suffered so much from the influx of journalists and other hacks who, eager to capture a market, all too often produced works based on little research and less understanding.[5] Military historians themselves have for too long concentrated on the description of battles and campaigns to the exclusion of almost everything else, producing the kind of stuff caricatured by Yaroslav Hassek in *Good Soldier Schweik*. There, cadet Biegler, a would-be famous military author, produced endless little descriptions of battles, all of which were exactly alike in that they were fought by armies having two wings and a centre between those wings. That such things should be widely regarded as intellectually unchallenging is not surprising (though it is well to recall Schlieffen's remark that 'yes, all it is about is this foolish business of winning'), and at least one well-known military historian once privately complained to me that the discipline does not require 'the same kind of high powered thinking' that (he believes) is demanded by economics, for example. Applied to military history as a whole, this is a cruel and unjustified remark. It is true, however, that more men of Schweik's intellectual stature are attracted to military history than to any other kind of history, and to the extent that military historians cater to this market, the contempt in which they are sometimes held may not be altogether unjustified.

The belief that economic and social factors are the true driving forces of human history; the rise of the *Annales* school; the trend towards quantification; and the fact that too much traditional military history has concentrated on 'simple' battles and campaigns (as if there were anything simple about the meticulous reconstruction of actions involving tens of thousands of men on each side) and thus isolated itself — all these have combined to create the crisis at present facing military history. This crisis has manifested itself in two ways. On the one hand, it is only necessary to look at news stands and supermarket shelves (where military history is the only kind of history, besides the juicier kinds of biography sold) to realize that wars continue to make rattling good history.[6] As has happened in other fields also, the attempt to substitute rigorous analysis for narrative has led to a divorce between academics and the general public. While the latter is being entertained with war films on television, the former go about their sometimes weird researches and meanwhile complain about being unable to make a decent living. However justified such complaints may possibly be when they come from scientists working in other fields, there can be no doubt that if military historians have succeeded in turning military history into a bore they only have themselves to blame.

The second result of the above-named trends has been the fact that, in recent decades, much of the best work on military history has been done not by experts on the history of war as such but by historians whose primary interest was in political science, sociology, economics, psychology, and administration. Claiming that it is impossible to understand the history of warfare without a thorough prior examination of the political, economic and social foundations on which it rests, these men have produced much outstanding work and considerably deepened our understanding of those factors. This 'socializing of military history', as the phenomenon has been called,[7] has even succeeded in restoring some of war's lost respectability as a field for academic study, as is made evident by the growing number of journals being published on 'armed forces and society'. At the same time, however, it faces the risk of throwing away the baby with the bathwater. To write about the economic, social, administrative, psychological, technological and other assorted bases of war is unobjectionable so long as one keeps in mind, with Clausewitz, that 'the soldier is levied, clothed, armed, exercised, exercised, he sleeps, eats, drinks, and marches, all merely to fight *at the right time and place*' [Clausewitz's emphasis].[8] On no account, otherwise expressed, should the attempt to broaden the basis of the study of military history cause one to forget that the purpose of armed forces is and should be to wage war or, in these days, to deter it; and that they can do the latter only through convincing others of their ability and willingness to go through with the former. To furnish just one example of where neglect of this elementary truth may lead, one well-known authority on civil-military relationships and the organization of armed forces has written that the skills demanded of the modern soldier are not very different from those of a crane operator. This rests upon the well-known fact that, in every modern army around the world, the proportion of soldiers engaged in operating and maintaining complicated technical equipment is constantly growing, and to this extent there is an element of truth in the statement; indeed, some soldiers today *are* crane operators. To regard their skill in handling cranes as their sole or even principal qualification as soldiers, however, is to completely miss the mark when writing about past wars and to risk the disintegration of one's forces — as actually happened to the Americans in Vietnam — when planning and waging current ones.

The hope of regaining for military history some of its lost academic respectability — God forbid that it should regain all of it — is therefore not entirely without foundation. In so far as this development can only rest upon the ability of military historians to take an increasingly interdisciplinary approach and incorporate the findings of as many other sciences as possible, beginning with cybernetics and ending with psychology and business administration, it is to be welcomed. Nobody can possibly argue against a broader, well-rounded, approach to the military affairs of the past. Care is to be taken, however, that writers active in the field know something of war, its nature and the way it is fought, or else foolish misunderstandings will ensue.[9] Nor should interdisciplinary studies be allowed to pull military history away from its true focus, which in this author's opinion consist of everything connected with the waging of past wars and preparations for them. War must be firmly anchored in its context, but, at least from the point of view of military history, it is the former and not the latter which is and must remain the most important thing. To behave otherwise, and this is a danger frequently faced by interdisciplinary studies, is not merely to risk confusion but also mistake lack of focus for depth.

From much of what has been said so far the reader may have gained the impression that this author believes in the values of military history as a guide for present-day military action, and such is indeed the case. While all history has always been studied partly in the hope of deriving 'lessons' from it, the pressure on military history to be not just entertaining but useful has been particularly strong. The conduct of war being an intermittent activity not infrequently divided by long periods of peace, the body of techniques which forms the 'know how' of other professions has always had some difficulty in developing; constant practice and feedback being, fortunately, unavailable, men professionally or occupationally interested in military affairs tend to fall back upon the more formalized study of history. Nobody has put the case in favour of this approach with greater force than did Napoleon Bonaparte:

Read and reread the campaigns of Alexander, Hannibal, Caesar, Gustavus, Turenne, Eugene, and Frederick. Make them your models. This is the only way to become a great general and to master the secrets of the art of war. With your own genius enlightened by this study, you will reject all maxims opposed to those of these great commanders.

Underlying this was a belief that there exists a substantial theoretical basis behind the conduct of war, a belief whose origins can be seen in the military intellectuals of the seventeenth and eighteenth centuries and which gained increasing currency during the nineteenth. To teach that basis became the task of the staff academies that began opening their doors during the seventeen sixties, to distill it from the conflicts of the past the task of military history writers. The founders of what was to become the German General Staff — including in particular Scharnhorst, Clausewitz, Boyen and Müffling — attached great importance to military history, producing many works both during the period of reform before 1815 and during the long years of peace and garrison life that followed.[10] In Helmut von Molke, its chief from 1857 until 1888, the German General Staff found a man who not only believed in the value of military history but practised it with a well-educated pen, helping to write the history of many a nineteenth-century campaign. The belief in the usefulness of military history probably reached its zenith during the half century following upon the spectacular German victories of 1866 and 1870-1871; it was in this period that every General Staff around the world established a Military History Department and set its best officers, from Schlieffen and Foch and Bernhardi downwards, to work in seeking lessons from the past. The result was that civilian writers were pushed into a corner — they could normally match neither the officers' access to source material nor their supposed expertise — while the General Staffs proceeded to pour out a vast amount of material, such as La Jonquerie's four volumes on the 1798-1799 Palestine Campaign or Alombert-Colin's five even bulkier ones on the Austerlitz Campaign of 1805. In their attention to detail and grasp of minutiae, those studies — usually centering on operations, but sometimes branching off into supply and intelligence as well — have been unequalled before or since.

During the interwar years from 1919 to 1939, military-professional interest in military history was kept alive, though perhaps less intensively so than before. Carried as much by the force of habit as by anything else, the German *Kriegsakademie* in particular continued to assign military history a place second only to tactics, much to the chagrin of those who believed that technical subjects should be allotted a more prominent place in the curriculum. The status of military history in those years was not enhanced by the publication of the various official histories, often seeking to make up in bulk for what they lacked in intellectual honesty and depth. During no other period, perhaps, was the study of military history — still assiduously striving to dig up lessons from the most trivial actions of the 'Great War' — so far removed from what historians in general wrote, read and thought.

The outbreak of the second world war, and even more so the nuclear device which brought it to an end, together produced a crisis in the writing of military history. The enormous outpouring of books on the war — by now they must be numbered in the hundreds of thousands — was accompanied by growing doubts as to whether history was of any use in a world subject to rapid and extensive technological change. The advent early in the nineteen-fifties of the nuclear balance of terror added another dimension to these doubts; now that the purpose of the most important forces was no longer to fight wars but to deter them, it appeared that the study of past conflicts had lost any usefulness it might ever have had. This point of view was put forward with particularly great force by Walter Millis, himself a first-class writer of military history:

> The military professional who must today preside over the design, production and employment of the giant weapons of mass destruction cannot really learn much from Napoleon, or Jackson, or Lee, or Grant — who were all managers of men in combat, not of 'weapon systems' about which one of the most salient features is that they must never . . . be allowed to come into collision . . . It is the belief of the present writer that military history has largely lost its function . . . the old tales are increasingly irrelevant to modern international politics, to modern war and modern citizenship . . . it is not immediately apparent why the strategy and tactics of Nelson, Lee, or even Bradley or Montgomery should be taught to the young men who are being trained to manage the unmanageable military colossi of today . . .[11]

The past having thus been rendered apparently irrelevant both by technological change and by the shift in the nature of the task facing the most important armed forces, it was thought that means other than the study of military history had to be found in order to provide guidance for action. Reflecting this belief, military history took a nosedive in the curricula of higher military training institutes, in many cases disappearing altogether. Its place was to be taken by a series of new disciplines apparently better suited to meet modern demands: operations research, systems analysis, business management, cybernetics, decision-making theory and game theory, most of which presented the additional apparent merit of being amenable to at least some degree of quantification and therefore to study by means of that prestigious new tool, the computer. To the extent that it remained of any interest at all, military history was increasingly regarded simply as a pool of data for these disciplines to draw upon. In the economically prosperous, intellectually confident Brave New World of the fifties and the sixties, guidance for military action was to be provided by analytical thought based on the new disciplines, not by the outmoded past. This approach enjoyed its greatest moment of triumph in 1960, when Robert McNamara, himself an expert of management and the handling of data, assumed power at the Pentagon. He brought with him a team of bright young men, the so called whiz-kids, who despised military experience (read: history) but seemed to know everything about economics, management, systems analysis, and computer science. Unfortunately, it soon turned out, they knew absolutely nothing of war.

Meanwhile, the belief that military history no longer possessed much relevance to the present was reflected in the way it was often being written. Reacting against the intellectual shallowness characterizing many of the attempts to seek 'lessons' from the past, and influenced by the new emphasis on interdisciplinary studies, there was a tendency to turn away from telling the stories of past wars and campaigns towards providing static pictures of economic-social-technical-military conditions at some time or place in the past. Such accounts often make interesting, even fascinating, reading, and in so far as they help clear up the background against which conflicts were fought, fitted in tolerably well with the *Annales* school. Seen from the point of view of somebody seeking guidance for action, such works had little to offer, however, their whole thesis being precisely that the wars of the past could not be understood except within the context of historical circumstances very different from those prevailing today, so that any possible lessons were *a priori* excluded. To study, for example, the technological, logistical, tactical and strategic factors which together governed the employment of fifteenth-century galleys in the Mediterranean[12] is an intellectual exercise of great intrinsic merit, but not one whose conclusions, whatever they may be, are easily applied to the present.

Nevertheless, the emphasis which the best contemporary military (and non-military) historical scholarship often places on the 'otherness' of the past appears misleading on two accounts. First, however much economic, social, technological and other circumstances may have changed, history and particularly military history remains the record of the thoughts and actions of organized groups of men whose basic needs, drives and passions have not changed since time immemorial; indeed, it might be argued that it was their failure to take cognizance of this fact that led to the disastrous failure of the above-mentioned analytical techniques during the Vietnam War. Second, it is a mistake to believe that something can be learnt only from cases whose circumstances are more or less similar, and that everything that took place before e.g the invention of the steam engine, quick-firing rifle, automobile, tank, aircraft, nuclear arms, or ballistic missile is therefore irrelevant. Rather, it is often a radical difference in circumstances which can lead to the most profound insights — provided, of course, that the differences are clearly recognized, and that a proper intellectual framework exists.

And this brings us to the last part of the present essay, namely a very personal statement by this author concerning the way in which military history should (and should not) be studied in order to regain some of the usefulness often attributed to it in the past and, at the same time, the respectable place which it deserves as an academic discipline. In making the attempt, some of the old platitudes need not be repeated except by the briefest of cautions. It is a matter of course that, to be useful, military history must first of all be valid. It is likewise a matter of course that no kind of history can possess any kind of validity unless the theories are made to fit the facts, instead of *vice versa*. Furthermore, to possess validity history should be based on the most thorough research practicable. On no account should the desire to derive some usefulness for the present lead to sloppiness in researching the past.

Before proceeding further, a word need be said concerning the *kind* of lessons which people, explicitly or implicitly, have usually hoped to derive from military history. These have assumed three distinct forms, none of them unproblematic.[13] On the most elementary level, there has been the attempt to learn from other people's experience: since General A took action B at place C in period D, and succeeded (or failed), similar action today is equally likely to result in success or failure. This of course suffers from the disadvantage that the lessons of the past are by no means always open to a single interpretation only, and also that it does not provide one with any guide as to which of the infinitely numerous examples of the past to emulate or to avoid. On a slightly more advanced level, military history has been used to extract 'the principles of war', the assumption being that the conduct of war for all its endlessly changing forms does rest upon certain eternal principles whose observation is essential to success and which cannot be violated with impunity.[14] Such an approach has much to be said for it (and much was said for it, especially between 1871 and 1914 when the principles of war enjoyed the heyday of their popularity), except that the principles themselves are few and simple to the point of banality. One does not, presumably, require to study the whole of military history in order to realize that banging one's head against a wall is usually futile and that surprise is an important ingredient in success. In so far as neither the nature of the principles of war nor their number (usually between four and nine) have undergone much change over the last century or so, it might be argued that any historical research done in this period has been wasted. Had the principles of war been the sole subject of this research, it would presumably have sufficed to have published them in condensed form, each followed perhaps by a brief discussion and an example or two, and have done with it.

The third way to use military history, like history in general, is to try and derive from it 'trends' and project those trends into the future. While a popular exercise, such use is notoriously dangerous in that the historian may easily end up in finding just what he was looking for. Even assuming that an 'objective' trend is identified, there is normally no way of knowing whether it will continue or come to an end (it might even be argued that the very fact that a trend has been identified as such by the majority of 'thinking people' is a sign that it is about to spend itself). Of the three ways of using military history, finding trends is the most ambitious; unfortunately, however, it is also the most dangerous.

Given these problems, what else remains? In groping our way towards an answer, the first thing is to realize that, in order to possess even a potential usefulness for the present, military history must put forward questions which are relevant to the present. This is to risk being accused of pandering to the needs of the powers that be, and also to go in the face of those who insist that past epochs can only be understood in their own terms; to both of which we might reply that, since the past itself is immutable, 'progress' in the writing of history consists precisely in postulating and answering new questions. For example, the pressing need to discover the 'secret' by which the French Revolutionary and Napoleonic armies had come close to overrunning the whole of Europe led men to delve deeply into the nature of moral force and of strategy, project those questions into the past, and come up with some of the most profound military writing ever. The obvious problems associated with the political standing of armed forces in the modern state and with the technical-economic background to warfare led to the outstanding work of Hans Delbrück, Joseph Schumpeter, and Otto Hintze during the early years of the present century. In the sixties and the seventies, the challenge presented by terrorism and guerrilla warfare led to searching investigations into the origins and development of these phenomena. As the seventies passed into the eighties and the threat posed to the peace of the world by those twins appeared to be receding (though it may be too early to tell), some of the most pressing problems that may be addressed by military historians included the relationship between technology and man in his capacity as a soldier on the one hand, and the growing difficulty and managing and commanding military forces of vast size and complexity on the other.

Whatever one's views of the nature of the past, the precise problems facing the present, and the actual and desirable relationship between historians and those who must make the decisions, the statement that one cannot even conceive of military history as being useful unless it poses questions relevant to the present remains axiomatic. The point of the exercise must therefore be to look at the past through the glasses of the present, then to use the past in order to gain a better understanding of the nature of those very glasses. All this must be done without imposing the frame of reference of the present upon the past, thereby sacrificing veracity and reaching false conclusions, but at the same time without using the otherness of the past as an excuse to retreat into an ivory tower. The final result should be a conscious locking together of past and present, enriching both by a thorough investigation of the similarities as well as the differences, the ephemeral as well as the eternal, and the way that these two interact.

Following from the above, there stems the conclusion that study of any one place or period in the past, however interesting as an intellectual exercise, can never be satisfying to those seeking guidance for the present. What we are after is not 'the experience of others', nor 'the principles of war', nor even 'historical trends', but insight into the nature of the various factors which together make up military reality, past and present, and the way in which they interact through change. To employ an analogy from chemistry, it might be argued (whether or not this is true from a philosophical point of view) that a material is the sum total of the ways in which it reacts with other materials. While experimenting with all possible combinations is not more practicable in history than it is in chemistry (and may be equally dangerous), this means that the former, like the latter, must proceed in width. Working either through space or through time, history to be useful must be comparative. It must compare historical times and places with each other, and also with the present.

The second *sine qua non* for making military history 'useful', is that it be studied in depth. In history as in other fields, it is only possible to compare things with each other or else with some 'objective' frame of reference. Had such a frame existed, our labour would have been enormously facilitated, but at the same time rendered somewhat superfluous. If history is to be of any help in this matter, the looked-for frame must be allowed to emerge of itself, so to speak, through and by means of a 'thick' comparison of different times and places with each other, and embracing as great a variety of factors as possible. Only when proceeding in this way can history even hope to arrive at its true goal, which is to understand 'what it is all about'.

Since limitations of time and space inevitably make 'width' and 'depth' incompatible with each other, it would appear that one of the best ways to derive guidance from military history is through detailed case studies. This immediately raises the question as to which cases are to be chosen. The only conceivable answer to this question is that the case studies must be so selected as to illustrate as many aspects of the problem as possible, yet without imposing a system of reference that will dictate the findings in advance. This is a matter which requires much thought, and often it will be found that the cases initially selected either shed insufficient light upon the problem under investigation or else predetermine its outcome. Such a situation inevitably leads to much labour being wasted and may indeed cause a crisis of conscience. If the crisis is honestly faced, however, the final product will probably be all the better because of it.

Thus, to the present author, the value of military history — even when regarded from a supposedly 'practical' point of view — lies less in the conclusions than in the discussion, less in final written presentation than in the process of study as such. That its value is not, consequently, subject to conclusive proof follows at once, but then this lack of demonstrability is shared by all the most important questions facing humanity from the existence of God downwards. As compared to personal experience of any of the more analytical disciplines, history when properly understood enjoys the tremendous advantage of dealing with the infinite variety of the human experience and should therefore be able to attain an intellectual richness which few if any of them can match. The frequently-heard demand that military history be 'useful', far from clashing with the demand for veracity and objectivity, should be understood as a challenge to come to grips with the present as well as with the past thus adding even further richess. The challenge is a daunting one, possibly more so than the one faced by many other kinds of historians; it is up to us to seize it.

Notes

1. See W. Hahlweg, *Die Heeresreform der Oranier und die Antike* (Berlin 1940), 11-17.

2. Interestingly, the antimilitary bent of much of the modern industrialized world was shared neither by Marx himself nor by his followers. Marx studied Clausewitz and occasionally produced a paper on military affairs, while Engels' knowledge of such matters was sufficient for his writings to be mistaken for those of a Prussian General. Some of the most famous names in the history of socialism, including Jean Jaures and Karl Liebknecht, wrote extensively and trenchantly on military affairs.

Trotsky even went so far as to call war 'the locomotive of history'. Present-day Soviet military history writings are nothing if not voluminous, and the Soviet Union is the only country that has PhDs in 'military science'. Partly perhaps for these reasons, there is some reason to believe that the Soviet leadership currently possesses a better understanding of the nature of war than do many members of Western 'defence communities'. See on this entire subject the recent work by B. Semmel, *Marxism and the Science of War* (Oxford 1981).

3. Normally, the more important the role played by technology in any form of warfare, the easier it is to quantify, and vice versa. This explains why air and naval warfare are much more easily quantifiable than is war on land, the former in particular being often waged at such speed that quantification (followed by automation) is the only way in which it can be waged at all. On the other hand, wars in which the political element is predominant — including in particular guerrilla warfare — are difficult to quantify, and attempts to do so may easily lead to a Vietnam-like situation where the Americans counted everything and understood nothing.

4. The people who have most consistently attempted to quantify warfare (except for those at the Pentagon), assigning numerical values even to such intangible qualities as morale, leadership and luck, are the war-gamers. Though their work is often based upon remarkably thorough historical research, as a group they have to day failed to win recognition from 'serious' academic historians. See on this question the article by Stephen Glick in this issue.

5. An excellent satire on how to write such military history is contained in N.C. Parkinson, *Inlaws and Outlaws* (London 1962), 22-23.

6. See the essay by M. Howard, 'The Demand for Military History', *Times Literary Supplement,* 13 November 1969.

7. C. Jones, 'New Military History for Old? War and Society in Early Modern Europe', *European Studies Review,* vol. 12, 1982, 97-98.

8. C. von Clausewitz, *On War* (London 1962 ed.) vol. i, 37.

9. A good example is N. Dickson, *The Psychology of Military Incompetence* (London 1976). This book certainly helps explain why a certain type of authoritarian person is able to climb the military ladder in peacetime, only to fail disastrously when reaching its apex in war. The author's lack of detailed knowledge of military affairs, however, causes him to lay too much emphasis on his heroes' stupidity and to neglect the objective problems of command, thus distorting the entire picture.

10. On the innovative use made by these men of military history see R. Höhn, *Scharnhorsts Vermächtnis* (Bonn 1952), 68-87; also P. Paret, 'The History of War', *Daedalus,* 100, 1971, 376-377.

11. *Military History* (Washington D.C., Service Center for Teachers of History, No. 39), 16-18.

12. See J. F. Guilmartin, *Gunpowder and Galleys* (London 1974).

13. For a somewhat more detailed discussion of these problems see M. van Creveld, 'Caesar's Ghost; Military History and the Wars of the Future', *The Washington Quarterly,* 3, Winter 1980, 67-75.

14. For a recent list of 'the principles of war', based upon rather more substantial research than most of its kind, see T. N. Dupuy, *The Evolution of Weapons and Warfare* (New York 1982), 323-24.

Martin van Creveld
is an Associate Professor at the History
Department, the Hebrew University,
Jerusalem. He is the author of *Hitler's
Strategy; the Balkan Clue* (Cambridge
1973), *Supplying War; Logistics from
Wallenstein to Patton* (Cambridge 1977)
and *Fighting Power; German and US Army
Performance, 1939-1945* (Westport, Conn.
1982).

Stephen P. Glick
and L. Ian Charters

War, Games, and Military History

Most works of military history succeed only in part in doing enough to enlighten the reader as to what actually occurs in war or in a given action. This stems from an insufficient appreciation of many of the elements of war on the part of most military historians. We propose the use of wargames as an additional tool to grant some further insights to the historian. After briefly explaining the history and types of wargames, specific elements of war, generally ignored by historians but encompassed in wargames, are examined. This is followed by a review of incidental benefits along with our conclusions.

I

Napoleon once said that 'to become a great general and to master the secrets of the art of war one must read and reread the campaigns of the Great Captains'.[1] Although the military historian is not supposed to want to become a great general (there is a lingering suspicion that this is sometimes not the case), the desire to master the secrets that Napoleon described is a part of the purpose of military history. So it follows naturally that the advice of Napoleon to his would-be emulators should likewise be of value to historians. By his command to read and reread, Napoleon did not mean the simple memorization of the forms and details of the campaigns of these masters, but the study and analysis of the hows and whys of their actions. However, the vast majority of military history is no more than narration of the various campaigns and battles with little of the critical analysis recommended in the Emperor's dictum.

This is not to belittle the importance of the narrative genre. Until comparatively recently it was the entirety of military history. In addition, the researches of these military historians provide us with a great amount of invaluable information necessary to proper analysis. Just the same, their contributions to the mastering of the

Journal of Contemporary History (SAGE, London, Beverly Hills and New Delhi),
Vol. 18 (1983) 567–582

secrets of the art of war have been considerably less than they might have been, given the quantity of material produced. Since the second world war, there have appeared two generations of military historians who have looked beyond simple battlefield narration to describe the inner workings of war. On the one hand these generations have drawn a great part of their roots from the important, though few, analytical works of histories that did exist.[2] On the other hand these new generations have, among their techniques, chosen to employ the tools of the other social 'sciences'.[3]

Along with the introduction of these new tools to military history has come the introduction of new approaches. These have come as studies on specific aspects of war which have received far less attention, if any, in the past than has been their due. The element of war benefiting the most from this new attention has been the field of military intelligence. Many important works detailing the functions and processes of military intelligence were produced by the mid-1970s.[4] Since that time, the baring of the existence and substance of the Ultra secret has spurred renewed attention and helped place intelligence in the context of war.[5] The study of techniques, tactical, operation, and strategic methods has advanced almost as much.[6] Even the fundamental but almost completely ignored key element of logistics has, through brilliant writing and careful selection of interesting topics, become 'sexy'.[7]

Still, the majority of contemporary military histories tend to be of the conventional narrative style, and could be enriched considerably through the incorporation of more detail concerning these and other elements of war into the fabric of their works. However, there are still a number of factors essential to war which are just beginning to receive attention from military historians. To study some of these as yet unappreciated elements, as well as to aid in the integration of a number of other elements into the fabric of one's understanding of war and military history, another device or tool is available, the wargame.

II

Wargames have existed in a recognizable form for over a century and a half. Abstract wargames like chess and Go have existed for millenia. In its modern form, the wargame was invented by Prussian Army officers in the early nineteenth century. Since that time, wargames have found their most appreciative audiences among various military staffs. There has also developed an entire hobby around them. For military officers and wargame has been an invaluable tool to assist in the preparation and testing of plans and methods and in the training of officers. To the hobbyist, wargames provide the pleasures inherent in a contest requiring skill and give something of the flavour of battle.

The attention given to wargames by the military as a planning tool makes it seem rather curious that military historians have paid so little attention to the wargame as a historical tool. In part this failure undoubtedly stems from the sheer size and complexity of military wargames, involving frequently a great many people and requiring considerable amounts of time and resources simply not available to the military historian. Further, the image of the hobby wargame as a somewhat disreputable thing of pleasure has precluded its use. But to an even greater extent this inattention has been due to the uncertain nature of the results of such games; the use of the so-called Monte Carlo technique in gaming.[8] What is perhaps overlooked is that military users of wargames have been using chance or Monte Carlo gaming techniques to determine combat results for nearly as long as they have been employing wargames. In this context it is important to remember how effective military wargames have been, when correctly designed and run, in predicting the outcome of campaigns.[9]

For the historian, the study of alternate possibilities, of what might have happened, is usually viewed as the realm of the novelist. This bias has kept the military historian from employing the wargame as a technique for examining the effects of an action upon a particular factor. It is in this manner that the wargame can greatly aid the individual's appreciation of the multitude of factors involved in the conduct of war. Of course no game, however sophisticated, can hope realistically to portray all of the myriad elements of the clash of states and civilizations, or even the small forces of armed men.

Fortunately no wargame attempts capture all of these elements on its map; although maps are not the only playing field currently utilized by wargaming. In fact the three major types of wargaming can be differentiated by their playing surfaces. The oldest school employs miniature models to represent the military forces involved and often makes use of highly detailed three-dimensional terrain models as playing fields. Most wargaming in miniatures simulates land combat, primarily, but by no means exclusively at the tactical level. Most current miniatures rules draw their roots from the techniques described in H.G. Wells' *Little Wars* (Boston 1913), and the handling of systems has not changed much since that time. The pieces are often quite expensive in numbers and a considerable part of the fascination this type of gaming holds for its adherents seems to be the detailed duplication of units' appearance by their models.

The next type of wargaming to establish itself among hobbyists was the map-based 'board-game'. This type of game currently possesses the widest audience, because of the flexibility and cost of the medium. With this in mind, our paper has addressed itself primarily to the characteristics and benefits of the board-game. The physical components are paper or cardboard maps and markers and are fairly inexpensive. The relative cheapness of manufacture and ease of modification to many different situations has aided in the popularization of this type of wargame. This has particularly helped in the large amount of design and modification work by players themselves, a characteristic that might also commend it to military historians. The cheapness of manufacture and widespread popularity has allowed a comparatively large amount of research to be funded by designers and this has been incorporated into game designs.

However, the computer gaming field is quickly matching the board-gaming school in terms of its ability to attract hobby game designers. This seems to be in great part due to a growing interest among designers to delve deeper into intelligence and other problems in game design and war that can be most easily handled by a computer. The marketability and quality of design of computer wargaming is being funded and fed by the rapid growth in 'computer literacy' that has attended the affordability of 'home' or 'personal' computers. Still, the initial expense of acquiring the basic equipment required for the play of computer wargames is daunting at this time, if the individual in question has no other intended application for the equipment. But, there is no doubt that the future of hobby wargaming resides in the chips of tomorrow's 'personal' computers. The reasons for this are compelling. As will be discussed in more detail later, the computer has the ability to act as both a second player and umpire. In addition to aiding in the handling of purely technical game or bookkeeping matters, such as handling intelligence and combat resolution, the computers' memory and the availability of telephone links have eased the problem of scheduling multiple player games, to the extent that a single wargame could be played by individuals all around the globe at their own convenience. These two factors, of convenience and factor sophistication, are joined by a third, insulation from the nuts and bolts of wargames that often are the bane of gamers; with this concern reduced, game designers can introduce even more sophisticated and detailed work into the subject.

It is the rare historian who can arrange for a military wargame to be held (as did the War Studies Staff at Sandhurst after the Second World War, a description of which appears in Richard Cox's *Operation Sealion,* London 1975). This leaves the historian at the mercy of the hobby wargamer's product. While costing a tiny fraction of the military simulation, even the simpler wargames can offer much to the military historian. And perhaps because the better wargame designers follow closely the latest advances in military history, their products incorporate the newly studied elements of war.

III

Before embarking upon the process of detailing the areas of military history in which wargames can be of assistance, it seems appropriate to mention briefly some, of the major systems that are employed in wargames to represent the elements of war. The two most basic are those employed to simulate the movement and combat of military forces.

The rates of travel of military units over a variety of landforms (or upon bodies of water or in the air), under various conditions are known. These rates are given values corresponding to the scale of the playing-field and the speed of time passage simulated in the game. The ability of the players to use the full potential 'movement allowance' of the markers representing their forces is modified by the type of terrain, the type of force, and in the more sophisticated designs further modified by any number of other factors, including but not limited to, weather, supply availability, unit density, command status, morale, and unit exhaustion.

Strengths of combat forces are quantified, often starting from the number of soldiers and/or guns, planes, ships, and so on present. These simple strengths may again be subject to modification on the basis of variables similar to those discussed under movement, in addition to others — the status of munitions supplies, for instance. These strengths are then compared and recourse is made to a matrix of combat results. After possible further modifications, such as leader effects, chance determines which of the results in the matrix represents the outcome of the combat. The matrix result not only decides the victor, but also the form of victory in terms of casualties and/or possession of territory. At this point, other sophistications present in a particular simulation may determine further consequences of that combat.

Beyond these two systems representing combat and movement, several others have made their appearance in various wargames. The next most common system used in the simulation of an element of war is that concerned with logistics. As has been discussed above, supply systems can be used to affect movement and combat. In more advanced game designs, it often has additional repercussions. Sometimes its expression is very simple, merely requiring the players to keep their markers no more than a certain distance from a particular location (supply depot), on the playing-field. Other designs utilize elaborate frameworks to represent very detailed effects of levels of various types of supply on a military situation, altering morale and unit capabilities, for example.

The most insightful and useful treatments of command, control, and communications (C^3), have come about in the last few years, interestingly enough arriving at about the same time that the subject became a major issue in American military circles. Those games involving smaller-scale engagements have tended to stress the effects of leaders in battle and upon the initiative and cohesion of the military units involved. Those involving simulations of operational level activity have tended to stress more the effects of commanders and their staffs in ensuring proper coordination of the forces assigned to them. Often incorporated in games at both levels are factors involving the employment of leaders to effect force morale and thus other capabilities in activities such as movement, combat, and so forth.

IV

One of the most important concepts that wargaming imparts to its players is the conflictual nature of war. Even the simplest hobby games simulate this basic aspect of war. It seems curious that so many historians writing of so many wars and battles should consistently fail to give to their readers an appreciation that a clash of wills was underway; that for every stratagem employed by one side and explored through its course in great detail by the historian, there might be another equally well-nurtured stratagem employed by the opposing side that was underway at the moment of the action, and that the success of one side was as much due to the failures of the other as to any action of its own. This despite the well-known saying, 'victory goes to the side which makes the fewest mistakes'. Seldom does the historian lay credit for victory upon the shoulders of the losing side. Instead, the readers are too often presented with the history of some force which encounters lifeless obstacles that appear to lie awaiting their arrival and attack. To borrow from Edward Luttwak:

> The situation is akin to that of an engineer attempting to build a bridge across a stream. He must consider the depth of water, its rate of flow, variations in those factors, the composition of the banks, the streambed, and the materials at hand. [10]

That is quite the spirit of the typical narrative military history. The plans are discussed, the obstacles are examined, the objectives are clear. Now, to add the remainder of the quotation:

> Now suppose the stream, instead of waiting passively for its bridging, begins to shift its course, alter its composition, seeking always to thwart the engineer, to undermine his plans for its bridging. [11]

That is war. A wargame forces the player to confront an opponent. Someone whose plans must receive as much consideration as one's own. Having once been placed in this position, particularly in a game in which one's knowledge of the enemy's forces is limited, the historian can more fully appreciate the anxieties that dominate the mind of the general commanding forces in the field. The situation brings home to the individual the truth of Napoleon's maxim, 'A commander-in-chief should several times a day ask himself, "If the enemy appears to the front or on my right or my left, what should I do?" If he finds himself embarrassed as to his reply, his dispositions are faulty, and he should correct them.'[12]

At this point the analytical player begins to acquire a sense of the importance of intelligence in the operations of military forces. Many hitherto obscure or pointless activities by commanders begin to assume purpose, revealing themselves to be efforts to improve flank or rear area security. Every consideration in war is given to grasping the purpose and plans of the enemy. Through playing even simple wargames the reality of war as a clash of wills becomes more readily apparent. Moreover, a sense of the uncertainties inherent in this most demanding of all human activities begins to reveal itself.

A second element of war present in wargames is chance. Its use is basic to resolution of combat. It has been employed to determine supply, movement, and a host of other activities. But although its place in wargames is so prominent, the recognition accorded it in military history has been almost nonexistent. This is rather strange given its role in the determination of so many campaigns and battles. An appropriate example is the advance of the Union army under McClellan to bring Lee's Confederate army to battle at Antietam Creek. The Union commander lost track of the Confederate force and only the accidental discovery of a copy of Lee's plans, which were found in a cigar box by a patrol of Union soldiers foraging through the remains of a Confederate camp, enabled McClellan to bring Lee's army to bay and halt the invasion of the North. This is but one example of where human luck had decisive consequences for a campaign, if not an entire war.

In real life, much of what wargames reduce to chance is the product of thousands of decisions by individuals at every stage of the action. Thoughts in the head of a private soldier as to whether to run or to fight, decisions where to place a headquarters, and so forth. Just as no historian would try to chronicle a battle by recounting every decision by every soldier on the field (although the study of the behaviour of the individual soldier in battle has proved of great value), so the game designer aggregates all such minor decisions into masses that can be dealt with through the application of chance and an outcome matrix; just as the military historian addresses events in terms of their aggregate effects, thereby giving you the 'big picture'.

A consideration of these myriad decisions and other incidents that actually determine the course of action in military campaigns brings us to that factor of war dubbed by Clausewitz as 'friction'.

To the readers of most military histories, actions seem normally to be carried out as ordered, and when this is not the case, the failure is only given attention by the historian if something rather spectacular results. The difficulties encountered during the conduct of military operations are rarely apparent. The verity is scarcely apparent that in conceiving and trying to follow a plan in war, a commander is trying not only to force his opponent to bend to his will, but is trying to impose his own sense of order upon a chaotic universe in which all the blunders and accidents that could happen seem to conspire against his purposes. General Stilwell, who met more than his share of difficulties operating in China and Burma said, '(The) Principal load (of a commanding general) is standing disappointment and upsetting of plans. Everything conspires against him; dumb execution, weather, breakdowns, misunderstandings, deliberate obstructions, jealousies, etc. (He) Must be prepared to accept fifty per cent results in twice the time calculated.'[13] The military historian describes occasional individual slip-ups that seem to have major effects upon important operations. But the everyday occurrence of those incidents which come together to provide the force of friction receives attention only from the occasional perceptive soldier in his memoirs.

Until recently, Clausewitz's friction was largely ignored in most hobby wargames. But its importance could be ignored by wargame designers for only so long. Yet their realization of the importance of this factor of war seems to have anticipated its incorporation into the works of military historians. This tardiness on the part of military historians amounts to a neglect of the inner workings of an army — the roles and continuous duties of members of the staff: planning operations, evaluating intelligence, arranging supply, coordinating forces, extracting and composing actual orders, replying to messages from subordinate units, keeping superior headquarters informed, checking and rechecking orders, trying to overcome the myriad of small problems that could bring the force to a halt, all while trying to avoid exhaustion and losing control of the situation. All this activity in order to fight the enemy. The difficulties overcome cannot be adequately conveyed to the reader of lines like, 'The general ordered the left wing division to proceed to attack'.

Some recent hobby game designs deal with this element of war with a certain degree of detail and respect. The difficulties are translated into the rules and certain penalties are imposed on the player's forces. Chance is usually given a role, often varying in significance over time. In the extremely complicated designs, even the distance between a force and its base of operations, or the amount of time a commander has been active without rest, can affect the ability of the players' forces to overcome 'friction'.

Along with this type of friction there is another. This is the attenuation of forces by efforts at movement, changing position, foraging, and by simply staying in one spot. This attritional friction was a more apparent factor in pre-twentieth-century conflicts, when it could waste an army to nothing over the course of a campaign. The enormous growth in support troops in armies has occurred chiefly to counteract the effects of this type of friction. A few designs deal with this, usually under the title of march attrition, often utilizing the distance travelled, troop morale, distance from bases, and force concentration among the modifiers in determining the wastage rate of the troops.

It must be understood that in the simulation of this element of war the game designer is particularly indebted to the military historian. The painstakingly researched works of many authors make possible the correct assessment of these effects. Unfortunately, the figures necessary to the development of tables of effects have needed to be gleaned from archives by wargame design research staffs themselves.

Another element of war susceptible to simulation in wargames is the so-called 'fog of war'. In certain respects the 'fog of war' is intimately connected with the friction of war. This is an outgrowth of having an active opponent in the battlefield, and the problems of keeping track of the location and conditions of one's own troops, and is seldom if ever discussed at length by military historians. On campaign, the general has only the faintest idea of what the enemy intentions are, where he can be found, and how strong he will be at the point of contact. A veil lies between the opponents, and each seeks to remove the veil in such a manner as to leave himself seeing, but unseen. To understand this phenomenon it is usually necessary to refer to the journals written by commanders while on campaign. Post-war memoirs and most narrative histories give little reflection of this desperate need to locate the enemy. Perhaps the first historian to realize the importance of this was Liddell Hart, who first saw it in a non-historical context. Writing a tactical manual for the British infantry,[14] he developed his 'Man in the Dark' theory, in whch he compared the small unit commander to a man preparing for and engaging in hand-to-hand combat in darkness. The unit manoeuvres, as the man does, to locate and come to grips with the opponent, all the time taking care to keep from being caught off balance himself. However, the analogy, although apt, has not struck a responsive chord among military historians.

Simulation of the 'fog of war' has been difficult for the hobby wargame to achieve. The ideal system practised by most military wargaming staffs is the umpired blind system. The two sides set up their forces on identical playing-fields isolated from each other. The umpire sets up another set of playing-fields and then shadows players' deployments and moves and other actions on it. Each side manoeuvres across the terrain, learning about its opponent's positions and forces solely through information passed by the umpires, who also resolve combat and other interactions between the opponents. The umpires control the flow of the conflict, although the two sides control most of the actions of their own forces. The accuracy of this type of simulation depends upon the depth of detail in the game design and the competence and impartiality of the umpires.

Hobbyists and historians cannot gather the necessary number of individuals to engage in wargames of the size and style of most military wargames. In this case, the next step downward in terms of complexity is the two sides playing on identical boards, separated by some opaque screen, passing sighting and other information back and forth, trusting each other's competence. Problems with this type of system include the 'leakage' of information that should not be exchanged that occurs with the passage of information that is required under the rules of the game system. It becomes somewhat cumbersome and, if there are sizeable numbers of discrete forces involved, begins to require a disproportionate amount of time. This problem can be abnegated by utilizing a third party to act as an umpire, forcing the acceptance of this additional demand in manpower.

Lately, the advent of the personal computer has eased this problem. With the entry of sophisticated game programmes into the market, the computer can take up the role of umpire. Programmes exist that reduce the manpower requirement of blind gaming further by enabling the computer to perform both the roles of umpire and opponent.

The more usual form of handling the fog of war involves the employment of one or more of the techniques grouped under the heading 'limited intelligence' systems. This involves both players utilizing the same mapboard and the employment of several devices to conceal information about one's forces out on the map. These can take the form of markers covering those representing one's own troops, the existence of dummy (fake) markers to mislead about the strength and location of forces and other similar measures. 'Hidden movement' also may be employed in which a portion, usually quite small, of each side's forces is kept off the map, with the responsible players taking considerable pains to ensure that all movement these units make is in keeping with the rules.

Chance plays a major role in war. Unfortunately it often does not appear in most works of military history. Even the best works giving subtle and sophisticated explanations often make events seem inevitable. This deterministic appearance is an inherent and thus almost unavoidable consequence of the narrative style of history. It is in precisely this respect, in their examination of the impact of chance on war that the wargames display their most fascinating quality. By exploration of the what-ifs or non-events of history (that plausibly could have happened), the wargame can be used to extend understanding of events, and perhaps provide a better picture of the options available to the battlefield commander or national leader.

Historians may be justifiably cautious of this, since here historical exploration nears fiction. This borderline must be determined by the individual historian, although there appears to be a growing number of volumes dedicated to the examination of why one or another event did not happen, and offering some commentary on what might have occurred had the event actually happened. However, wargames do offer the military historian the opportunity to test his pet theories as nothing else can. The 'turning points' of history can be examined and judged to see if they are as advertised. The historian has the occasion to follow the flow of history around and through the events and non-events that have shaped it and gain insight into the shaping itself. Many operations suggest themselves to the military historian. A fine example of such an operation is the timing of Hitler's invasion of the Soviet Union. A great deal of ink has been spilled over the effects of the Balkan incursion upon Hitler's plans and the resulting lack of success of the first year's campaign in Russia for the German army. Consensus among historians seemed to be that the Germans would have won if they had not delayed their attack and overstrained part of their force in the attack on the Balkans. More recently, evidence has been presented to indicate that the delay had considerably less influence on the readiness of the German army to commence Operation

Barbarossa than had been believed. Still, that does not make it clear that the additional weeks of good campaign weather available to the German army might not have turned the tide of the campaign in their favour. With a suitable wargame and some time, the historian could examine the effects of an early invasion, an altered force composition, or whatever, on the outcome of the campaign.

Obviously, this question is still of interest even after forty years. For the military historian the opportunity to explore these what-ifs might lead him to conclude that the commonly attributed reasons were not the real ones for the results of a conflict. With the ready availability of games covering many major campaigns and battles in history, as well as many of the minor ones, the military historian need not seek very far to find one suitable for his wishes. Many of these are not terribly sophisticated, but enough are so that many of the interesting problems of military history can be tackled with a fair degree of confidence in the validity of the results. Utilizing these occasions the historian can perhaps locate the factors that propelled history to flow in the fashion it did. With wargames and careful employment of the proper modifiers and conditions the military historian has many opportunities to learn to appreciate the importance of the what-ifs and non-events in history.

The hobby wargame has provided a partial answer to one of the most serious weaknesses of military history: the absence of constantly updated maps. With the exception of the works of Vincent Esposito,[15] combining text and maps, there are few volumes of military history that possess enough maps of sufficient quality and utility to convey the flow of events clearly. This is undoubtedly partly due to the high cost of reproducing maps for books, but we feel that this is an insufficient excuse for the present state of affairs. Most books of military history provide just brief glimpses of the scene where the action occurs, instead of steadily unfolding the movement of forces and events to show the balance of forces over space and time, as a wargame in play does. An analogy could be seeing the maps in most volumes as being frames in a comic strip in comparison with the wargame that is a movie with some sort of mechanism to control the speed of presentation, enabling detailed scrutiny at will.

The wargame, with its precise rules and defined playing area serve to keep the observer's attention on the dominant physical features of the action. This is often not the case in military histories. Although terrain may dominate, unless it is the actual location of a good part of the fighting, it will receive far less attention than it should and than actually was given it by the commanders of the forces engaged.

V

In addition to the benefits that can accrue to the military historian through his own gaming (or better through his own game designing), the wargaming hobby has produced benefits for the entire field. One of the most valuable of these has been the original archival research that has gone into the design of some games. This has resulted in the increased availability of order of battle information in particular, to the extent that publishers now offer books of such data. The existence of such a large market for wargames has encouraged the growth of a number of magazines dealing with wargaming topics which has resulted in the publication of great quantities of military history.

Another 'public good' resulting from wargaming has been a sizeable increase in the audience for military history, despite the Vietnam War. Along with the increase in the breadth of the audience there has come an increase in its depth as well. The wargames have generated an interest into why battles and campaigns turned out the way they did and this has resulted in a more informed audience, conscious of the complexities of war and seeking to understand their interactions. This has resulted in a more critical reader looking for higher quality in his historical reading.

In addition to these general benefits, there are others of which we are less sure. One of these addresses a worry of the military historian that has existed for some time, but which has seemed particularly acute since the coming of the Vietnam War, that has been a general turning-away not only from war, but from an interest in any things military or security-related by many people. We feel that the interest that hobby wargames has engendered has helped to counteract this trend, a trend which might have very dangerous and grave results.

And lastly, it is our feeling that careful study of properly constructed games can yield some insights into the complexities and truths of war. And it is our hope that such insights might be of help in the formulation of approaches to military problems in the future, whether they concern weapons procurement decisions or the formulation of a national security policy.

Notes

1. Maxim 78, *Napoleon and Modern War* (Harrisburg 1943).

2. The major analytical works were: Hans Delbrueck, *Geschichte der Kriegskunst in Rahmen der Politischen Geschichte* (Berlin 1921); Charles Oman, *A History of the Art of War in the Middle Ages* (London 1924); and Robert Albion, *Forests and Seapower: The Timber Problem of the Royal Navy 1652-1862* (Princeton 1927).

3. A few examples are: sociology in Morris Janowitz, *The Professional Soldier: A Social and Political Portrait* (Glencoe 1960); psychology in S.L.A. Marshall, *Men Against Fire* (Moren 1947), and John Keegan, *The Face of Battle* (New York 1976); political science in Edward Luttwak and Dan Horowitz, *The Israeli Army* (London 1975), and Samuel Huntington, *The Soldier and the State* (Cambridge 1959).

4. Albert Wohlstetter, *Pearl Harbor, Warning and Decision* (Stanford 1962), Barton Whaley, *Codeword Barbarossa* (Cambridge 1973), and David Kahn, *The Codebreakers* (New York 1974) are particularly noteworthy.

5. The best volume to date integrating Ultra into operations in the war is Ronald Lewin, *Ultra Goes to War* (London 1978).

6. Robert Smail, *Crusading Warfare* (Cambridge 1956), David Chandler, *The Campaigns of Napoleon* (New York 1966), Edward Luttwak, *The Grand Strategy of the Roman Empire* (Baltimore 1976), and others.

7. Martin van Creveld, *Supplying War: Logistics from Wallenstein to Patton* (Cambridge 1977), and Donald Engels, *Alexander the Great and the Logistics of the Macedonian Army* (Berkeley 1978).

8. Monte Carlo merely refers to the determination of outcomes on a random basis through such means as dice, roulette wheels, etc.

9. The most famous example is the Japanese planning wargame for the battle of Midway, in which close to real-life results were obtained, but invalidated by the umpire, who insisted upon giving the Japanese player an unwarranted victory, thus encouraging the very defeat foreseen in the wargame.

10. From a lecture at Georgetown University in February of 1981.

11. Ibid.

12. Maxim 8, *Napoleon and Modern War*.

13. Quote from Vincent Esposito and John Elting, *A Military History and Atlas of the Napoleonic Wars* (New York 1964), the Leipzig Campaign.

14. Eventually published in Basil Liddell Hart, *Science of Infantry Tactics* (London 1921).

15. Vincent Esposito, *The West Point Atlas of American Wars* (New York 1959) and with John Elting, *A Military History and Atlas of the Napoleonic Wars* (New York 1964).

Stephen P. Glick
is currently a military analyst with the
American Israel Public Affairs Committee
in Washington, DC. He has written widely
on military topics and is presently working
on a monograph concerning possible Israeli
provision of Medical Care for an American
Rapid Deployment Force in the Middle
East.

L. Ian Charters
is a writer and analyst in the field of
military and strategic studies, based in
Washington, DC.

Dennis E. Showalter

Army and Society in Imperial Germany: The Pains of Modernization

Current images of the Imperial German army depend heavily on a mixture of Eckart Kehr and Karl Marx. Concentration on the primacy of domestic politics combines with emphasis on the class struggle to produce interpretations of an institution committed to traditional militarism, yet striving to maintain and enhance its position in a transitional society. Such accounts often seem to assume that every German officer from the Chief of Staff to the newest lieutenant had as his first thought on arising: what can I personally do today to fix the yoke of decaying Junker feudalism on the necks of the emerging proletariat?[1] More prosaically, they describe an army concentrating on preserving social and political privileges at the cost of operational efficiency, failing to keep pace with technical progress, concentrating instead on plans to suppress internal dissent by force.[2]

This position is so general that any reinterpretation must meet and refute the charge of seeking cleverness at the expense of accuracy. Yet recent research also, albeit indirectly, encourages evaluating the German army of the Second Empire as an instrument not of reaction, but of modernization. The process can best begin with the work of Michael Geyer. He argues convincingly that the Reichswehr sought to remedy what it regarded as the flaws of the pre-1914 military establishment, in particular to make the army an integral part of society, to prepare in peacetime the human and economic conditions for victory in modern total war.[3]

To Geyer only the shock of defeat propelled the German military into the twentieth century. He presents the First World War as a watershed. Yet the German army's performance in that war suggests that openness to new ideas was more than just a reaction to disaster. Evaluations by non-German sources of the German army's fighting power in that war are uniformly high. The nature of that praise is also significant. Words like 'flexibility',

Journal of Contemporary History (SAGE, London, Beverly Hills and New Delhi), Vol. 18 (1983), 583–618

'adaptability' and 'initiative' dot the pages. Commanders are presented as willing to listen to subordinates and learn from experience. Officer-man relationships are favourably compared with British, French, even American counterparts. Even in its domestic policies the High Command proves surprisingly flexible, preferring compromise and negotiation to brute force.[4]

A certain degree of continuity, in short, exists between the attitudes of the first world war and the policies of the 1920s. And this in turn suggests the logic of extending this search for continuity one more step backwards, into the pre-1914 era. Modernization, particularly in its German context, is generally presented in terms of traumatic upheavals and painful shifts, of dramatic, visible breaks with past traditions, attitudes, and behaviour generating corresponding resistance and hostility. Yet in practice, modernization can also occur when institutions and values are restructured to meet new needs. This is more than uneasy compromising with what cannot be helped. Traditional organizations can be extremely flexible — and this includes armies, whose primary declared mission of implementing state policy by force involves a corresponding need to keep up with the military Joneses. As they commit to innovation, such organizations can provide the coherence necessary for quick, successful change in their societies at large. The Japanese factory system, for example, has been described as a translation of feudal patterns of rewards, leadership, and loyalties into the terms of modern industry. On a smaller scale, a social history of the Bon Marché department store presents a process of identifying family relationships and a sense of community with the functioning of an impersonal, bureaucratic institution.[5]

In this context the German army was peculiarly, perhaps uniquely, well-adapted to serve as an instrument of modernization. Since the Era of Reform the Prussian army and its liberal critics had accepted similar logic about the relationships between a strong army and a healthy society — albeit from strikingly different premises.[6] And it was this army whose size and reputation set the standard for the Empire's other contingents. For all the sound and fury about William II's navy as the symbol of the new Germany, moreover, the army exercised a direct influence over a far broader spectrum of society. Politicians might debate the cost of battleships. Intellectuals might exchange polemics on the nature of *Weltpolitik*. But every German male of twenty faced his own personal rendezvous with the state in the form of a conscription notice. For the overwhelming majority of them, that meant at least the possibility of two or three years in an army barracks.

Any study of the German army as an instrument of modernization must begin by considering its primary institutional function: preparation for war. Recent analyses present a military anachronism dominated by an establishment unwilling to risk losing its special place by opening its eyes. Twentieth-century war demanded the radicalization of an institution committed to sustaining itself as part of a traditional, autocratic state structure. Faced with this choice, the German army preferred to place its strategic faith in a short, decisive war based on the gambler's gambit of the Schlieffen plan. Its approaches to tactics were similarly retrogressive. Taking counsel from neither the lessons of contemporary wars nor the comments of foreign critics, the German army emphasized formal discipline and parade-ground drill, denied the effects of firepower, and ultimately drove massed formations of human cattle into the slaughter-pits of 1914.

A comprehensive critique of this evaluation is beyond the scope of this essay. It is therefore appropriate to consider its strongest specific point: the evolution of infantry assault doctrine between 1871 and 1914. The nature of the first world war was ultimately shaped not by strategy, not by logistics, not even by technology, but by tactics. Specifically, the armies of Europe went to war convinced that good infantry could capture and consolidate enemy positions, not necessarily as a matter of course, but with something approaching regularity. If this could be done, then entire offensives could make the kind of progress that rendered 'breakthrough' and 'exploitation' meaningful concepts.[7] Was this a reasoned conviction in Germany? Did bemedalled aristocrats and pseudo-aristocrats offer hecatombs of trusting civilians in uniform on the altar of caste pride? Moreover, and more significant for an essay on modernization, prior to 1914 the infantry *was* the German army. Over two-thirds of the men on active duty at any time were assigned to its ranks. Its training and the principles behind that training were likely to have the most general social effect of any of the military establishment's specific internal procedures.

This essay begins by presenting the development and implementation of the German army's doctrines of attack. It moves from the lesser to the greater world by exploring the effect of these doctrines on the army's personnel policies. It argues that these policies represented not merely a means of social stabilization, but a coherent response to the greatest single challenge of modern war: its demands on the individual soldier. And finally, it suggests that the military modernization of the German army facilitated its role as an instrument of social integration for an empire by no means as ramshackle as its critics have asserted.

The difficulties accompanying the tactical offensive were recognized and accepted in Germany long before the first rounds were fired from the guns of August. Even in the 1850s Helmuth von Moltke had argued that the best way of meeting the challenge of modern weapons on the battlefield was to force the enemy to assume the offensive, then counterattack once his charge was broken.[8] It was a pattern which proved exceptionally successful for the Prussian army in 1866, and whose utility had little to do with whether the national strategy was offensive or defensive. It had only one flaw. No army, however confident in its generals' abilities, could afford to base its doctrines on the assumption that its enemies would be obliging enough to dash themselves to pieces on one's own rifles, artillery, and machine-guns. Sometime, somehow, it would be necessary to go forward — to go through.

Since the seventeenth century, a concept of battle had been developing in Europe and Germany — a concept too often submerged under vitalist rhetoric about battles of annihilation and the mystique of cold steel. Simply expressed, the aim of combat was to destroy the enemy's army at the lowest cost to one's own. The deficiencies of drawing up masses or lines of men to mow each other down had been plain since the days of Gustavus Adolphus. Even at its most effective the process resembled a duel at ten paces with submachine guns. Victory was meaningless if its price became too high; even Napoleon's conscripts were not an infinitely self-renewing force.

Instead of killing an enemy in place, the essential craft of war involved convincing him to run and *then* killing him. To achieve this, it was necessary to concentrate superior force at one point. 'Force' in this context meant in the German army a combination of firepower, physical presence and moral superiority. Experience indicated that all three were required. Specifically, during the Napoleonic Wars the fire fight had become an essential element of battle, no longer a mere preliminary. By itself, however, fire action was not decisive. Infantry skirmishers could wear down an enemy. They were as a rule unable to do more for a very human reason. Once an advance stopped and men spread out to fire their weapons, it was difficult, if not impossible, to get them moving again. This was particularly true of the half-trained conscripts who filled the ranks of the Prussian army during the Wars of Liberation.

Yet move they would have to. A line of skirmishers, improvising cover and taking their own ranges, blazing away at well-armed defenders increasingly likely to be concealed behind improvised fieldworks, was an open invitation to attrition on the wrong side of the balance sheet — and to the drawn-out murderous, indecisive battles increasingly characteristic of the Napoleonic Era or the American Civil War. The problem was exacerbated as improved weapons made such manoeuvres as the cavalry charge, or the concentration of masses of guns to blow apart an enemy's front at close range, less and less feasible alternatives to the forward movement of the infantryman.[9] Contrary to their historical image, the generals of Imperial Germany were not bloodthirsty savages. Apart from purely professional questions, they perceived that the best way for them to maintain and enhance their class position was to win any future war decisively, while spilling as little German blood as necessary. The best way to do this was to produce infantrymen able and willing to advance on the modern battlefield.

The nineteenth century was an age of applied science, and the German army entered this era on a broad front from ballistics to horse-breeding. Specifically, it began turning to the study of military history as something more than a series of war stories. Twentieth-century scholars are quick to condemn the ten-dentiousness of works which allegedly mined the past for arguments to support existing doctrines. Yet particularly in analysing the course of battles at company and battalion level, the historians of the General Staff and such mavericks as Hermann Kunz and Fritz Hoenig established patterns of research which remain useful a century later. In the process they provided support for the argument that successful infantry attacks remained possible.[10]

These military scholars presented coherent and convincing arguments against being excessively influenced by set-pieces, particularly those drawn from the earlier battles of the Franco-Prussian War. Images of thousands of men crammed into the ravine at Gravelotte, of the Prussian Guard marching to destruction on the slopes of St. Privat, were warnings — but not more than that. Troops poorly commanded or improperly committed could get out of hand under any circumstances. An unsupported attack against unsuppressed defensive fire could be smashed by bows and arrows. One Prussian division went into action at Gravelotte in closed columns, bands blithely playing. The Guard had taken similar mass formations into the killing zone of French rifles, and seen them shot to pieces.[11]

Less than three months later, however, some of these same guardsmen were ordered to attack the fortified village of Le Bourget, part of the defence system of Paris. Supported by thirty guns, nine battalions of the 2nd Guard Division crossed the open ground in front of the village. But this time they took pains to offer a small target. Long skirmish lines went forward in sections, covering each other by rapid fire. The Prussian cannon helped keep French heads down until the guardsmen were close enough to storm Le Bourget from three sides. Of the six thousand infantrymen who went into the fight, four hundred and thirty-three were killed or wounded — a loss rate of just over seven per cent. On 18 August thirty per cent of the corps had fallen at St. Privat.[12]

Le Bourget was considered a useful model for several reasons. It had not involved an exceptional amount of artillery support — indeed, more guns were available than were used. Nor had the French garrison panicked and run. Instead they had fought it out from house to house even though surrounded. On another level the Guard tended to be the cynosure of the Prussian/German army. Its proximity to Berlin made it, both before and after 1871, a logical test bed for proposed innovations in tactics or armament. More to the point, the Guard was resented as well as admired by the lesser beings of the line. It did not have the mystique attached to such twentieth-century élites as paratroopers or commandos. No officer was likely to concede, at least in public, that the Prussian Guard could do something his regiment, battalion, or company could not.

Le Bourget, moreover, was by no means an exception. Operational analyses of the Franco-Prussian War were influenced both by wishful thinking and a certain amount of *post hoc, ergo propter hoc* reasoning. Nevertheless as German formations gained experience on the breechloading battlefield, an increasing number of regimental and battalion-level actions suggested that infantry attacks remained possible even under modern conditions. They posed a comprehensive challenge to all levels from commanding general to rear-rank private. They required preparation: coordinating troop movements and artillery support, timing attacks precisely, providing adequate reserves. But above all, a successful attack demanded striking an exact balance between dispersion and control in order to maintain momentum.

No-one in Germany between 1871 and 1914 seriously challenged the argument that soldiers were less vulnerable to bullet or shell when they were lying down and far apart. The problem was that men so disposed could achieve nothing except perhaps to pick off a few of the enemy before they were shot themselves. On the other hand tactical theorists like Jacob Meckel, whose *Summer Night's Dream* argued for the necessity of mass formations able to provide moral support for weaker vessels and carry positions by sheer weight, were an isolated minority. 'Winter Day's Reality' involved sober recognition of the fact that even a too-strong skirmish line was nothing more than a target.[13] And the steadily-improving range and killing power of modern weapons made maintaining the momentum of an advance once begun even more urgent. To remain passive invited destruction; to retreat invited massacre. Experience in 1866 and 1870/71 had only reinforced the truism that the heaviest casualties were suffered when an attack stalled, then broke under the fire of a triumphant enemy.

The problem was compounded for German tactical theorists by the increasingly influential concept of biologically-determined national characteristics. Across the Rhine writers stressed the Frenchman's natural élan, his genetic fitness for the bayonet charge. Republican mythologists supplemented this by insisting that the spirit of the nation in arms was enough to overcome material obstacles. If nothing else, it made soldiers more willing to die for *la patrie*. German observers were not so optimistic. The Teuton, they argued, was more phlegmatic than his southern neighbours, and at the same time more reflective than the Slavic peoples. He was difficult to exalt; he was equally difficult to drive forward. The German was at his best holding ground; given the slightest encouragement to entrench or seek cover, he would do so, and the spirit of the offensive be damned. When the German was brought to emotional heights, his response was likely to be a berserker's fury taking him beyond any control. Instead of resorting to his bayonet he turned to the German's instinctive weapon, the club, and lashed about him in all directions with his rifle butt.[14]

Twentieth-century observers, conditioned to dismiss such military genetics as pernicious nonsense, tend to overlook the fact that these biological theories were at the cutting edge of the nineteenth-century's intellectual life.[15] Accepting and acting on them involved a commitment to the up-to-date, an abandonment of the seemingly-discredited eighteenth-century notion that all men were identically suitable raw material for the drill sergeant. These generalizations, moreover, tended to provide a 'scientific' matrix for demonstrable facts. German troops from all contingents had shown that they knew well enough how to seek cover under fire. They knew even better how to bunch together and be shot down. What they needed to be taught was how to keep moving. It was beyond question that many of them would be killed or maimed in the process — but their sacrifices would at least serve a purpose.

Armies, like other institutions, seek to handle problems in detail rather than as a whole. Certainly Germany produced no influential theorists who stepped back from the issue of advancing against modern weapons on a modern battlefield, who sought to develop alternate patterns, entirely new ways of thinking about the subject. But on the other hand, technical developments between 1871 and 1914 were also incremental. There were no seminal innovations to match the breech-loading small arm or the rifled cannon. Weapons improved by degrees, and invited a correspondingly limited effort to solve the problems they posed — which in turn were often highly ambiguous. The magazine rifle, for example, might be hyperbolically described as being to the single-shot rifle what the single-shot was to the muzzle-loader. In fact, the range, accuracy, and rate of fire of the magazine rifle were on a continuum with the needle gun or the *chassepôt*. The weapons were essentially similar, in ways a breech-loading rifle and a muzzle-loading musket were not. They posed essentially similar challenges and opportunities. The magazine rifle, above all, was still a one-man weapon. Its efficiency ultimately depended on the nerve and skill of its user. If he were shaken, confused, or incompetent, it did not matter how many rounds per minute he could fire. None would do any damage except by accident.[16]

An even better illustration of the incremental nature of military technology after 1871 is the machine-gun. The German army was well aware of its potential. As early as 1874, military journals were speaking of the *mitrailleuse* or Gatling type of gun as a useful weapon, particularly for defensive operations in woods, villages, or redoubts — anywhere its relative bulk could be concealed. The introduction of the automatic machine-gun generated even more interest. Its utility in defence was never doubted, despite periodic questions about mechanical reliability and ammunition supply. One of them was worth at least fifty riflemen — perhaps more, since a machine-gun was 'nerveless'. But defence was not the German army's overriding concern. It might be useful to have a quick-firing addition to the rifles and the cannon. The cavalry in particular was interested in the machine-gun to supplement its relatively weak dismounted fire-power. But the overriding question was what other sacrifices should be made to introduce on a large scale a weapon reinforcing what was already generally recognized as quite the strongest tactical form of warfare. Especially as successive navy bills ate into the defence budget, the German army initially saw no more need to equip itself comprehensively with machine-guns than a man wearing a belt normally feels to don suspenders as well.[17]

Institutionally, the army's concern was with developing machine-guns as an offensive weapon. Here, too, legitimate questions of size and vulnerability were repeatedly raised. If an individual rifleman was dangerously exposed on the modern battlefield, what was the likely fate of a machine-gun crew? And even on a tripod or sled mount, how could a weapon weighing more than a hundred pounds be moved under fire? Both questions were to be answered by experience in the twentieth century as the water-cooled machine-gun became increasingly obsolescent. What nevertheless caught the German army's eye was the machine-gun's potential for supporting an attack. After the turn of the century, an increasing number of voices suggested that this 'concentrated essence of infantry' be massed at divisional or regimental levels, a reserve of fire-power at the disposal of higher commanders, either to enable riflemen to be concentrated for an attack or to support that attack by concentrating fire on selected positions. Some descriptions of how this manoeuvre should be executed read like a revival of Napoleonic techniques, using machine-guns on wheeled carriages as the Emperor used cannon. But others stressed the value of the extremely accurate Maxim-model guns in providing support for an attack once the artillery had to cease fire for fear of destroying its own men. Given suitable enfilade positions, machine-guns could play on an objective until the very moment an assault was pushed home. And still other military futurologists foreshadowed use of machine-guns for offensive barrages in the way best developed by the British army in 1917/1918: firing indirectly on ranged lines, borrowing techniques of observation and control from the artillery.[18]

Another clear indication of the German army's appreciation of the potential of massed small-calibre fire-power is its organization from the beginning of machine-guns in company strength. This process also favoured indirectly the development of machine-gun doctrine. A captain exercising an independent command, responsible only to his regiment's colonel, was more likely to influence tactics than the junior lieutenant in charge of a two-gun section in a French or British battalion.[19]

Machines, however, were not enough to make attacks under modern conditions possible. In this context it is necessary to pay some attention to the often-derided 'spirit of the bayonet'. What it meant in Imperial Germany was a corporate will to force an adversary off his ground by closing with him. This was, and is, by no means a retrograde concept. In V.G. Kiernan's words, facing 'stabbing weapons' seems to require 'bravery of a special kind, different from that of the soldier exposed to missiles; however deadly . . . the psychology — or physiology — of such reactions deserves more study'.[20] But for every fire-eating essayist arguing for 'lively' instruction on the use of the bayonet, there were a dozen dry cynics arguing that bayonet drill was essentially a means to an end, an elaborate form of gymnastics designed to increase the soldier's self-confidence. 'Fixing bayonets' was a gesture — important, to be sure, but still a gesture. There was no need to perform it as soon as a formation came under fire. And the bayonet itself should be slight and short, perhaps able to perform other, homelier functions as well.[21]

The German army emphatically rejected any argument that a successful modern attack could be a product of *élan vital* alone. The attack was a science, requiring scientific preparation. Periodic arguments were made in favour of lightening the infantryman's load, of giving him laced boots and puttees in place of the familiar shaft boots, of making his uniform looser, more comfortable, and less visible. When field grey was finally introduced, no voices were raised to argue that 'the blue tunic is Germany'. Organizationally, the German army was reluctant to form specialized élite formations. Within the battalion, the practices of ranking men by height for the sake of appearance, or putting the ablest soldiers in the third rank as skirmishers, gave way to a policy of distributing the skillful, the clever, and the aggressive throughout an organization, using them as a leaven for the rest.[22]

Such housekeeping measures, however, were futile without corresponding improvements in tactical doctrine. Above all this meant absorbing, systematizing, and institutionalizing the battlefield lessons of 1866 and 1870/71. Experiment and improvisation in open-order tactics had historically been fostered by a general, if unsystematic, belief that skirmishing was somehow more 'natural' than other forms of combat, that its demands could not be codified without introducing a fatal degree of artificiality. But civilized men, in the words of one critic, had goals in war as well as peace. And they could work towards these goals as cooperating individuals. Open-order tactics were not the caperings of an armed mob.[23] Particularly since experience on both sides of the Atlantic indicated that deployed lines of skirmishers were the only viable attack formation, the German army needed to adapt to the new way of warfare, and to the extraordinary demands it would make on the ordinary soldier.

The industrial revolution, with its unique challenges to human flexibility, offered grounds for optimism. If the sons of men conditioned for generations to the plough or the artisan's bench could be socialized by the hundreds of thousands into mills and factories, then surely civilians could be taught in two or three years how to use terrain, estimate ranges and respond to orders even on the empty modern battlefield. Images of the nineteenth-century industrial worker frequently suggest or imply that factory routine itself dulled the mind. The reverse was far more likely to be the case. Participation in a modern industrial plant demanded degrees of alertness and cooperation that were mentally and physically exhausting. The miner, the mill-hand, the iron-worker, could rarely afford the luxury of detaching his mind from what his hands did, or from what his workmates were doing.[24] And what civilian employers and foremen could do, the German army saw itself as being able to do even better.

For forty years after the Peace of Frankfurt, German theorists addressed themselves to the problem of bringing the largest possible number of men as close as possible to their enemies with the lowest possible casualties. They worked at two levels. One involved improving the individual skills of the ordinary soldier. Gymnastics, historically an important part of infantry training in Prussia, was supplemented by field sports in an effort to improve agility and teamwork — despite some incongruous criticism of football as too dangerous, costing too much training time. Since men would seek cover under fire no matter what, they should be taught to seek positions from which they could fire and move. No wise officer confused instruction in using terrain properly with a lack of aggressiveness.

Allowances of practice ammunition were steadily increased — and here, too, for a purpose anticipating the fire tactics of a century later. German doctrine favoured using the magazine rifle much in the fashion of a modern assault rifle. Individual aimed shots were less important than concentrated, controlled bursts at the right time. This was not merely a manifestation of scepticism at the prospect of turning the average German conscript into a Daniel Boone. Field tests, even under artificial peacetime conditions, demonstrated time after time that an exaggerated emphasis on individual marksmanship, the approach fostered by Imperial awards to the army's best shots, was less important than volume of fire, with the first round placed somewhere near the target.[25]

A series of instructions, many of them tested and refined on the manoeuvre grounds of Potsdam by, the often-derided Prussian Guard, culminated in the revised Infantry Drill Regulations of 1888. This document, despite numerous significant weaknesses, established the rifle as the principal weapon of the modern infantryman, and open order as his principal formation. He was expected to combine fire and movement, advancing steadily from fire position to fire position towards his assigned objective. Columns, close formations of any kind, were described as useful only to support and reinforce the skirmish line, or to hold troops in hand until they were needed.[26]

Nor was the infantry expected to advance alone. German artillery steadily evolved after 1871 as an instrument for preparing and supporting attacks. Its gunners might debate the relative merits of neutralizing the enemy's fire and seeking to destroy his positions. They tended, however, to agree on practical points: the worth of heavy guns for field operations; the value of deluging an enemy's position with concentrations of shell and shrapnel; the advantage of being able to shoot *over* the hill, searching out covered positions and reserves. As early as 1872, isolated voices advocated adding a 12-centimeter field howitzer to the artillery's inventory. An increasing number of artillerymen criticized even the 10-centimeter howitzer adopted at the turn of the century as too light to be effective against modern positions. As for those dashing advocates of galloping into position in the open to support attacks directly, they were frequently reminded that dead gunners could support nothing. Successive artillery regulations stressed the utility of concealed positions and indirect fire — scientific gunnery as opposed to Napoleonic heroics.[27]

The Germans, in short, considered the problem of attacking on the modern battlefield in coordinated fashion. This does not mean they prefigured twentieth-century combined-arms tactics. Communications technology was too primitive to permit any but the most general co-operation between infantry and artillery. Even in 1870/71, messengers became casualties or simply got lost — and the despatches they carried, written in the heat of battle on anything from wrapping-paper to visiting-cards, often lacked such vital information as place, time, and signature. It therefore remained difficult in practice to concentrate fire in support of an attack without concentrating men as well — which in another context had become the army's principal training problem.

Regulations and periodicals might stress the importance of dispersion, the utility of initiative and flexibility. In the field, exercise after exercise indicated that a formation deployed in open order tended almost immediately to slip out of the control of its leaders. Even against blank ammunition men became lost, or huddled in heedless groups, or ran eagerly forward in columns or flocks, with no more ultimate effect than a handful of peas thrown at a window. Neither bugles, whistles, nor shouted commands were enough to keep the rank and file responsive. The platoon, company, or battalion held in close formation to the rear too often became the only troops a commander could use to influence a mock battle. And this was under the inevitably artificial conditions of peacetime, with establishments little more than half what they would be in war. What would be the result when thousands of mobilized civilians were involved?

In the face of constant exhortation to train their men to move in deployed lines and advance by rushes in controlled small groups, officers continued to encourage their men to mass by failing to discourage them. What began as skirmish lines commonly ended as assault lines, running forward shoulder to shoulder, led by sword-waving lieutenants. As combat experience diminished with the retirement or promotion of 1870's veterans, it was increasingly difficult to convince freshly-commissioned subalterns of the risks incurred by any sort of upright movement on the modern battlefield — particularly when the alternative to heroic theatrics was far too often an embarrassed confession to higher authority that one was not quite sure where one's platoon or company had gotten to, Sir.[28]

Almost every full manoeuvre offered at least one major illustration of the aphorism that numbers serve only to perplex and embarrass, especially in open order. Yet at the same time, the rapidly-increasing projected size of future field armies meant that the breakthrough battle, the direct advance on enemy positions, acquired corresponding importance. The German army's experiences in 1866 and 1870/71 had shown the vital importance of coordinated frontal and flanking attacks. But if armies still were, in the words of Confederate General James Longstreet, 'as sensitive about the flanks as a virgin', the truism was meaningless if the enemy for practical purposes had no flanks.[29]

Nor was Germany's strategic position congenial to a detached rethinking of tactical doctrine. Whatever the diplomatic weaknesses of the Franco-Russian alliance of 1894, no German general could accept it as anything but the kind of threat obviating the possibility of sacrificing the initiative on any level. No matter how the war began, the German army would have to end it — and ultimately that meant advancing.

In war, as in so many other human endeavours, the necessary tends to become the possible. But in fact, nothing in South Africa, Manchuria, or the Balkans indicated that infantrymen could no longer attack successfully under modern fire-power. Inadequate preparation, clumsy formations, and one-sided reliance on enthusiasm brought defeat to British and Japanese, Bulgars, Serbs, and Greeks, indiscriminately. The Boers demonstrated everything Germans had been saying for decades about the value of initiative and the necessity to take account of terrain. But their experiences illustrated even more clearly the problems of controlling an attack, of maintaining its momentum once begun. Perseverance under heavy fire was not a Boer strong point. As for the Japanese, they spent thousands of lives rediscovering lessons the Germans had been taught in 1870. By the end of their war they too had learned the value of advancing in small groups, each under its own leader, in open, flexible formations offering small targets for a limited time. [30]

No-one argued after 1905 that the process of advancing was easy — only that it was still feasible under the right conditions. To an increasing extent these conditions were seen as psychological. German analysts emphasized the morale engendered in a Japan where mothers committed suicide if their sons were found unfit for service, where wives celebrated their husbands' funerals before seeing them off to war. This wisdom, however, was another dead end except in patrioteering rhetoric. The revised German drill regulations of 1906 recommended in paragraph after paragraph the need to develop 'inner assertiveness' and a need to reach an objective before one's neighbours, to charge to the music of bugles and shouts of 'hurrah!'. But Germans were not and could not be made into Japanese — nor, indeed, were Japanese bullet-proof. [31] The Boer War, the Russo-Japanese War, and the two Balkan Wars suggested that the real key to a modern attack was not the spade, the hand-grenade, the cover of darkness, or even fighting spirit, but rather articulation. Concentrating on the individual soldier's morale and training had been a step in the right direction. What was necessary now was to integrate him into a combat team small enough to survive on the battlefield, yet large enough to be tactically effective — if not by itself, then through cooperation with similar groups. [32]

Hindsight makes this point far more obvious than it appeared either to theorists concentrating on the morale and the military skills of the individual, or to practical soldiers conditioned to regard a company, or perhaps just a platoon, as the smallest feasible tactical unit. But the process involved far more than simply making sections or squads combat units as well as administrative formations. It involved more than giving sergeants and corporals increased paper authority. In this context, far from being stagnant or retrograde, the German army recognized more clearly than most of its critics the single most difficult problem of modern warfare: getting soldiers not only to advance under fire, but to accomplish something by advancing. It was fortunate in not facing the distractions of colonial or frontier warfare, where morale and mystique could acquire disproportionate importance. German planners knew their enemies would be from the world's first team: highly skilled and highly motivated. Against such opponents, doctrinal subtleties and tactical gimmicks were likely to be of at best marginal value.

The craft of war in the twentieth century, at least as practised in the western world, has increasingly been devoted to sidestepping this problem by substituting the internal-combustion engine for men's legs. Tanks, personnel carriers, or helicopters, all have the same purpose: to bring soldiers into contact with the enemy without overstraining either physical or moral possibilities. Yet without human will and human skill, the machines remain useless. It was not romanticism, but hard, practical considerations that led the Kaiser's army to concentrate on human relationships: to seek the creation of a disciplined, consciously committed military community.

The Prussian/German army's approach to its conscript rank and file is generally presented in terms of a coherent attempt to socialize them into the existing order: to generate enthusiastic acceptance of the values of capitalism and Christianity, to inspire support for monarchs and aristocrats and contempt for businessmen and politicians. It is not necessary to challenge this interpretation in order to suggest an extra dimension to the patterns of socializing recruits. Between 1871 and 1914 it seemed increasingly apparent to the military that the virtues of the modern soldier were so intertwined with those of the citizen that it was impossible to separate them, or to tell where one set began and the other ended. But the army's basic task was to emphasize their military aspects. Discipline imposed from above was not enough to enable men to function on a modern battlefield. They needed instead what F. Scott Fitzgerald was to describe as a 'whole-souled sentimental equipment' — an equipment easier to describe than to develop in the context of an increasingly-sceptical age. Whether the modern infantryman was seen as pressing confidently through the smoke of battle even when separated from his comrades, or closing in on the regimental colours as men fell in windrows about him, he was seen as requiring conscious motivation.

A more practical reason for accepting this concept involved the German army's command structure. A rifle company at full war strength had a maximum of five officers for over 250 enlisted men. A single lieutenant was expected to control a platoon of eighty rank and file. This was a legacy from the Napoleonic era, of little significance in an era of mass formations, but extremely important on a skirmish line. Under anything approximating post-1871 combat conditions, no officer could hope to lead that many men personally and directly. And a hero's death was pointless unless it brought results. Even in the Franco-Prussian War, King William had enjoined his officers against risking their lives merely to inspire the troops. Increasing the ratio of officers to men was hardly likely to interest an army already reluctant to grant commissions to social undesirables and political unreliables. Like it or not, the company officer of the German empire had to be able to trust his men. He had to depend on their intelligence and goodwill in a way unknown to his Frederician or Napoleonic predecessors.

One way of ensuring this was by pre-induction screening. The army's well-documented failure to keep pace with Imperial Germany's population growth meant that a universal military obligation did not bring universal military service. Those men deemed politically, physically, or psychologically unsuitable could be shuffled into the reserve. If British regiments had to take what the recruiting sergeants sent, if the French manpower shortage was so acute that by 1914 men barely able to march were being assigned to regimental service companies, the German army could count on suitable human material as defined by the army itself.[33]

Warm bodies, however, were only the beginning. To train the modern German soldier also required a significant evolution in the army's concept of obedience. The often-criticized *Kadavergehorsamkeit* of barracks and drill-field was a means to an end. It was not purely a structure for limiting human rights, or creating obedient citizens uninterested in demanding social changes. Formal discipline was rather the first step in maintaining control on the battlefield — in making patriotism and enthusiasm into military rather than martial virtues. The killing-zones and killing-power of modern weapons made rapid movement and rapid decision essential. There would be no time for debate or reflection. Men had to be conditioned to respond promptly under extreme stress: stress, moreover, with no civilian equivalent. This was the ultimate purpose of the German army's particularly rigorous close-order drill. A conscript, citizen army after a long period of peace would have no combat veterans able to inculcate the utility of conditioned response by osmosis. The process must therefore be theoretical, despite its constant abuse by officers afflicted by a fondness for precision drill as a military absolute, despite the certainty of criticism by civilians and enlisted men who saw the whole process as anachronistic.

Emphasis on conditioned obedience was also designed to help soldiers cope with the emptiness of the modern battlefield. Theory and experience alike indicated that even the bravest of men could be shocked into incoherence by modern fire-power. Even the most willing could become lost or confused, dropping behind cover, straggling to the rear, or appearing on the objective after the fighting was over. Casualties and confusion, moreover, could play havoc with command structures. No modern soldier could count on remaining part of a familiar group, or receiving orders from a familiar leader. He must learn to respond to ranks, not men — to accept as a rule of thumb that his superior was better fitted to cope with a military situation because he was a better soldier.

This concept is easily — and cheaply — challenged by offering case studies of incompetence. The German army was clearly not prepared to defend as an abstract truth the assertion that rank determined ability — all the more so since its archives and its gossip-structure alike were replete with accounts of junior leaders who had saved situations over the protests of inefficient or disoriented superiors. But no better reasonable, pragmatic solution to the tactical demands of modern war at company and platoon levels had, or has yet, been developed. Indeed, the broader cross-section of men in the ranks and the social expansion of the officer corps made such conditioning imperative. An army recruited from social outcasts, or even peasants and labourers, and commanded by men conditioned from birth to exercise authority, had no real problem with deference. An army which conscripted the intelligent and articulate must be prepared to cope with their inevitable challenges. And that could not be done by discipline alone. Discipline at best secured submission. The lessons of 1866 and 1870/71 suggested that only conscious commitment to a collective brought favourable results in modern war.[34]

The military system's negative sanctions posed a real threat to this perspective. Here the scholar encounters a paradox. On the one hand the Empire's records are replete with horror stories indicating tolerance, indeed acceptance, of harsh treatment escalating into obscene brutality. On the other hand, most of those same records were generated by the army's efforts to solve the problem of mistreatment of enlisted men.

The issue was a natural focus for interest-group conflict. The army's claim to be a training-school of the citizen made it correspondingly sensitive to charges of failure in that respect. For socialists in particular, tales of brutality illustrated the essential corruption of the militarist system. In an open society increasingly interested in scandal and exposé, human-interest anecdotes of suffering while in uniform sold books and papers. The army for its part tended to respond to such accusations with a mixture of flat denial and unctuous boys-will-be-boys declarations that a barracks was not a young ladies' seminary — not an approach calculated to enhance credibility. Official denials, however, were matched by orders urging fair treatment of recruits, by investigations producing a high rate of court-martials and convictions, and above all by a process of administrative discipline intended to separate flagrant offenders from the service quietly but permanently. The war ministries of Germany sought to engage the loyalty and inspire the enthusiasm of their soldiers — not break their bodies and spirits. Indeed, officers and non-commissioned officers of the imperial army were not infrequently reminded even in their professional literature that men brutalized on the drill-field could hardly be expected to follow their tormentors in battle.[35]

Despite this apparent institutional commitment to abolishing brutality, it remained a persistent thorn in the army's side. One explanation is to dismiss the orders and exhortations as mere window-dressing. A somewhat more fruitful approach involves examining the army's ambiguous structural position in Imperial Germany. On the one hand it assumed the role of a primary social institution, demanding ultimate loyalty from and control over its personnel while on active duty — a state within a state long before Hans von Seecht. But the army was also a secondary institution in that its basic justifying function was instrumental. It existed not merely to guarantee the welfare of its subjects, but to do something. In secondary institutions — armies, hospitals, even universities — abstract claims of justice tend to be balanced against a pragmatic need for results. The ultimate question becomes not 'What is right?' but 'What is required to complete most efficiently the task for which we are here?'

The imperial army's link between its two worlds was its non-commissioned officer corps. And evidence suggests that an ongoing, successful attempt to modernize that body generated the unwelcome side-effect of virtually institutionalizing physical and emotional abuse of the rank and file.

Since well before 1871 the armies of Germany had suffered from a shortage of non-commissioned officers. The traditional sources of these men, the peasant and artisan classes, were steadily declining relative to the size of the various conscript contingents. In a generally expanding economy, the careers open to talent were numerous and attractive enough to discourage many a bright young man from spending his life in uniform. Those who stayed were often enough unwilling to face civilian life: the stupid, the lazy, the alcoholic, the vicious. Neither pay nor fringe benefits could be improved steadily enough to ensure an ability to compete in purely economic terms with private employers. The officer corps was unwilling to open its ranks to enlisted men whatever the grade. The problem lay, therefore, in finding men who would neither become objects of scorn as incompetent misfits like their French counterparts, nor exercise authority by consensus like the NCOs of the Russian peasant army. Recruitment, moreover, was only half the problem. Experience in 1866 and 1870/71 indicated that rejuvenation was also necessary. Men in their late thirties or early forties were regarded as less suited to the enhanced demands of modern war than their younger colleagues. Even field training could be a challenge to a man with the beginnings of rheumatism, arthritis, or a beer paunch.[36]

The German army solved both problems through the *Zivilversorgungsschein*. Often presented as a means of permeating civil society with military values, it was also a means of first attracting, then removing non-commissioned officers. Instead of expecting to spend his life in uniform, the typical NCO looked forward to completing twelve years of service, then moving on to a post in the state or local civil service. The army was for him a stepping-stone.[37] What was important was keeping one's stripes and earning the good opinion of one's superiors long enough to move into the second career that would absorb twenty-five or thirty productive years. And that was not an easy process.

A non-commissioned officer in the imperial army was judged by results. If his squads drilled poorly, if the rooms in his charge were untidy, if his recruits appeared improperly uniformed, he could be refused the right to complete the years of service necessary to apply for the *Zivilversorgungsschein*. Or his efficiency reports could be so poor that his chance of receiving decent employment on discharge were minimal. Junior non-commissioned officers almost inevitably received the least likely recruits. A man whose competence was questionable would be assigned an awkward squad of the clumsy or the incorrigible as a test. It was hardly surprising that they tended to transfer their sense of pressure to the men they trained.

The process was further complicated by the fact that regulations forbade a non-commissioned officer to punish a soldier on his own responsibility. That was the duty of an officer. In theory, the system was designed to limit abuses of power. But to report a soldier meant establishing a record in the company punishment book. In an army based on the premise that its rank and file served willingly, a captain who ordered too many extra drills or three-day arrests ran the risk of blotting his own copybook with his superiors. Correspondingly a corporal who played strictly by the book, reporting minor performance failures and breaches of discipline to his superiors as prescribed by regulations, was likely to be encouraged to settle his own problems. Should he be unable to do so he might be recommended for an alternate career behind a plough, or on the wrong end of a shovel. [38]

The NCO of the Imperial German army emerges as a peculiarly modern figure, comparable in many respects to the growing class of white-collar workers and similar *Angestellten*. His career depended on results. His relationship to the system depended on production of the 'goods' demanded by the system: trained and obedient soldiers. To do that, he might have to bend or break rules — and bodies — in a way the officers who both incorporated and administered the system might tolerate, but could not sanction. But to go too far, as defined by one's superiors, meant arrest, imprisonment, the ultimate disaster of premature discharge. It is scarcely remarkable that this double bind proved too much for many of its victims. Alcohol abuse and efflorescent sadism are alike well-documented. Even more suggestive is the fact that the German army's suicide rate was highest among non-commissioned officers in the first half of their twelve-year service. Percentagewise, it was not the soldiers who made away with themselves — it was their drill instructors. And the reasons most often given in the investigations involved some form of stress. [39]

The non-commissioned officers' position as the army's enforcers in turn restricted their utilization to improve the army's articulation. Historically, the armies of Germany had fought in formations controlled by officers. The NCO's perceived role had been that of a disciplinarian rather than a junior leader. The image, common in western cultures, of the sergeant whose harshness is acceptable because it manifests experience won the hard way is in Germany a product of the twentieth century. Prior to 1914,

Schleifer or *Soldatenschinder* were more common epithets for men who had never faced anything deadlier than a beer mug.[40] Breaking platoons into sections and squads, in short, was only part of the problem. It was also necessary to convince the rank and file that the men who led them in the field had meant only the best for the men they harassed in the garrison.

One means of compensation involved encouraging the German soldier to accept the army's discipline as an element of the army's comradeship. The military functions of this approach were at least as important as its social utility. Close-order drill was considered particularly useful as a means of developing group consciousness while retaining a sense of individuality. For the exercises to be performed satisfactorily, each man had to play his own personal role properly. Formal parades and reviews, singing on the march, *Bierabende* in the canteens — all were designed to inculcate a sense of *Geborgenheit* that would encourage cooperation in battle even if no superior was at hand. Similarly the reserve associations were more than a means of influencing the civilian community. In wartime their members, at least the young ones, would be drawn back into their old units, or assigned to entirely new reserve formations. Even more than active soldiers, they must feel accepted; they must feel that they belong.[41]

Such internal approaches, however, smacked too much of the improvisational. They were criticized for paying too little attention to generalized moral values able to sustain men even after their discharge. Initially, religion seemed to be a promising supplement. The German army cherished, at least officially, its legacies of piety from the days of Frederick William I and Frederick the Great, of regiments marching into battle chanting hymns, of officers and men raising victory chorales around campfires. To an officer corps whose religious observances were increasingly conventional, to an Evangelical church increasingly concerned with finding new ways of reaching an indifferent population, the incongruities of seeking a direct, emotional link between Mars and Christ were outweighed by the perceived advantages.[42]

Generations of earnest chaplains laboured over tracts and sermons designed to convince twenty-year-olds of the importance of obeying their superiors, writing their mothers, and avoiding pleasant vices.[43] The results were so marginal that even during the

1870s, critics suggested the policy be abandoned. Its survival owed more to institutional inertia than to positive belief that traditional religion mixed well with modern soldiering. Even during the *Kulturkampf,* officers questioned the wisdom of offending the Catholics who filled the ranks of so many regiments. Others challenged the legitimacy in a constitutional state of forcing anyone's conscience. But too-harsh criticism meant the risk of being branded irreligious by the pious or the hypocritical. Moreover, the sharpest critics of religious indoctrination were also the army's sharpest critics: the Progressives and the Social Democrats. If they wanted it abolished, that was all the more reason to sustain it, whatever its effect. In practice, however, regimental and company commanders tended to regard the process as a waste of already scarce time, something to be scheduled for rainy days and assigned to any officer unlucky enough to be handy. Certainly the Imperial chaplains never became the equivalent of the Nazi party's leadership officers.

A similar fate awaited the second possibility for generating enthusiasm: civic instruction. This is usually presented in the context of the empire's continuing campaign against Social Democracy. Its failure becomes, correspondingly, the triumph of an emerging class-consciousness over obscurantism and reaction. But the policy also collapsed because of the army's enduring refusal to take it seriously. At bottom, this reflected the army's failure to take socialist ideology seriously. The military's programme assumed the ultimate goodwill of its subjects. Socialist recruits in general tended to be described as led astray by a bad environment, temporarily corrupted by ideas impossible for any reasonable man to believe. A victory or two, as one optimist put it, would mean the rapid abandonment of Marx.[44]

Organized socialism, for its part, took an increasingly temperate attitude towards the ground forces, as opposed to the navy. August Bebel's periodic reaffirmations of the SPD's patriotism were reflected on practical levels by a negative: the absence of any significant organized programme of undermining the army from within. It was a pointless risk both before and after socialism became a legal political movement. The factory and the tavern were far more useful forums than the barracks; courage of conviction did not demand a heedless thrusting of heads into the lion's mouth. Individual resistance, 'job actions' or 'slowdowns', were seen as harming both the individuals involved and the socialist movement as a whole. The self-interest of the typical socialist conscript also suggested the wisdom of serving one's time, keeping a clean conduct sheet, and resuming any interrupted political activity once safely beyond the clutches of military discipline. Indeed, not a few of them ended their active service as lance-corporals — to the subsequent consternation of high military authority.[45]

For all that it maintained its policy of religious instruction and patriotic lectures, the army in practice came increasingly to regard systematic indoctrination as a time-wasting distraction from training programmes already criticized for putting too much pressure on recruits. It could also be a serious risk in a constitutional state. After 1890, numerous Imperial edicts forbade the discussion of party politics — an elastic term at best, particularly as interpreted by a critical journalist or politician. Imperial Germany was, moreover, a *Rechtsstaat* even for its private soldiers. Searches for socialist propaganda in the barracks could lead to full-panoplied investigations — investigations which embarrassingly often indicated that the men involved had been using the offending newspapers as wrapping-paper, or that they could not be proved to understand the Aesopian language of a poem.[46]

Despite the elaborate instructions on holding and winning an audience published in military periodicals, the average lieutenant or NCO remained an uninspiring speaker whose knowledge of specific political or social problems was likely to be at best superficial. His lectures put his men to sleep. His question-and-answer sessions were likely to generate the risk of being tied in knots by a clever private whose motivations might be political, but were just as likely to involve pleasure at throwing a superior for a mental loss. An instructor who was by chance intellectually sophisticated enough to discuss current events ran the risk of introducing soldiers to problems they might not even have considered — with the accompanying risk of side-choosing. An instructor who tried to liven his sessions by a bit of personal philosophy, or by talking to the troops on what he considered their level, could also find himself in trouble. For example, Lieutenant von Forstner, the central figure of the Zabern affair, was quoted as having informed recruits in one of these sessions that any of them was welcome to shit on the French flag. Such sentiments passed unnoticed in the officers' mess at midnight. Reported to a journalist, a Reichstag deputy, or even a colonel, they might bring their author attention he neither needed nor welcomed. The unfortunate Forstner found himself the centre of a brief international incident when the French government complained about his choice of images.[47] It was far safer to stick to platitudes.

The audience for the lectures, finally, was kept busy from dawn to dusk in a combination of intense physical activity and a fairly demanding intellectual programme requiring memorization of ranks, orders, responsibilities, and weapons nomenclature — all likely to be completely unfamiliar. Formal instruction in religion or civics tended to become an excuse for an hour's uneasy dozing, or to generate a dull indifference not to be overcome by spot quizzes — which themselves inspired protests that the army was not supposed to be a school of the nation in quite such a literal sense.

The army and its uniformed critics, in short, on the whole achieved a working relationship far smoother than the rhetoric of either party would suggest was possible — or that the mythmakers of either camp readily accepted. The army for its part put increasing pressure on civilian society, specifically the schools, the patriotic societies, and the veterans' organizations. The perceived success of Japan in creating patriotic warriors at primary-school level encouraged drawing contrasts to a German flabbiness which allowed young men to be corrupted by secularism and socialism long before they reached the regiments. The army also advocated pre-military training to bridge the gap between elementary school and barracks — that time when youth, left to its own devices, could so easily go astray. These complex efforts produced a great deal of sound and fury, but less in the way of concrete results. The conscripts of 1914 entered the army with no more of the martial virtues than their grandfathers of 1871.[48]

This in turn led to a growing emphasis on internal possibilities. The German army had a strong self-image of paternalism. In part this reflected feudal/Frederician myths of the officer as a chieftain leading his tenants and followers into battle: visions filtered through romanticism in defiance of often brutal realities. In part it reflected the army's growing internalization of a more modern myth: military service as a socializing and maturing experience for the youth of Germany. In part it reflected pragmatic necessity. Because the German army was a national, short-service force, money for amenities was seldom easily come by. The average barracks was a human warehouse, neither attractive nor comfortable, easily rendered uninhabitable without strict attention to personal hygiene and collective order. Youths away from home for the first time, coming from a society which emphasized women's responsibility for even the simplest domestic chores, often required systematic, patient instruction in the techniques of living in a group.[49] With messing a unit responsibility, officers were likely to spend a great deal of energy on housekeeping details. Officers whose caste honour theoretically forbade dealing with tradesmen except at arm's length boasted in their professional journals of saving a few pfennigs per ton of potates by buying wholesale, of improving their men's diet by investing in small cooking utensils instead of one large stewpot, of cultivating battalion gardens and introducing exotic spices into the bland government rations. Well-kept account books could be as important in promotion recommendations as a reputation for dashing conduct on manoeuvres.[50]

On a slightly higher level, the army encouraged its regiments and battalions to establish libraries and canteens for men wishing to relax after a day's drill. This policy was and is described by its critics as part of a desire to control the soldier even in his off-duty hours by confining his reading to approved literature and keeping him away from socialist taverns. It is not necessary to deny this point to assert another, significant dimension to the army's desire to keep its men close to the barracks. Ideological corruption might be important in the minds of most commanders — but so were the risks generated by bad liquor and cheap women, which were far more likely objects of men on pass than Social Democratic pamphlets.

A significant number of establishments placed out of bounds as socialist haunts during the army's various anti-radical campaigns seem to have begun as dives which attracted socialists because soldiers were known to frequent them. Others appear to have turned a suspiciously blind eye to the presence of prostitutes, or to excessive drinking, in order not to discourage their uniformed customers. An academic tendency to take socialist political oratory at face-value oversimplifies an issue which was often far from the party's image of young men forbidden to seek innocent amusement and political enlightenment by military reactionaries. Alcohol abuse and venereal disease were matters of increasing concern to Imperial society at large — and likely to be of even more concern to an army whose institutional image of its soldiers emphasized their callowness. More specifically, the army's stress on formal discipline involved an ascending series of draconic punishments for lapses. Relatively few officers took pleasure in filling their orderly rooms with twenty-year-olds who failed to salute because they were too intoxicated to focus. Even fewer found abstract enjoyment in spoiling a conscript's record for alcohol-induced offences, or discharging a man infected with syphilis during his active service.

Indiscriminate off-duty mixing of soldiers and civilians, or even soldiers of different regiments, enhanced the possibility of brawls over turf and women. Complaints from civilian authorities or outraged citizens could mean questions raised at corps headquarters, in state assemblies, even in the *Reichstag* itself. And though the army stood staunchly beside its own officially, though even the Kaiser might applaud an officer defending 'military honour' against mere civilians, experience and rumour alike suggested that such publicity was a significant ultimate risk to one's career. The German army had a plethora of undesirable stations and dead-end assignments for those who contributed to its public embarrassment. It seemed safer by far to keep the rank and file firmly under control — particularly since the army's junior officers were such a continually fruitful source of incidents.[51]

This paternalism, with its mixure of institutional myths and pragmatic self-interest, was increasingly reinforced by professional considerations. In part this reflected the growing *embourgeoisement* of the German officer corps — a process which generated a corresponding professionalization of the craft of leadership. A born aristocrat might accept the concept, however inappropriate, that the 'von' in his name conveyed a genetic ability to give orders in a way that ensured obedience. But the very enthusiasm with which middle-class youths copied and exaggerated what they considered to be aristocratic styles of behaviour bespoke a certain underlying insecurity. The '*Simplicissimus* lieutenant' of the turn-of-the-century comic press was essentially the product of role-playing. And he had a serious side.

More and more officers argued that their task was to do, not merely to be. A German officer should set such an example of efficiency and character that even convinced socialists might accept the army's value system. At the same time, he must be realistic enough to see that even the best military 'work environment' was temporary, and not likely to alter firmly established world views. But how important was socialism in practice, after all, as long as the socialist obeyed orders? Instead of playing the Grand

Inquisitor, a company officer should concentrate on performing his duty so well as to inspire his subordinates to emulation. Win the confidence of your men, the subaltern was urged. Participate in their sports and recreations. Bridge class-gaps on a human level — not only as an exercise in social evolution, but as a means of ensuring cooperation in battle. In this way soldiers would evolve a personal attachment to their officers which would evolve into a general commitment to the military system.[52]

The conscious cultivation of leadership as a professional craft epitomizes the German army's role as an instrument of modernization. The military's function as an integrative force in a Germany socially and politically fragmented from its creation is well-established. As a symbol of the new empire it eventually overcame even the jealously-guarded military particularism of the lesser states. At the same time, the army was anything but a collection of sullen conscripts marking time until discharge. It may never have become the school of the nation and the hammer of socialism envisioned by idealists. It did, however, develop into a significant rite of passage for males in a society where change had invalidated many of the more traditional forms.

Even the harsh discipline contributed positively to this process. A familiar contemporary joke involved a recruit asked by his regimental commander, 'Who are the father and the mother of your company?' He gave the expected answer: 'The captain and the *Feldwebel*.' When asked what he would like to become in the service, he promptly answered, 'An orphan'. But an easy rite of passage is a contradiction in terms. In western societies since at least the Renaissance, if not the Age of Pericles, males in particular have been conditioned against accepting the verdict of Lewis Carroll's Caucus Race: everyone has won and all must receive prizes. The fathers, uncles, and older brothers of Imperial Germany may have enjoyed telling horror stories about their time 'with the Prussians'. They did not significantly discourage the new generations of conscripts. Between 1871 and 1914 the everyday routine of peacetime service was not regarded as an unbearable strain on the average man in his early twenties. Exceptions only validated the generalization.

These and similar points, however, involve roles assigned to the military by the wider society: a form of competence by definition.

The German army was significantly committed to positive modernization as well. A cynic — or an accurate observer — might suggest as obvious examples of modernity the army's growing sensitivity to external pressure; its tendency to clean house internally while steadfastly denying any shortcomings; above all its capacity to function effectively on two levels, the official and the real. More than attitudes, however, were involved in the process. This essay has demonstrated that the German army's concepts of man management, of training and discipline, reflected a coherent sense of the demands of modern war, as opposed to being primarily a means of social stabilization. The army was willing to test, modify, and for practical purposes abandon unproductive approaches to the problem. It was consistently unwilling, moreover, to sacrifice efficiency for principles in terms of making soldiers of its rank and file.

The ultimate test of the army's commitment to modernization remains the efficacy of its preparation for the first world war. While the German army was by no means as good as its press releases, it had in fact kept steady pace with developments in material and doctrine. It had paid close attention to the lessons of the world's battlefields. If its conclusions were often debatable, certainly the German army òf 1914 had not gone down the operational dead-end of the French in 1940, or the United States in Vietnam. Above all it clearly recognized an uncomfortable ultimate: victory in war depends on advancing. And unlike the British, with their anti-intellectual empiricism, unlike Republican France, whose soldiers were expected to replace skill at arms with patriotic zeal, the Germans attempted to produce men with both the psychological and the professional equipment to survive on the modern battlefield. Theoretical emphasis on dispersion and articulation put the German army on the right tactical track, even if it was not sufficiently developed to antedate directly the infiltration and storm-troop methods of the world war. Moreover, the Imperial Army's effort to create a disciplined, committed *Wehrgemeinschaft* was the remote source both of the *Reichswehr's* and the *Wehrmacht's* interest in a more comprehensive *Volksgemeinschaft,* and of that cohesion in combat which so impressed Germany's enemies throughout the second world war.[53]

It is, however, possible to take the argument a stage further and suggest that the German army's training approaches and tactical doctrines were exercises in the impossible. The First World War demonstrated that the critics of Europe's conscript armies had been right, but for the wrong reasons. Where they had concentrated on moral and morale deficiencies, the shortcomings of mass man in uniform proved to be technical. War had become so exacting in its demands, so alien to the routines of European society, that only small numbers of men could cope effectively with its demands from the beginning. What the German army expected its rank and file to achieve could not in fact be done without levels of material support depending on major developments in transportation and communications technology. And those developments in turn have arguably brought armies even closer to the dead-end postulated by John Keegan. The machines that assist men to move against fire have themselves begun to make physical and moral demands for which even the best training cannot compensate.[54] Ironically, the Imperial German army's ultimate role as an instrument of military modernization may prove to be the initial and involuntary steps it took towards the abolition of battle itself.

Notes

The author wishes to thank the Alexander von Humboldt Foundation for the fellowship sponsoring a year's research in Germany in 1979-80, which provided the groundwork for this essay. The Foundation is in no way responsible for its contents or interpretations.

1. What might once have passed as sarcasm became embarrassingly literal with Bernd Schulte's insistence that the German army's emphasis on the strategic and tactical offensive reflected its commitment to prompt, decisive action against domestic enemies in case of civil war! *Die deutsche Armee 1900-1914. Zwischen Beharren und Verändern* (Düsseldorf 1977), 535 ff.

2. The best of the frequently-cited surveys developing this interpretation are Manfred Messerschmidt, 'Die Armee in Staat und Gesellschaft', *Das kaiserliche Deutschland*, ed. M. Stürmer (Düsseldorf 1970), 89-118; and Wilhelm Deist, 'Die Armee in Staat und Gesellschaft, 1890-1914', ibid., 312-329; Martin Kitchen, *A Military History of Germany* (Bloomington, Ind. 1975), 131 *passim*; and John Gooch, *Armies in Europe* (London 1980), 114 ff. are familiar general studies

accepting the same line of argument.

3. Michael Geyer, *Aufrüstung oder Sicherheit. Die Reichswehr in der Krise der Machtpolitik 1924-1936* (Wiesbaden 1980). Cf. also Ernst Hansen, *Reichswehr und Industrie* (Boppard 1978).

4. Timothy T. Lupfer, 'The Dynamics of Doctrine: The Changes in German Tactical Doctrine during the First World War', *Leavenworth Papers,* 5 (Ft. Leavenworth KS, 1918); and G. C. Wynne, *If Germany Attacks* (London 1940), are among the best presentations of the army's operational flexibility. For its approach to domestic affairs cf. Gerald Feldman, *Army, Industry, and Labor, 1914-1918* (Princeton 1966); and Martin Kitchen, *The Silent Dictatorship* (New York 1976).

5. Cv. J. G. Abegglen, *The Japanese Factory* (Glencoe, Ill. 1958), 131; and M. B. Miller, *The Bon Marché: Bourgeois Culture and the Department Store* (Princeton 1918), 11.

6. This argument is best developed in the work of Alf Lüdtke. See particularly 'On the Role of State Violence in the Period of Transition to Industrial Capitalism. The Example of Prussia, 1815-1848', *Social History* 4, 2 (1979), 175-221; and "Wehrhafte Nation" und "innere Wohlfart": Zur militärischen Mobilisierbarkeit der bürgerlichen Gesellschaft, Konflikt und Konsens zwischen Militär und ziviler Administration in Preussen, 1815-1860', *Militärgeschichtliche Mitteilungen* 30 (1981), 7-56. Reinhard Höhn, *Verfassungskampf und Heereseid. Der Kampf des Bürgertums um das Heer (1815-1850)* (Leipzig 1938), remains useful for ideological questions.

7. Paddy Griffith, *Forward into Battle: Fighting Tactics from Waterloo to Vietnam* (New York 1981), 43.

8. Helmuth von Moltke, 'Bemerkungen vom Jahre 1865 über den Einfluss der verbesserten Feuerwaffen auf die Taktik', in *Militärische Werke*, 2 Abt., *Tätigkeit des Generalstabschefs im Frieden*, 3 vols., ed. Gr. Generalstab (Berlin 1892-1906), II, 45 ff.

9. Steven T. Ross, *From Flintlock to Rifle: Infantry Tactics 1740-1866* (Rutherford, NJ 1979), surveys this problem.

10. Cf. Joachim Hoffmann, 'Der Militärschriftsteller Fritz Hoenig', *Militärgeschichtliche Mitteilungen* 7 (1970), 5-26; and Reinhard Brühl's DDR study *Militärgeschichte und Kriegspolitik. Zur Militärgeschichtsschreibung des preussisch-deutschen Generalstabes 1816-1945* (Berlin 1973), 116 passim.

11. Harry Bell (ed.), *St. Privat. German Sources* (Ft. Leavenworth, KS 1914), offers a convenient cross-section of this critical literature. The General Staff analysis, *Der 18. August 1870, Studien zur Kriegsgeschichte und Taktik,* 5 (Berlin 1906) is particularly scathing.

12. The most complete account of the German attack on Le Bourget is Hermann Kunz, *Die Kämpfe der preussischen Garden um Le Bourget während der Belagerung von Paris, 1870/71* (Berlin 1891). For the defender's perspective, see A. A. Ducrot, *La Défense de Paris, 1870-1871*, 4 vols. (Paris 1875-1878), II, 14 ff.

13. Jacob Meckel, *Ein Sommernachtstraum. Erzählt von einem älteren Infanterist* (Berlin 1888); 'Die Infanterie-Taktik im Traume und in der Wirklichkeit', *Jahrbücher für die deutsche Armee und Marine*, 66 (1888), 102-222 (hereafter cited as *JAM*); and 'Rauhe Wirklichkeit', *Militär-Wochenblatt* 1887, 106 (hereafter cited as *MW*).

14. For the French approach cf. Douglas Porch, *The March to the Marne: The French Army, 1871-1914* (Cambridge 1981), 214 ff.; and Joseph C. Arnold, 'French

Tactical Doctrine, 1870-1914', *Military Affairs* 43, 2 (April 1978), 61-67. For a representative example of the German attitude see Prince Krafft zu Hohenloe-Ingelfingen, *Militärische Briefe*, Vol. II, *Ueber Infanterie*, 2nd ed. (Berlin 1886), 19 passim.

15. But see Grady McWhiney and Perry D. Jamieson, *Attack and Die: Civil War Military Tactics and the Southern Heritage* (University Ala. 1982), which links Confederate preferences for the assault to 'Celtic' elements in Southern culture.

16. 'Die Mehrlader', *MW* 1883, 81; 'Wird die Taktische Offensive durch die Tragweite und Präcision der modernen Feuerwaffen erleichtert oder erschwert?' *MW* 1885, 27; Petermann, 'Welchem Einfluss hat die Einführung der neuen Kleinkalibergewehre auf die Taktik?' *JAM* 77 (1890), 148-158.

17. 'Ueber den Werth der Mitrailleusen', *JAM* 10 (1874), 303-323. 'Zur Geschichte der kleinkalibrigen Schnellfeuergeschütze', ibid. 88 (1893), 196-215; Loyutz, 'Zur Frage der Verteilung und Verwendung der Maschinengewehr', *Kriegstechnische Zeitschrift*, 8 (1905), 26-35 (hereafter cited as *KTZ*).

18. Beckmann, 'Zur Maschinengewehrfrage', *JAM* 134 (1908), 384-407, 463-473, 571-587; 'Die Notwendigkeit der Maschinengewehre', *KTZ* (1904), 530-537; A. Fleck, *Maschinengewehre, ihre Technik und Taktik* (Berlin 1914); and Krieger, *Das Gefecht der Maschinengewehr-Kampagnien* (Oldenburg 1913).

19. Cf. Shelford Bidwell and Dominick Graham, *Fire-Power: British Army Weapons and Theories of War, 1904-1945* (London 1982), 55.

20. V. G. Kiernan, *European Empires from Conquest to Collapse, 1815-1960* (Leicester 1982), 35.

21. Cf. 'Der offensive Geist und seine Pflege bei der Infanterie', *MW* 1881, 8-10; with 'Das Bajonettfechten', *MW* 1881, 5; 'Bayonett und Feuerwaffe', *MW* 1871, 23; or 'Feuerwaffe und blanke Waffe', *MW* 1872, 36. One ultimately unfortunate result of this latter recommendation was the development of a bayonet with a saw-toothed blade for use by pioneers. During the first world war this tended to be interpreted by Allied troops as an example of Hun frightfulness, deliberately designed to enhance the suffering of its victims. Prisoners taken with such a bayonet in their scabbards frequently received short shrift.

22. 'Zur Frage des Gepäcks des Fussvolkes', *MW* 1883, 86; 'Betrachtungen über Gepäckerleichterung und Fusspflege bei der deutschen Infanterie', *JAM* 60 (1886), 61-71. 'Marschleistungen, Marschausrüstung und Marscherleichterungen', ibid. 138 (1910), 178-192, 259-274. 'Bedenken wider eine Grössen-Rangirung durch das Bataillon bezüglich Regiment', *MW* 1871, 90.

23. G.V. Marées. 'Die Offensive und Defensive dem verbesserten Feuerwaffen gegenüber', *JAM* 11 (1874), 205-210. Cf. F. Knott, 'Die Ausbildung der Infanterie zum Gefecht', ibid., 16 (1875), 89-97.

24. Peter Stearns, *Lives of Labor: Work in a Maturing Industrial Society* (New York 1975), is a useful survey. His *Be a Man! Males in Modern Society* (New York 1979), 59 ff., focuses more sharply on the development of new bonding and coping patterns in industrial Europe.

25. Wichert, 'Der Sport in der deutschen Armee', *KTZ* 10 (1907), 'Deckung', *MW* 1897, 35, 37, 302, 305. Reisner Frh. v. Lilienstern, 'Kriegsmässiges Schiessen', *JAM* 125 (1903), 325-338; 'Prüfungsschiessen und Königsabzeichen', *MW* 1896, 102-103; are typical of the literature on these and related subjects.

26. Joachim Hoffman, 'Die Kriegslehre des Generals von Schlichting', *Militär-geschichtliche Mitteilungen* 5 (1969), 5-36, is a useful background study on the

revised regulations. Cf. also 'Das neue Infanterie-Exerzier-Reglement auf dem Uebungsfelde', *MW* 1890, 65-66; 'Bericht über die Taktik der Infanterie, 1888', *Jahresberichte über die Veränderungen und Fortschritte in der Militärwesen* 15 (1885), 303-308; and 'Bericht über die Taktik der Infanterie 1893', *Von Loebells Jahresberichte über die Veränderungen und Fortschritte im Militärwesen* 20 (1893), 299-302.

27. 'Ueber die künftige Bewaffnung der Feld-Artillerie', *JAM* 4 (1872), 40-63; 'Wurffeuer im Feldkriege', *MW* 1890, 49; Braucht die Feldarmee eine Haubitze?' *KTZ* 6 (1903), 185-196; 'Feldhaubitzen', *JAM* 121 (1901), 204-207; 'Wirkung geht vor Deckung?' ibid. 132 (1907), 522-530.

28. Cf. inter alia. A. v. Brygalski, 'Die deutschen Kaisermanöver', *JAM* 36 (1880), 316-334. S. v. Schlichting, *Taktik der drei Waffen im Uebungsjahr 1892 beim XIV. Armee-Korps* (Karlsruhe 1893); 'Die Infanterie im Manöver 1893', *MW* 1893, 100; Frh. v. Falkenhausen, *Rückblick auf die Ausbildung des Armee-Korps im Uebungsjahr 1899-1900*, 4 Teilen (Stuttgart 1900). Spohr, 'Wie können wir die Zweckmässigkeit unserer Feuertaktik im Frieden prüfen?' *JAM* 92 (1894), 68-84; and 'Manöver-Feuer und scharfes Feuer', *MW* 1901, 96, are among many perceptive treatments of the problems of inculcating a sense of the power of modern weapons on the manoeuvre field.

29. An early discussion of this problem is Maschke, 'Die Operationen mit Massenheeren in den Kämpfen zu Anfang und in der Zweiten Hälfte des 19. Jahrhunderts', *JAM* (1894), 16-45, 147-160, 265-293.

30. Arnold Möhl, 'Der deutsche Infanterieangriff und der Buren-Krieg', *MW* 1903, 33, 34, 35, 38. Cf. Stieler, 'Die sogennanten Burentaktik', *JAM* 123 (1902), 365-376.

31. Hermann Müller, *Die Erziehung der Truppe zum Moralischen Wert in Deutschland, Russland und Japan* (Berlin, n.d.); 'Zum Infanterieangriff', *JAM* 130 (1986), 170-188; *Exerzier-Reglement für die Infanterie von 29. Mai 1906*, rev. ed. (Berlin 1909), esp. pars. 265, 327, 347; and Balck, 'Das Exerzierreglement für die Infanterie von 29. May 1906', *JAM* 131 (1906), 111-135.

32. Von der Goltz, 'Deutsche Infanterie voan!' *JAM* 127 (1904), 323-339. Wolf, 'Die Infanterie der Zukunft', ibid., 134 (1908), 144-150; Otto Schulz, 'Gruppenkolonne und Kompagniekolonne', ibid., 136 (1909), 35-38.

33. The accurate observation that the army preferred rural recruits as less likely bearers of radical ideas is frequently presented in an over-simplified manner. Men from nineteenth-century urban environments were in fact significantly more likely than their country or small-town cousins to fail the increasingly-strict physical examinations, or to score low enough to justify their assignment to the reserve, without need to pay much attention to their political beliefs. The city-bred recruit, moreover, tended to be regarded as generally less tractable than men from a more stable or deferential environment — an opinion common in the military establishments of industrialized countries, and having less to do with politics than with attitudes. Cf. Ludwig v. Seckendorff, *Die Allgemeine Wehrpflicht und ihr sozialer Wirkungsbereich in den Jahren 1888-1914* (Neustadt 1934); and Hermann Gauer, *Von Bauerntum, Bürgertum und Arbeitertum in der Armee* (Heidelberg 1936). A critical summary from a DDR perspective is Dieter Fricke, 'Militäristische Soldatenerziehung im preussisch-deutschen Heer zu Beginn der Imperialistischen Epoch', *Militärgeschichte* 11, 4 (1972), 423-434.

34. Cf. inter alia 'Ueber die Kunst des Befehlens', *JAM* 1 (1871), 328-333;

'Gedanken über die Grundzüge unserer militärischen Erziehungs-Systems und sein Verhältnis zur infanteristischen Ausbildung', ibid., 98 (1896), 194-202. Blume, 'Der Werth des Drills und seine Grenzen', *MW* 1902, 91, 98, 107; Falkenhausen, 'Exerzieren und Fechten', *Vierteljahrsheft für Truppenführung und Heereskunde,* 4 (1907), 464-487; H. v. Angeln, *Moderne Soldatenerziehung* (Munich 1913). Joseph Halgus, 'The Bavarian Soldier, 1871-1914: Efforts to Use Military Training as a Means of Strengthening the Consensus in Favor of the Existing Order', Ph. D. Dissertation, New York University 1980, 159 ff., is perceptive, but concentrates on the social function of discipline to the virtual exclusion of its worth for military purposes — a common weakness of the 'new military history'.

35. Representative admonitions include 'Soldatenmisshandlungen und öffentliches Gerichtsverfahren', *MW* 1892, 6; von Kessling, 'Massnahmen für Hintanhaltung von Misshandlungen sowie vorschriftswidriger Behandlungen überhaupt', *JAM* (1903), 623-630; Pelet-Narbonne, 'Die Einfluss von Offizier-inspektionen bezw. Offizier-beritts auf die Misshandlungen', ibid. 130 (1906), 188-191. Hans Rau, *Der Sadismus in der Armee* (Berlin 1904), incorporates a cross-section of contemporary case studies. Halgus, 174 ff; and Martin Kitchen, *The German Officer Corps, 1890-1914* (Oxford 1968), 183-186, offer summary discussions of a problem which deserves systematic scholarly consideration.

36. 'Ueber die Mittel, den Mangel an Unteroffizeren zu heben', *JAM* 7 (1873), 259-266; 'Zur Erziehung des Unteroffizier-Korps', ibid; 95 (1895), 75-82; Adolf Streit, *Das Unteroffizierkorps des Deutschen Heeres* (Hagen 1905). For the status of the French NCO cf. Terry Strieter, 'The Sous-Officers of the French Army, 1848-1895: A Quantitative Study', PhD Dissertation, University of California, Santa Barbara, 1977; and the more impressionistic treatment in Porch, 196 ff. John Bushnell, 'Peasants in Uniform: The Tsarist Army as a Peasant Society', *Journal of Social History* 13, 4 (Summer 1980), 565-576, suggests that the real internal structure of that army was a network of *artels,* which the average NCO had neither the will nor the competence to dominate.

37. 'Militärdienst und Zivilversorgung', *MW* 1899, 2-3.

38. There is no modern analytical history of the Imperial Army's NCO corps. Werner Lahne, *Unter-offiziere Gestern-heute-morgen,* 2nd ed. (Herford 1975); and *Die Geschichte des deutschen Unteroffiziers,* ed. F. v. Ledebur (Berlin 1939), contain useful information in highly-tendentious frameworks. The discussion in Wiegand Schmidt-Richberg, 'Die Regierungszeit Wilhelms II', in *Handbuch zur deutschen Militärgeschichte,* Vol. V (Frankfurt 1968), is slightly better balanced, but derivative and uncritically sympathetic.

39. Cf. inter alia, 'Die wichtigsten Krankheiten in der Armee', *JAM* 56 (1888), 317-329; and 'Die Psychologie in der militärischen Erziehung', ibid., 97 (1897), 98-104.

40. The literary example most familiar outside of Germany is Unteroffizier Himmelstoss of Erich Maria Remarque's *All Quiet on the Western Front.* Among many contemporary treatments cf. J. Buleck, *Der Soldatenschinder und sein Ende. Original-Erzählungen aus der Gegenwart* (Munich 1893); and Oswald Bilse, *Aus einer kleinen Garnison* (Vienna 1904).

41. 'Die Disziplin des Preussischen Heeres und die formalistische Methode', *MW* 1884, 81; O. v. Uechtritz, 'Gedanken über Kameradschaft', *JAM* 77 (1890), 62-77. 'Armee und Volkserziehung', ibid. 112 (1895), 58-72; Paul von Schmidt, *Die Erziehung des Soldaten* (Berlin 1894).

42. Reinhard Höhn, *Die Armee als Erziehungsschule der Nation. Das Ende einer Idee* (Bad Harzburg 1963), remains the most complete general survey of this issue.

43. A good example is C. Th. Müller, *Wir Männer in des Königs Rock,* 2nd ed. rev. (Berlin 1912). Cf. also v. Kreitschman, *Für den deutschen Soldaten* (Berlin 1894).

44. Cf. 'Sozialismus und Heerwesen', *JAM 89*(1893), 263-282; and Konrad Lehmann, 'Die Erziehung des Soldaten', ibid., 137 (1909), 279-289, 405-415.

45. On this issue cf. Reinhard Höhn's monumental compendium, *Sozialismus und Heer,* 3 vols. (Bad Homburg, Bad Harzburg, 1961-1969); and the specific studies of Albert Lotholz, 'Die Haltung der Sozialdemokratie in den Heeres-Flotten- und Weltmachtsfragen', PhD dissertation, Freiburg 1954, and Walter Wittwer's DDR study, *Streit um Schicksalsfragen. Die deutsche Sozialdemokratie zu Krieg und Vaterlandsverteidigung, 1907-1914* (Berlin 1964).

46. Halgus, 209 ff., offers several interesting case studies. It must of course be remembered that legal exoneration for this military offence did not preclude continued persecution, outside the regulations — a point stressed in Fricke, 'Militärische Soldatenerziehung'.

47. This particular aspect of the Zabern affair is discussed in David Schoenbaum, *Zabern 1913: Consensus Politics in Imperial Germany* (London 1982), 103-104, 113-114; and somewhat more ponderously in J. G. Morrison, 'The Intransigents: Alsace-Lorrainers against the Annexation, 1900-1914', PhD Dissertation, University of Iowa, 1970, 411-412.

48. K. Saul, 'Der Kampf um die Jugend zwischen Volksschule und Kaserne', *Militärgeschichtliche Mitteilungen* 9 (1971), 94-143; and W. Bethge, 'Bestrebungen der herrschenden Klassen in Deutschland zur Militärisierung der männlichen Jugend in den Jahren 1910 bis 1917/18', Diss. Päd, Potsdam 1965.

49. For a good description of the housekeeping responsibilities of an officer see 'Einiges aus der Militär-Gesundheitspflege für den Offizier von Kompagniechef abwärts, *MW* 1899, 50-51.

50. 'Ueber Truppenverpflegung im Frieden', *MW* 1885, 80. 'Ueber Truppenmenagen', ibid., 1878, 93; 'Verpflegung des Soldaten in der Kaserne', ibid., 1882, 80; 'Ein Wort über den Werth von Gewürzen und Konserven für Truppen und Truppenmenagen', ibid.

51. Schoenbaum, *Zabern 1913,* is a perceptive illustration of this pattern at work even in a notorious case of civil-military conflict.

52. The most familiar spokesman for this position was Edward Preuss. See particularly *Die höheren Aufgaben des jungen Offiziers für Armee und Volk,* (March 1960); and 'Erziehung und Bildung im Heer', *Deutsche Schulerziehung,* 2nd ed, ed. W. Reen (Munich 1907), 485-502. Cf. also such works as Julius Hoppenstedt, *Sind wir Kriegsfertig?* (Berlin 1910); R. Zangguth, 'Die erzieherische Aufgabe der Offiziere', *MW* 1903, 68-70, and P. v. Schmidt, 'Der deutsche Offiziertum im Kampf gegen den Umsturz', *JAM* 110 (1899), 261-276.

53. Cf. Manfred Messerschmidt, 'The *Wehrmacht* and the *Volksgemeinschaft*', last article in this issue; and Martin van Creveld, *Fighting Power* (Westport, Conn. 1982).

54. John Keegan, *The Face of Battle* (New York 1977), 325ff.

Dennis Showalter
is Associate Professor of History at The
Colorado College, Colorado Springs. He is
author of *Railroads and Rifles: Soldiers,
Technology and German Unification*
(Hamden, Conn. 1975), and *Little Man,
What Now? Der Stürmer in the Weimar
Republic* (Hamden, Conn. 1982). He is now
completing a history of the German army in
the Second Reich and a monograph,
Tannenberg: Clash of Empires.

Mira Beth Lansky

'People's War' and the Soviet Threat: The Rise and Fall of a Military Doctrine

A reasonably clever anecdote was circulating in Eastern Europe after the Yom Kippur War in 1973; like most such dry political humour in unofficial circles, it dumped on the Soviet Union and its clients.

> One Pole asks a co-worker: 'Friend, do you know why the Arabs lost their war against Israel?'
>
> Second Pole: 'Of course! Everyone knows they lost because they used Soviet weapons and material.'
>
> First Pole, triumphantly: 'No, no, that wasn't the key factor at all. They were defeated because they used Soviet strategy!'
>
> Second Pole, puzzled: 'Soviet strategy?'
>
> First Pole, smugly: 'Yes, lure the enemy deep into your own territory,' he paused, 'and wait until winter.'

The Soviet withdrawal into the interior during the second world war was not exactly voluntary, nor was it without staggering cost. Such inconvenient details notwithstanding, the practice enjoyed continued favour where it had been adopted independently of the USSR for use in insurgencies, civil wars and wars of resistance, as in what was to become the People's Republic of China. Under the name of 'luring-in-deep', this 'strategy' of withdrawal was until recently a prominent fixture of Chinese military doctrine. Currently, however, luring-in-deep and other concepts appear to be the casualties of a thoroughgoing revision of Chinese military doctrine, paralleling the process of 'de-Maoization' in the political sphere. This article will discuss the most significant of these changes, placing them in historical context.

The significance of the question of Chinese military doctrine becomes apparent when its role in the Chinese leadership's assessment of the balance of forces between China and the Soviet

Journal of Contemporary History (SAGE, London, Beverly Hills and New Delhi), Vol. 18 (1983), 619–649

Union is considered. Military doctrine can act as a 'multiplier' on 'static' measures, such as numerical comparisons. Thus, a superior doctrine can offset other weaknesses: under certain circumstances, *how* forces are used can be almost as important as the quantity and quality of the weapons and material disposed of by the forces.

The conclusions arrived at by the Chinese leadership in their assessment of China's ability to withstand Soviet attack will help determine whether relations with the USSR will be maintained at the level of controlled hostility, or whether China will feel compelled to execute a preemptive rapprochement with her primary adversary. With as many as fifty-one Soviet divisions on the Sino-Soviet border that could be redeployed to the Central Front in Europe or elsewhere during a period of relaxation, it is obviously in the interests of Western security to avoid a Sino-Soviet accommodation. As a factor in this equation, the question of Chinese military doctrine, is, therefore, of more than academic interest.

Over the past couple of years the doctrine of 'People's War' has been dislodged from the pantheon of Chinese orthodoxy, although evidently it is still felt necessary to make a ritual bow in its direction by referring to the very different concepts now prevailing as 'People's War *under modern conditions*'. Despite the former pre-eminence of People's War, its tenure was not without repeated and serious — although until now unsuccessful — challenge.

The debate surrounding the changes that are now being implemented is but the most recent manifestation of a recurring dispute over the nature, source, and immediacy of the most severe threat facing China, and over the military strategy and corresponding doctrine to meet that threat. Such disputes are also the overt manifestation of internal competition for personal power. Before treating current developments it is necessary, therefore to elaborate briefly the two contending doctrinal 'lines', since these are the source of the 'operational code' or vocabulary in which such policies are discussed and debated.

Some distortion is probably unavoidable, since information must be obtained from content analysis of the polemics traded by the competing factions; the participants feel compelled, moreover, to delegitimize opposing arguments by depicting these as aiding and abetting enemies of the state. Nonetheless, by comparing the highly formalized statements employed by the proponents and detractors of a particular 'line', it is possible to gain some insights into their respective views, although the evidence is necessarily fragmentary. In comparing the two lines it will be simplest to proceed by identifying the different responses to the following questions:

— where the enemy is to be engaged: whether he is to be intercepted either outside Chinese territory or close to the frontier, or not engaged until he is well inside Chinese territory;

— the role of territory and fortifications: whether a partially positional defence should be conducted in order to hold assets and exact enemy attrition, or whether territory should be traded for time;

— the nature of Chinese deployments: whether forces should form a forward line or zone, perhaps along major axes of enemy advance, or whether they should be held well back from points of entry into Chinese territory;

— the type and composition of the Chinese forces employed: whether these will be regular forces disposing of whatever heavy weapons are available, or the more numerous and lightly armed militia; also the nature of the relationship among the various types of forces;

— the 'style' of warfare to be employed: whether battles using major regular force formations are permissible, or whether irregular, guerrilla warfare will be conducted while avoiding major engagements, and develop into 'mobile warfare' of hit-and-run attacks on weak or isolated enemy detachments;

There are other differences of opinion concerning:

— the timetable of mobilization;
— the proper role of modern material and technology;
— the acceptability of foreign aid and models and joint operations, as opposed to 'self-reliance';
— the pace of modernization.

Two caveats are in order: there is obviously a measure of overlap among these questions, so that in the body of the discussion there will be some shifting back and forth between questions when necessary for clarity's sake; also, space does not permit an exhaustive treatment of every question at issue in this debate. Yet even a cursory survey of current Chinese military doctrine suffices to disclose two contending schools of thought.

These opposing lines are frequently known as 'active defence' and 'passive defence', at least by adherents of the former. This terminology may be misleading: no revolutionary worth the red star on his cap would willingly use the term 'passive' — a term of opprobrium tantamount to the dire and horrible sin of 'tailism' or even, *horribile dictu*, 'capitulationism' — to apply to himself. It is only in the articles and statements attributed to the 'guerrillas' or 'Maoists', who arrogated to themselves the banner of 'active defence', that the deprecating term of 'passive defence' is used to describe and attack the competing line advocated by the 'professionals' or 'modernizers'. For reasons of legitimacy the latter also employ the term 'active defence', but define it differently. (Indeed to some observers it will appear that reversing the labels would more accurately describe the characters of the two lines.)

Although the terminology of 'active' and 'passive' strategies appears to date from the height of the Great Proletarian Cultural Revolution (GPCR), the dispute itself originated at least as far back as the Chinese Civil War, during the Kuomintang (KMT)'s fourth encirclement campaign in 1932-33. While Mao Tse-tung (Mao Zedong) advocated following the 'guerrilla' strategy of 'luring-in-deep', or withdrawing before the advancing enemy rather than attempting to engage him immediately and halt his advance, Chou En-lai and Liu Po-ch'eng prevailed with a plan for 'halting the enemy beyond the gate'. Following the latter plan, the Communists' main forces engaged one of the advancing KMT columns and destroyed its two divisions. When the KMT mounted another assault this was also thwarted and Mao's 'line' fell into disfavour.[1]

When the issue surfaced again during the GPCR it was in the context of the 'Strategic Debate' of 1965-66 over whether the United States or the Soviet Union was to be regarded as the 'principal adversary', and over the nature and immediacy of the threat each posed. If the US posed the greater threat and if that threat was military and immediate, then rapid modernization of the Chinese People's Liberation Army (PLA) was necessary, and this could only be accomplished through reliance on the USSR and under the protective cover of the Soviet nuclear umbrella; this also implied that joint action with the USSR to aid North Vietnam (this being the period of US military involvement in Southeast Asia) was permissible. Alternatively, if the USSR posed the greater and more immediate threat, and if that threat was primarily political rather than military in nature (i.e., interference in China's domestic affairs), then rapid modernization of the PLA was unnecessary — People's War would suffice — and reliance on the USSR for anything was out of the question. The implications of this debate for Chinese grand strategy and foreign policy have been dealt with at some length by other writers,[2] and so the present discussion will limit itself as far as possible to the military implications of the debate. A clear demarcation between the two sets of implications is, of course, impossible.

The 'professionals' or 'modernizers' were grouped around the Chief of the PLA General Staff, Lo Ju-ch'ing (Lo Ruiqing),[3] while the 'guerrillas' or 'Maoists' gathered under the banner of the Minister of Defence, Lin Piao (Lin Biao). Also included as a target of the latter group's denunciations was Marshal P'eng Teh-huai (Peng Dehuai), whom Lin replaced as Minister of Defence in 1959. At the time he was purged in 1959, P'eng appears to have been part of a group of military professionals who argued that Mao's doctrine of guerrilla warfare was outdated, especially in the nuclear era, that the next war was unlikely to be a protracted one allowing for post-attack mobilization, and that therefore rapid modernization and professionalization of the PLA was necessary in an atmosphere free from the meddling of party functionaries.

P'eng's purge was preceded by a series of denunciations of unnamed persons who held 'purely military views' which 'one-sidedly stress the suddenness and complexity of modern warfare . . . [and] assert the system of Party committees will impede the better judgement and concentration of command . . .'.[4] Furthermore, as a later article charged, these miscreants were 'one-sidedly stressing the role of atomic weapons and modern military techniques'. Most serious of all, they 'stood for mechanical application of foreign [read: 'Soviet'] experience'.[5] The articles appeared in *Chieh-fang-chün pao* (Jiehfangjun pao — *Liberation Army Daily*) and *Jen-min jih-pao* (Renmin ribao — *People's Daily*) in the wake of an unusually prolonged conference of the Military Committee of the Chinese Communist Party (CCP) Central Committee in May-June 1958, suggesting that a sharp debate over the questions outlined above took place at that conference. The reader should remember well the wording of the above denunciations: the exact same formulations were used when the debate was rekindled during the 1960s; and as the Soviets are fond of saying, 'it is no accident, comrades'.

Having set forth some of the background necessary for the interpretation of the material on military doctrine that emerged in the course of the 'Strategic Debate' and the GPCR, the discussion will proceed with an analysis of the two 'lines' of 'active' and 'passive' defence by comparing their different responses to the questions of military doctrine outlined above.

As will be readily apparent, the sources frequently employ the technique of 'waving the red flag to oppose the red flag', or as Donald Zagoria has called it, the 'of course . . . but . . .' technique; this consists of making a ritual obeisance to a formulation — usually an unassailable orthodoxy — used by the opposition, but following this affirmation with a different stress or definition, or placing it in a different context in order to indicate the author's disagreement, but according to the accepted ritual.[6] To wit, the article on the 'Basic Differences Between the Proletarian and Bourgeois Military Lines' (hereinafter 'Basic Differences') flourishes a section heading in bold-face type reading:

> Active Defence and Passive Defence Are Two Diametrically Opposed Principles of Strategic Guidance Between Chairman Mao's Military Line and the Bourgeois Military Line.[7]

In constrast, Lo Jui-ch'ing's article, 'Commemorate the Victory Over German Fascism! Carry the Struggle Against U.S. Imperialism Through to the End!' (hereinafter 'Commemorate the Victory'), contains a section heading which reads:

> The historical experience of the Anti-Fascist War also teaches us that the strategy of active defence is the only correct strategy for the socialist countries in fighting against imperialist wars of aggression.[8]

Whereas in 'Basic Differences' it is Mao who is the source of the active defence doctrine, and the article continues to cite examples from the Chinese 'War of Resistance Against Japan', for Lo the source of active defence is the 'Anti-Fascist War' (of the USSR against Nazi Germany) thus employing a Soviet model, and it is 'the only correct strategy for the *socialist countries,* plural, i.e., there is more than one socialist country, implying that the Soviet Union is still socialist, as opposed to 'revisionist'.

In case the reader has any doubts as to how Lo defines the doctrine of active defence, he discusses '[the] strategy of active defence *applied by the Soviet Supreme Command headed by Stalin* . . .,'[9] which was very different indeed from the guerrilla warfare envisaged by Mao; Soviet-style active defence involved a defence-in-depth of successive fortified lines as the 'shield', and large, armour-heavy force formations as the counter-attacking 'sword' within, which then engaged the forces that had pushed through the fortifications.

Even in the initial stages of rapid Nazi advance and envelopment of Soviet forces at or near the frontier, although the Soviets sustained staggering losses, these were not the Soviets' best forces, and some of these did escape to fight again, denying the Germans their sought-after decisive engagement; such forward deployments also may have slowed the invaders somewhat and cost them men, ammunition, and POL (petrol, oil, and lubricants). Within six weeks of the invasion, the Soviet High Command, applying some of the harsh lessons learnt in that early period, began building field fortifications in depth and deploying mobile reserves behind them, which, although they were overrun, gained time for the Soviets to develop the defence-in-depth around Moscow and to regroup.[10]

As to the conflicting uses to which the phrase 'passive defence' is put, the 'Basic Differences' criticizes

Lo Jui-ch'ing [who] has always opposed Chairman Mao's strategic concept and stood for passive defence. As early as the War of Resistance Against Japan, he followed P'eng Teh-huai in opposing Chairman Mao's correct policy of boldly arousing the masses and starting up guerrilla war independently in the enemy's rear . . .[11]

However, in Lo's discussion of the 'active defence applied by the Soviet Supreme Command' during the second world war, he defends the concept against 'gross distortion and slander', asking what alternatives there were: '. . . Or should the Soviet Union's strategy have been one of passive defence, of simply waiting to be attacked? This was obviously not to its advantage . . .'[12] Perhaps this was Lo's way of pointing out that it is the Maoist/guerrilla variant of active defence that is in fact passive, since it involves withdrawing before the enemy rather than contesting his entry into Chinese territory. This essentially passive approach is especially pronounced in the Maoist/guerrilla response to the question of where and when the enemy is to be engaged.

While the Maoist/guerrilla 'active defencists' appear to confine their discussion to operations within Chinese territory and bristle at any who would 'negate the historical experience and fine tradition of our army' — which of course is largely relevant to *civil* war and to resistance — they and the professionals/modernizers appear to agree that the latter have a different territorial focus. Indeed, 'Basic Differences' charges that 'Lo Jui-ch'ing maintains that with new technical equipment "any invading enemy can be annihilated on the sea, in the air, *or at the base from which it launches its attack*"'.[13] Obviously, engaging an invader decisively at the base from which it launches its attack is very different from waiting until he is already on Chinese territory — an unheard-of concept in the doxology of People's War. In 'Commemorate the Victory', Lo himself envisaged a strategic pursuit phase of carrying the war out of the country to the territory of the aggressor:

> The strategy of active defence does not stop with driving the aggressors out of the country, but requires strategic pursuit to destroy the enemy at his starting point, to destroy him in his nest. As Stalin put it, we must not allow a wounded beast to crawl back to recuperate; we must follow on its heels in hot pursuit and finish it off in its own lair.[14]

The question of where the enemy is to be engaged is closely related to a second question: whether territory should be traded for time, or whether a partially 'positional' defence should be conducted in order to hold assets and exact enemy attrition.

In response to this question the two groups battle over the competing doctrines of 'luring-in-deep' and 'halting the enemy beyond the gate', a dispute that dates back to the 1930s (*supra*). The Maoist/guerrilla variant advocates trading space for time by withdrawing before the invader's advance, thereby inducing him to penetrate deep into the country's interior so that Chinese superiority in manpower can be brought to bear, and forcing him to overextend his logistical lines of communication (LOCs), which would then be vulnerable to interdiction. A partisan of this group wrote in a 1965 *Peking Review* article, 'Strategically Pitting One

Against Ten, Tactically Pitting Ten Against One: An Exposition of Comrade Mao Tse-tung's Thinking On the Strategy and Tactics of the People's War', that during the Third Revolutionary Civil War Period:

> At the start of the war the Kuomintang reactionaries gathered together more than 1,600,000 troops to launch an all-out offensive against us. Our army then put into practice the principle of active defence, that is, it made rapid withdrawals and advances over great distances, abandoning on its own initiative some cities and places so as to *lure the enemy in deep* and then, concentrating an absolutely superior force and selecting weak and isolated units of the enemy, wiped these out one by one while they were on the move . . .[15]

An obvious and fatal weakness of 'luring-in-deep' is that it depends entirely on the assumption that the invader has unlimited objectives and can indeed be induced to penetrate deep into the interior in an (ill-advised) attempt to subjugate the entire country. If, however, the invader has only *limited* objectives, such as partially dismembering China and seizing an outlying province or two, this could possibly be achieved *before* the invader's logistical LOCs are overstrained, and before China's superiority in manpower could be brought to bear. In order to withstand attack by superior forces with limited objectives it would be necessary to force them to sustain a high rate of attrition from the outset and to prevent them from achieving their objective rapidly, i.e. within their logistical limits. This could be achieved by creating a dense network of self-contained and mutually supporting positional defences blocking invasion routes; these hard-points would have to be reduced by the invader; otherwise they could interdict LOCs not only for logistics but also for second echelon forces or reserves being sent either to exploit a successful axis of advance or to support a flagging one, depending on the invader's 'style' of warfare.

These measures presuppose at the very least a willingness to build and man fairly extensive static defences at forward locations — a disposition that is nowhere evident in the Maoist/guerrilla outlook. Indeed, the Maoist/guerrilla group, in its preoccupation with luring-in-deep, subjects any suggestion of measures designed to slow the invader's progress to withering criticism. 'Basic Differences' attacks those who, like

. . . China's Khrushchev [Liu Shao-ch'i] said: 'Hold the enemy back' and 'it will
be bad if the enemy comes in'. Lo Jui-ch'ing also said: 'New conditions are
different', and that the only method to be used was that of '*blocking the water*'.
Such absurd statements are nothing new, they are simply the same trash of
passive defence, of '*engaging the enemy outside the gates*', which was criticized
by Chairman Mao as early as the thirties.

Acting according to this wrong policy would inevitably lead to the *building of
defensive works everywhere and wide dispersal of forces to man them*. In this
way, we would always be in a passive position and this would lead finally to the
wreck of the proletarian regime. This is the psychology characteristic of the
successors to Khrushchev revisionism . . .[16]

A corollary to the opposition to 'the building of defensive works
everywhere and wide dispersal of forces to man them' is the role of
city-defence. Consistent with the Maoist/guerrilla belief that
holding territory is not of primary importance, cities, even major
ones, should likewise be traded in return for the dispersal of enemy
forces that would be necessary in order to garrison them.
Abandoning cities also serves to avoid a major encounter with the
enemy on terms thought to favour the latter, as might occur in a
siege in which the defenders are inadequately armed. Li Tso-p'eng,
in 'Strategically Pitting . . .', maintained that:

. . . the outcome of a war does not depend on the seizure or loss of a city or place
but on the decrease or increase of effective strength of the belligerents . . .
Facing the attacks of a powerful enemy, in order to concentrate our troops to
annihilate the enemy forces or *to prevent the main force of our army from being
compelled to engage the enemy* and suffering his attacks, it is not only
permissible to abandon some places temporarily, but also necessary to *give up
places in exchange for the dispersal of enemy troops,* thus making the enemy sink
ever deeper into the sea of the people.[17]

From a close reading of Lo Jui-ch'ing's 'Commemorate the
Victory', it appears that he did indeed envisage a response to
external threat very different from that advocated by the
Maoist/guerrilla group, particularly with regard to the above
questions. There are several indications that this was the subject of
a heated intramural debate. The publication in the same issue of
Peking Review of a *Jen-min jih-pao* (JMJP) editorial, 'Unrivalled
Power of the People's Revolutionary War' side-by-side with Lo's

piece and an opposing *JMJP* editorial which also seemed to take issue with Lo's views ('The Historical Experience of the War Against Fascism') is especially revealing. The piece on the 'Unrivalled Power' employed a curious rhetorical device in which it summarized and counterposed the contending viewpoints thus in bold-face type:

> . . . But no matter how many warships and aeroplanes US imperialism may use, the people's revolutionary war has its own style of fighting. *You may seize cities while I occupy the countryside. You may dig yourself in while I wage guerrilla warfare everywhere. You may count on your up-to-date weapons while I rely on the politically awakened masses.* It can be boiled down to this: you fight in your fashion and we fight in ours.[18]

The unnamed 'you' being taken to task here is undoubtedly Lo Jui-ch'ing and his functional adherents. As in the arcane art of Kremlinology, when two or more articles expressing different views on the same subject are published in the same journal or newspaper within a fairly brief interval, it is usually an indication of the existence of a factional dispute; when the articles appear in the same issue of the same journal or in different publications on the same day it is *a fortiori* a signal — an intentional one — that such is the case.

As discussed above, Lo employs the technique of 'waving the red flag to oppose the red flag' in advocating a doctrine of active defence *not* as defined by the Maoist/guerrilla group according to Chinese experience, but as applied by the Soviet Union in the second world war, which is an entirely different concept.

Lo also waves the red flag to oppose the red flag where he reiterates the orthodox (i.e. Maoist) dictum on the role of territory:

> Operationally, the strategy of active defence should not have the holding or capturing of territory as its main objective. It should be to concentrate superior forces to destroy the enemy's effectives [sic].

With the very next sentence, however, he begins his rebuttal:

> It was *precisely* by adopting this strategy in the anti-fascist Patriotic War that the

Soviet Union forced Hitler to halt his troops before *high mountains* and *outside fortified cities* along the far-flung battle*line* stretching from Leningrad, Moscow and Stalingrad to the Caucasus, so that they were *caught in an impasse,* unable either to advance or to retreat, and suffered tremendous losses.[19]

Where he speaks of halting the enemy 'along the far-flung battle*line*', Lo appears to conceive of the theatre of operations in linear terms, i.e., as characterized by an extended and identifiable front separating the opposing forces; this is a markedly different conception from that of the Maoists, in whose view there is no clear demarcation between front and rear, as is to be expected in an insurgency or civil war situation in which there is no permanently held territory.

This does *not* necessarily mean that Lo was arguing for a *linear defence,* which consists of concentrating all available forces in a single frontal belt and attempting to forestall enemy penetrations. Against an attacker employing a manoeuvre doctrine — as in Lo's example of the Nazi German invasion of the USSR — once a breakthrough of the defensive line is achieved and exploited, severing the defender's communications and supply, the entire defence is disrupted; in short, the game is up. This was not, however, the case in the example cited by Lo. In a defence-in-depth, such as that organized by the Soviets, the battlefield may be described as 'granular' or 'cellular' rather than linear. Here, successive and mutually-supporting lines or 'hedgehog'-like cells disposing of anti-tank weapons and artillery are arrayed in depth to form a 'grid'. These units are not themselves disrupted by envelopment, since they are at least temporarily self-sustaining; instead, they disrupt the enemy attack by separating its components. Although many tanks can bypass the hedgehogs, the tanks' unarmoured or less heavily armoured support elements, the infantry and supply, cannot follow since they are highly vulnerable to artillery fire from the hedgehogs. Those forces that have not been trapped in the interstices of the defensive grid — either between the successive lines or in the gaps between hedgehogs — and emerge on the other side will be weakened and unbalanced, having been deprived of their support. They can then be engaged by defending mobile forces that have been held farther back.

Lo's reference to halting the enemy 'before high mountains and outside fortified cities' should be viewed in the above context. The phrases used suggest that he favoured the construction of fixed defences with the flanks covered by natural barriers and the intervals filled with obstacles, such as those ringing Moscow and the other cities he names, and that these were to be located 'along a far-flung battleline . . .'. This interpretation is supported by Lo's point, after explaining the '[it] was precisely by adopting this strategy' that the Soviet Union forced the German forces to a halt before these natural and man-made obstacles along an extended front, 'so that they were *caught in an impasse, unable either to advance or to retreat,* and suffered tremendous losses'.[20] The reference fits the Soviet-style defence-in-depth described above, and may allude to how in this model the enemy forces, unable to bypass strong points, are caught between successive fortified lines and destroyed.

Lo's emphasis on the Battle of Stalingrad is also significant in the following regard: 'Over 300,000 German fascist crack troops were encircled and annihilated in the Battle of Stalingrad, which marked the turning-point of World War II.'[21] Aside from underscoring the positive role of city-defence, the reference to the loss of General Paulus' Sixth Army may be the author's way of discussing that phase in defence-in-depth in which the defender's mobile reserve engages the enemy forces that have pushed through the static defences. In a slightly different context the reference to encirclement suggests that under certain circumstances it is permissible and even desirable for the defender's main forces to engage even a formidable enemy directly in a major battle — a tactic upon which the Maoists have pronounced anathema. 'Basic Differences', for example, castigated Lo and P'eng for having 'had the presumption to concentrate the main forces of the Eight Route Army for a war of attrition with the Japanese invaders'.[22]

The order in which Lo then arranges the defence's objectives is also meaningful. His article, after commenting on the Battle of Stalingrad, continues:

In the subsequent counter-offensives the effective forces of the aggressor were successively wiped out in large numbers. Such was the brilliant strategy that brought Hitler to his doom. Experience shows that only by wiping out the enemy's effectives [sic] is it possible successfully to change the military situation, *to defend cities and other places* and *finally* to defeat the aggressor.[23]

It is significant that Lo refers to the *defence* of cities 'and other places' and not to their surrender and eventual recovery, as do the Maoists, who do not use the word 'defence'in conjunction with fixed assets. The latter also argue, in reverse order, that 'only' by 'annihilating' the aggressor's 'effective strength' is it possible to defeat the aggressor (one) and thereby 'hold' cities and other places (two), whereas the professionals/modernizers exemplified by Lo argue that 'only' by wiping out the enemy's 'effective forces' is it possible *successfully* to change the relation of forces, to defend cities and other places (one), and 'finally' to defeat the aggressor (two). For Lo, it appears that the defence of 'cities and other places' is both a means to the end of defeating the enemy and an end in itself; for the Maoists, consistent with the doctrine of luring-in-deep, the concept of city defence doesn't really exist — at most it is incidental to the enemy's defeat.

In the strategic debate of the mid-sixties between the professional/modernizers faction and the Maoist/guerrilla faction, the latter had the last word. For ten years the PLA was involved in anything but the military profession: the military academies were closed down, teaching materials destroyed, no large-scale exercises were held, and the guerrillas' emphasis on ideological fervour 'turned the People's Liberation Army into the only army in the world which "studied culture only but no military affairs",' as a 1981 *Junshi Xueshu* (Military Science) article put it.[24]

With the accession to power of Teng Hsiao-p'ing (Deng Xiaoping) and the rehabilitation of several prominent victims of the Cultural Revolution who were associated with the professional/modernizer faction, there began what is developing into a radical revision of People's War. The revisions under way are largely concerned with the Maoist doctrine of 'active defence', discussed above, although they include related questions of force structure and command-and-control.

Among the victims of the Cultural Revolution who have been rehabilitated are two figures with whom the reader is by now familiar: Minister of Defence Marshal P'eng Teh-huai and PLA Chief of Staff Lo Jui-ch'ing. Both Lo and P'eng, as we have seen, were identified with the views of military 'professionals' seeking the rapid modernization of the PLA and the employment of operational and tactical doctrines different from those favoured by the 'Maoist' guerrillas. P'eng's rehabilitation in December 1978 was posthumous. Since the beneficiary was already dead and rehabilitation could do little to ameliorate this circumstance, it may be assumed that the intention of the rehabilitation was largely symbolic. When Lo was rehabilitated, however, in 1975, he was still very much alive and received a post on the Party Politburo's Military Affairs Committee, where as of 1978 he was reportedly working with Army General Su Yü, a vice minister of defence, on a study of the PLA's 'war-fighting ability'.[25] Given his doctrinal predilections, Lo's involvement in the study suggests the locus of current Chinese concerns about weaknesses in PLA doctrine as well as capabilities. More recently, at the national Military Academy, Su reportedly said that rote repetition of Mao's dicta had 'greatly hampered the development of military thought'.[26]

As in the political sphere, for reasons of regime legitimacy — and perhaps because there are still many PLA figures whose careers flourished during the tenure of the Maoist/guerrilla faction and who would actively resist a frontal assault of their positions — 'Mao Zedong's military thinking' cannot be abandoned entirely. Instead, a re-evaluation of the Great Helmsman is taking place, like that promulgated in the 'Resolution on Certain Questions in the History of Our Party Since the Founding of the PRC' adopted at the Sixth Central Committee Plenum in 1981, which is calculated to displace Mao from his pre-eminent position in the Chinese Communist calendar of saints, not by decanonizing him, but by canonizing others. Since Mao's successors have no alternative source of legitimacy, they are compelled to posture themselves as Mao's coadjutors.

In order to introduce changes in Chinese military doctrine without appearing to challenge Mao directly, it is affirmed that 'Mao Zedong's military thinking will still develop', that Mao himself never intended that his 'thought' be applied inflexibly, and that there are several aspects of Chinese experience of which 'it was a pity that Comrade Mao Zedong had no time to make a systematic summation' — a task that presumably will be carried out by his successors. In order further to legitimize what from the standpoint of People's War would be unorthodox concepts, not least since they were associated with persons disgraced in some purge or anti-this-or-that campaign, it is stressed that a number of 'revolutionary martyrs and comrades who are still living' have made 'important contributions to creating and developing our party's military theory. In fact, they directly participated in activities of creating Mao Zedong's military thinking . . .'[27] (At the head of the list is

Comrade Peng Dehuai, about whom there has developed something of a cult.) Thus, Mao Zedong's military thinking has been defined as the product of a collegial effort, as 'The Crystallization of the Collective Wisdom of the Whole Party and the Whole Army'.

In summary, it is stated that 'we must adhere to the basic tenets and most of the principles of Mao Zedong's military thinking but should also supplement them in accordance with new situations'. People's War will become People's War Under Modern Conditions. 'Under modern conditions', however, 'there are many aspects in a people's war which differ from the people's war of our army's history.'[28]

Persons haven't been the only objects of rehabilitation: this state of grace has also been extended to several military doctrines. Among the aspects of people's war under modern conditions that are markedly different from the version of people's war that has prevailed until the present, is the expected duration of the war. It appears that the 'protracted' is being taken out of the Maoist 'theory' of 'Protracted War'. That is, there seems to be an increasing appreciation of the potential decisiveness of what the Soviets term 'the initial period of war'. (Indeed, there is even an important Soviet textbook on military history with that title.) There are numerous Chinese references to 'the first stage of war', and to tactics in 'an initial battle to gain a favourable position'. In an account of a major military exercise, Zhang Zhen, deputy chief of the PLA General Staff, told the Chinese press agency *XINHUA* that 'the ground, naval, and air force adopted campaign training for senior and medium-grade officers last year', with '. . . concentrated training of senior officers conducted in north China . . . The practice proved a good combination of training with solving practical questions *arising during an initial battle*.'[29] These are phrases that would have been considered heretical not long ago, since they undermine the very basis of People's War: its protracted duration, allowing the entire nation to be mobilized, which in turn is supposed to endow the struggle with a popular — as opposed to elite, or professional — nature. Rather than being protracted, however, it is now held that 'future war has the characteristics of being abrupt, flexible, intense, continuous, in great depth and three-dimensional; the course of war and the time of battle may be shortened and the high-speed nature of it may be enhanced'.[30] This characterization itself entails revisions in several other areas: operational doctrine (grand tactics), force structure, and command-and-control. It was probably prompted in part by the recognition of several fatal weaknesses in the Maoist doctrine that could redound to an invader's advantage if the invader has limited objectives, and by the conclusion that while applicable to an *insurgency* or revolutionary war situation in which there is no permanently controlled territory, the doctrine was completely inapplicable to the defence of a *state*.

It now appears that luring-in-deep has fallen into disfavour. In a 1979 speech before a Military Academy audience, Colonel General Xiao Ke — presently the commandant of the Academy of Military Sciences and a member of the Party Central Committee (CC) and the Standing Committee of the CC Military Commission — read an obituary for luring-in-deep. He prefaced his remarks by stressing the necessity of studying modern strategy, tactics and military science and technology, and noted critically that 'in the past, we did not dare to study and discuss strategy and campaigns, and when we talked about strategy we limited ourselves by referring only to the "problems of strategy in China's revolutionary war" . . .'. Xiao then stated in no uncertain terms that:

> *To follow the method of 'luring the enemy in deep' used by the Red Army during the Jiangxi period and to apply it mechanically today would be absurd.* At that time, we occupied no cities and had no modern industry: we took everything we needed from the enemy, and when the enemy came, we 'strengthened our defences and cleared the fields to lure the enemy in deep, throwing open our arms and inviting him to come in.' Therefore, we must study new ways of war in accordance with the developing situation.[31]

This is logically consistent with the view that 'future war' will be anything but protracted. If the war is to be decided within a short period of time, it would be folly to retain a 'method' of defence which both requires an extended period of time for its implementation and which itself shortens the period of decision by facilitating the enemy's achievement of his objectives.

The weaknesses of luring-in-deep cited by Xiao — surrendering cities and modern industry — are particularly acute in the case of Manchukuo (Manchuria), which forms a salient, bounded on three sides by Soviet or Soviet-controlled territory, and which the USSR seized in 1945 in a ten-day lightning campaign. Despite some measure of dispersion of industry introduced fairly recently, the highest concentration of Chinese heavy and defence-related industry is still in Manchuria, which is also covered by a well-developed road and railway network (in fact, the Chinese Eastern Railway is a spur of the Soviet Trans-Siberian Railway), and has several principal oilfields and refineries. In the event of a Soviet invasion, were the Chinese to act according to luring-in-deep, they would effectively surrender these assets, thus denying themselves the means to continue anything but a symbolic resistance.

Along the Sino-Soviet border the USSR has, according to Chinese and Japanese sources, at least fifty-one divisions deployed,[32] of which a minimum of thirty-nine are located in the Transbaykal and Far Eastern Military Districts (MDs).[33] The major invasion routes into Manchuria are located in these MDs, as can be seen by consulting any decent map of the area. The Soviets have also created the specialized command-and-control infrastructure necessary to control a limited land-grab in this area — the same command that was used to control the Soviet invasion of Manchuria in 1945.[34] These developments are doubtless of great concern to China, and Chinese statements on defence matters should be read with this concern in mind.

The significance of dropping luring-in-deep from the Chinese doctrinal inventory is heightened when it is considered in conjunction with other modifications: it appears that the Maoist injunction against city defence has also been rescinded. Whereas it had been an article of faith that abandoning cities 'and other places' would cause the enemy to disperse his forces, leaving him with fewer disposable forces to employ against the defenders, and that to do otherwise was tantamount to conducting a 'passive' defence, such is no longer the case. A September 1981 *Junshi Xueshu* (Military Science) article, reprinted in *Hongqi* (Hung-ch'i — *Red Flag*), the main party theoretical journal, after mentioning several past practices that are now 'absolutely impermissible', noted ever so delicately that 'the principle of "not making the preservation and capture of a city or place the main objective" is also not wholly applicable to future wars'.[35] That the 'preservation and capture of cities' may in some cases constitute a main objective begs the question of how this is to be implemented. A likely technique is suggested in the statement of one observer of the Chinese military that 'plans have been made for the defence of certain key cities, with civilians and military admonished to turn them into "Stalingrads".'[36]

It is unlikely that the reference to the Stalingrad model is accidental. It is interesting that the same formulation was employed by Lo Jui-ch'ing in his *Peking Review* article, 'Commemorate the Victory Over German Fascism . . .' analysed above; it is likewise curious, then as now, that the speaker does not recoil from overt reference to a *Soviet* model.

In the context of the Stalingrad model, the retrieval of positional defence from the dust-bin to which it had been consigned by the guerrilla faction is also significant. The *Junshi Xueshu* article cited above stresses that

during the first stage of a war, *we should mainly use positional defensive warfare, with powerful support and coordination of mobile warfare* and guerrilla warfare in order to gradually consume and annihilate the enemy's strength and bring about a change in the balance of strength between the enemy and us.[37]

This formulation — the use of positional defences supported by mobile forces — resembles Lo Jui-ch'ing's use of the Stalingrad model of a defence-in-depth. The resemblance is reinforced by the statement in the same paragraph of the *Junshi Xueshu* article that in the course of 'adhering to the armed forces system of integrating field armies, local armies, guerrillas and militiamen, we should establish garrison forces and reserve forces adequate for the fighting tasks'. As has been shown, the word 'garrison' is not to be found in the Maoist/guerrilla vocabulary. Indeed, the garrisoning of positional defences was roundly criticised as an attribute of 'passive defence', as in 'Basic Differences Between the Proletarian and Bourgeois Military Lines' (1967): 'Acting according to this wrong policy would inevitably lead to the building of defensive works everywhere and wide dispersal of forces to man them. In this way we would always be in a passive position.'[38]

In a defence-in-depth, however, 'garrison forces' would be needed to man fixed defence works arrayed in depth, and mobile 'reserve forces' would be held behind the successive fortified lines or hedgehogs, in order to engage whatever enemy armour had pushed through the fortified zone. The reference to 'reserve forces' is also significant. In Maoist/guerrilla usage, 'reserves' refer to using the people's militia to replenish the ranks of the main forces or field armies; in the present context, however, the word is apparently used to mean *standing* reserves, i.e. additional echelons of regular forces.

From the *Junshi Xueshu* article it does not appear that the linear/preclusive defence denounced by the Maoists — 'defensive works everywhere and wide dispersal of forces to man them' — is contemplated. Instead, in implementing

> a positive defence, we cannot fully practise quick-decision warfare on exterior lines in campaigns and operations *but* should practise instead *defensive warfare of strong positions in a certain direction or at a certain place together with the field armies' quick-decision offensive warfare* on exterior lines in order to keep the stability of the defence.[39]

Whereas a linear-style defence collapses once the defender's line is breached, since this will sever lines of communication and support, the defence-in-depth is designed to continue functioning in the event of multiple enemy breakthroughs; in fact, it is only by permitting such penetrations that it is possible to unbalance the enemy force by separating its components. The armour will be separated from its less well-protected infantry and other support as the enemy columns push their way through the defender's successive fortified lines, or find their way between mutually supporting hedgehogs. These 'hedgehogs' ('strong positions') are at least temporarily self-sustaining, so that they will not be cut off from their support, even if surrounded. Whether successive lines or staggered hedgehogs are used, these are not arranged in a continuous line following the contours of the border as this would sacrifice depth for frontage, but cover likely axes of enemy approach ('certain directions' — 'direction' can be another word for 'axis', as in Soviet military parlance), or valuable fixed assets such as industrial or other installations ('certain places'). Mobile armour-heavy reserves capable of engaging enemy armour ('the field armies'* quick-decision offensive warfare') once the latter is deprived of its support, are held behind the zone of field fortifications.

---

*For 'field armies' read 'main forces' (MF) divisions, to which all armoured assets are reserved.

This division of tasks optimizes the capabilities of the different types of forces available to the defender. Furthermore, this scheme permits a materially and technologically inferior defender to deny a superior invader fighting according to a manoeuvre/shock doctrine the advantage of fighting on its own terms. The defence-in-depth is thus well-suited to China's defence against the USSR, since the Soviets employ the manoeuvre style of warfare characteristic of armoured forces, which is devastatingly effective against a defence lacking depth and coherence (even one vastly better equipped and trained than the Chinese, as were the French and British forces overrun at the outset of the second world war by the numerically and technologically *inferior* Nazi forces employing *Blitzkrieg* tactics). The defence-in-depth would also exploit to the fullest China's strength in manpower and tend to minimize its inferiority in manoeuvre capability.

Soviet doctrine calls for the rapid advance into the enemy's depth simultaneously along multiple and sometimes converging axes. Advancing units seek what Liddell Hart called the 'line of least resistance', bypassing centres of strongest enemy resistance;[40] in its Soviet incarnation this tactic appears as the reinforcement of success. This is made possible by the echelonning-in-depth of well-balanced forces: Soviet force structure is characterized by the integration of tanks at all levels (divisional, regimental, and battalion) with supporting infantry riding in infantry-fighting vehicles and with self-propelled artillery; the mechanized infantry and artillery reduce the vulnerability of the armour to the defender's anti-tank weapons by suppressing the latter's fire.

In order to unhinge this style of offensive it is necessary to change the nature of the battlefield, so that it will not be the highly fluid one in which superior Soviet manoeuvre forces have the advantage. This change is also necessary to unbalance the Soviet forces by separating their components from one another. These are the goals that the defence-in-depth is designed to achieve.

In order to change the nature of the battlefield, the necessary changes in military doctrine must be complemented by suitable changes in force structure. To date, the Chinese PLA force structure has been over-compartmentalized and unbalanced, resembling the Soviet Red Army of the pre-world war two period. (The Soviets, of course, have since applied the lessons learnt from the Nazi *Blitzkrieg* and have replicated as far as possible the well-balanced and highly manoeuvrable composition of the latter's *Panzerkampfgruppen*.) According to the *Military Balance* published yearly by the International Institute for Strategic Studies (IISS) in London, the PLA is organized into tank divisions, infantry (non-mechanized) divisions, anti-tank and anti-aircraft artillery divisions.[41] While there is some integration of arms at the divisional level — tank divisions, for example, dispose of one infantry regiment, and infantry divisions dispose of one tank regiment — it is limited in extent, and (also unlike the latter-day Soviet model) does not extend to lower echelons. That is, at the regimental, battalion, and company level the units are incapable of the independent action necessitated by the modern, highly fluid battlefield. Aside from the heightened vulnerability of each component when it is not part of a combined-arms team, such a compartmentalized structure means that the task of coordinating the different arms is left to the highest command levels; this arrangement is simply too unwieldy to meet the exigencies of modern battle — a weakness that was highlighted in the Chinese pedagogical exercise in the Socialist Republic of Vietnam.

There are indications that this approach is being substantially revised in favour of the combined-arms concept. Probably this is due to the Chinese realization that, as an article in *Jen-min Jih-pao* (Renmin Ribao) noted, 'future war already presents itself as "manoeuvrable", characterized by offensive military operations with rapidly changing lines of front'. This statement was quoted by a Soviet observer in a 1979 *Voyenno-Istoricheskiy Zhurnal* (*Military-Historical Journal*) article; the author also indicated that this marks a departure from earlier concepts of 'partisan war'.[42] The changes underway are apparently of sufficient moment, therefore, to have caught the attention of Soviet military analysts and to have received mention in open Soviet sources.

No doubt in order to create a more flexible structure better suited to the rapid tempo and fluid character of modern manoeuvre warfare, the PLA has reportedly been experimenting since about 1978 with integrating armoured units with selected infantry; copies of a Soviet BMP (an armed and armoured infantry-fighting vehicle) that would greatly enhance the mobility of infantry on the battlefield have also been observed.[43]

This putative shift has also been reflected in Chinese press coverage of recent large-scale exercises, which were held in Northern China in September 1981. Early in 1982, *XINHUA* cited the deputy chief of the PLA General Staff as having disclosed that the 'Chinese People's Liberation Army improved its military training last year by shifting the stress from infantry to tank warfare, *from single service to combined units* and from fighters to commanders'.[44] In an earlier article, 'Sketch of a Military Training Ground in the North', the authors described the mock attack of a 'blue' tank army with bomber and attack plane (close air) support on a 'red' army in positional defences laying down cannon and rocket fire. An anti-tank guided missile, 'Red Arrow', was also described, as was the air-dropping of mines, poetically described as like the 'heavenly maiden scattering flowers'. From the context it may be surmised that the attacking tank-heavy 'blue' forces represented the Soviets and the defending 'red' forces in positional defences represented the Chinese. (Although not the only reason for this inference, it is inconceivable that self-styled revolutionaries would cast themselves as anything but 'red'.) Significantly, two participants in the exercise were quoted as stressing

'. . . Look, to totally wipe out this many armoured reptiles so forcefully required the integrated striking power of a combined-arms force!' (Narrator:) a cadre at his side took up the thread of the conversation:
'In the past, once modern warfare was mentioned one thought of an attack by a concentrated group of tanks — a dark mass of tanks shoving its way forward! Therefore, *some people* felt that we lacked the means to do this. That was because . . . *we had long been confined to our own little world of a single service arm,* thought only of the weapons at hand, *and could not see the power of combined operations.*'[45]

Quaint phraseology to the contrary, this is a not unsophisticated observation.

The new emphasis on combined-arms operations is apparently of sufficient interest and duration for it to have been discussed in the Hong Kong communist media. A *Ta Kung Pao* article on PLA Army Day, 'The PLA Enters Three-Dimensional Warfare Training — China's Military Affairs Take a New Step Toward Modernization', observed that:

The characteristic that has drawn most attention in the PLA's training in recent years is that all branches of the armed forces have carried out training in three-dimensional warfare called in China 'training in synthetic warfare'. This means that the army, navy and air force and the missile units, tank units, antichemical units and so on all closely coordinate in training . . . This has brought about a great change in the former practice of training each branch of the armed forces alone.[46]

This emphasis on training would have been inconceivable during the tenure of the 'guerrilla' faction: it would have been denounced as 'bourgeois' at the very mildest. The charges levelled against Lo Jui-ch'ing to justify his purge (retroactively) are a case in point. As stated in a 1967 *Peking Review* article, 'Hold High the Great Red Banner of Mao Tse-tung's Thought, Thoroughly Criticize and Repudiate the Bourgeois Military Line' (Chinese polemics are not known for their analytical detachment):

> On his own authority Lo decided to make a big show throughout the army of military skills. He made great efforts to ensure top priority to military affairs and technique . . .[47]

Furthermore, as the 'Basic Differences' article published in the same journal later that year charged,

> Lo Jui-ch'ing used contests in military skill to obstruct politics and disrupt the study of Chairman Mao's works. Vice-Chairman Lin Piao promptly corrected this mistake and again issued instructions to put politics to the fore. But Lo Jui-ch'ing still resisted desperately and talked such nonsense as: 'Military training itself is politics, the biggest politics'. This argument which puts politics and military affairs on a par and replaces politics with military affairs is an out and out bourgeois military viewpoint.[48]

From the perspective of the military professionals the results of 'putting politics to the fore' were disastrous. As the present commandant of the Academy of Military Sciences observed critically, the Maoist/guerrilla group exemplified by Lin Piao and the 'Gang of Four' 'did not allow the military academy to teach military affairs, saying that to teach military affairs was to pursue a purely military viewpoint and had all military teaching materials destroyed'.[49] The commandant made it clear that this policy has been reversed.

The acceptability of military professionalism is closely linked with the question of PLA regularization, as opposed to remaining an irregular, or guerrilla force. Obviously, both factors help determine the nature of the command-and-control infrastructure. As with other shifts in policy, Mao's authority is cited to legitimize placing the PLA on a regular footing. *Junshi Xueshu* pointed out that during the period of the Red Army Mao stressed its guerrilla nature:

> *but* near the end of the war of liberation, he put forth the demand that we 'should further regularize all the field armies'. During the early stage after the founding of the PRC, he again asserted that we should overcome 'the phenomenon of no centralism, no unity, lax discipline, oversimplification and guerrilla practices', and decided on the task of 'building a regular and modern army for national defence'.[50]

Regularization, of course, implies reliance on the field armies (sometimes called main forces), rather than the militia. This emphasis constitutes a frontal assault on traditional People's War: reliance on the 'people's' militia to immobilize an invader by 'conducting guerrilla warfare everywhere' is a fundamental tenet of traditional People's War. Thus, 'Basic Differences' took Lo Jui-ch'ing to task on the grounds that: 'He opposes arming the masses, opposes the people's militia system and opposes Chairman Mao's great strategic idea of a people's war'.[51] The accused was probably guilty as charged: in his own article, 'Commemorate the Victory Over German Fascism . . .', Lo stressed the need for 'close co-operation among the different armed services, *of which the ground forces, and particularly the infantry, are primary*'. He made no reference whatever to the militia in this context.[52]

The question of the role of military commanders and the extent of their independence from political control in the person of the political officers is another expression of the chronic conflict between advocates of 'regularization' on the one hand and 'putting politics to the fore' on the other, or, as the conflict is more popularly known, between 'reds' ('guerrillas') and 'experts' ('professionals'). Under traditional People's War 'reds' enjoyed unquestioned precedence over 'experts'.

It was more important that the PLA be ideologically pure than that it be able to fight. Apparently this stress resulted in a pattern in which all authority rested in the party committee, which became the locus of all decision-making. The pervasiveness of this practice understandably had a paralytic effect on command-and-control. A 1965 *Peking Review* article directed against the pro-fessional/modernizer faction in the course of the 'strategic debate' criticized those who believed that 'only those commanders and technical experts who had undergone strict professional training were to be depended on'. This grievous error was even more serious than it might appear to the uninitiated, however:

> In the name of building a modern regular army, they advocated the abolition of the Party committee system in the army, which in reality meant abolishing the Party's leadership over the army, weakening political work and negating the democratic tradition and mass line of our army. This represented a vain attempt to push the People's Liberation Army on the bourgeois road of army building.[53]

This verdict too has been overturned: it is now held that while party committee meetings have a role to play, 'working methods must be subordinated to the needs of war unconditionally . . .'. In wartime, if time permits, the committee meeting may be held; if there is no time, command initiative will be relied upon. Since

> future war has the characteristics of being abrupt, flexible, intense, continuous, in great depth and three-dimensional; the course of war and the time of battle may be shortened and the high-speed nature of it may be enhanced. Under these circumstances, what should be stressed is that the commanders should calculate the timing accurately, make correct resolution without losing a moment and act correctly and resolutely according to their own discretion.[54]

This statement envisages a degree of autonomy for commanders that would have been considered scandalous not long ago.

The final modification in the doctrines of People's War concerns the acceptability of foreign models. Under traditional People's War it was permissible to cite only Chinese Communist experience, while reference to foreign models was frowned upon. It was difficult, however, to assess this prohibition accurately since it was bound up with the question of reference to foreign — largely Soviet — influence and, indeed, direct interference in China's internal affairs. That is, over-reliance on 'foreign experience' is *sometimes* used as a codeword for pro-Soviet leanings. Attitudes towards foreign models divided along factional lines, according to each faction's assessment of the nature of the threat facing China: all factions agreed that both the US and the USSR posed threats to China; they disagreed over which was the most serious and what was its nature. 'Moderates' saw the USSR as posing the most serious military threat; the nature of this threat was military and external, making a tactical rapprochement with the United States desirable. The military 'professionals' or 'modernizers' saw 'US imperialism' as the chief external threat, which implied that a tactical accommodation with the USSR, as the only available source of military aid and protection, was necessary in order rapidly to modernize the PLA. The 'radicals' or 'guerrillas' also saw 'modern revisionism' (the USSR) as posing the most serious threat to China, but in their view this threat was not external, but *internal*: it was a threat of subversion, a threat that the US, however dangerous in other ways, was incapable of posing. The radicals' emphasis on the internal nature of the Soviet threat may partially explain their preoccupation with the PLA's ideological loyalty rather than war-fighting ability. Their viewpoint is now, of course, in deep disfavour.

Although not without continuing debate and dissension, the prohibition on learning from abroad has been replaced with a lively interest not only in foreign technology and material as exemplified by Chinese 'window-shopping' for arms in Western Europe and the United States, but also in foreign 'experience'. Commandant Xiao Ke enjoined his Military Academy audience to consider

> Our attitude toward foreign military as well as our own experiences in running academies and schools . . . we must do away with the closed-door policy on military affairs, have the courage to learn from foreign armies, particularly enemy armies, 'take the enemy as our teacher and make it suit our purposes'.[55]

In summary, the 'professionals' or 'modernizers' faction appears to have carried the day: 'luring-in-deep' has been replaced with the idea that territory and fixed assets are indeed important and should be defended; the prohibition on city defence has been reversed; the injunction against positional defence has also been reversed, all of which suggests that a defence-in-depth is contemplated; in addition, emphasis has shifted from the militia to the main forces (field armies); emphasis has also shifted from the single service arm to combined-arms operations; the concept of the battlefield itself as it is conventionally understood in more advanced regular armies has been introduced, symbolizing the People's Liberation Army's shift from an irregular (guerrilla) to a regular footing. These are modifications that will enhance China's modest ability to withstand a Soviet attack of limited scope. These modifications must also be implemented in advance of any arms acquisitions or technology transfers from Western suppliers in order for such acquisitions to be effective.

Such is the Chinese PLA's 'new look'. Given the congenital instability of a political system that does not provide for a regularized succession, however, any resolution of the military debate and of the accompanying factional competition must be considered provisional: it may resurface as soon as the next succession crisis arises. Any resolution of the intramural conflict is also partial as the author of a 1981 article in *Junshi Xueshu* (*Military Science*) noted cryptically: 'To date, there are still a lot of questions on which a unified understanding has not been reached'.

Notes

1. See Jerome Ch'en *Mao and the Chinese Revolution* (New York 1967), 177.

2. See especially Uri Ra'anan, 'Peking's Foreign Policy "Debate", 1965-1966', in Tang Tsou (ed.), *China in Crisis,* Vol. 2 (Chicago 1968); Donald Zagoria, 'The Strategic Debate in Peking', ibid.; Harry Harding and Melvin Gurtov, *The Purge of Lo Jui-ch'ing: the Politics of Chinese Strategic Planning* (The Rand Corporation, R-548-PR, 1974); Thomas M. Gottlieb, *Chinese Foreign Policy Factionalism and the Origins of the Strategic Triangle* (The Rand Corporation, R-1902-NA, 1977).

3. Where the Wade Giles spelling is used in the text, the Pinyin spelling is provided in parentheses.

4. *Chieh-fang chün-pao, 1 July 1958;* Survey of the China Mainland Press (hereinafter SCMP) 1881, 24 October 1958, 4, in Donald S. Zagoria, *The Sino-Soviet Conflict 1956-61* (Princeton 1962), 191.

5. *Chieh-fang chün-pao,* 1 August 1958; SCMP 1881, 24 October 1958, 2; ibid., 191.

6. A fascinating passage from Czeslaw Milosz' *The Captive Mind* illuminates this milieu: 'Whoever would take the measure of intellectual life in the countries of

Central or Eastern Europe from the monotonous articles appearing in the press or the stereotyped speeches pronounced there, would be making a grave error. Just as theologians in periods of strict orthodoxy expressed their views in the rigorous language of the Church, so the writers of the people's democracies make use of an accepted special style, terminology, and linguistic ritual. What is important is not what someone said but what he wanted to say, disguising his thought by removing a comma, inserting an "and", establishing this rather than another sequence in the problems discussed. Unless one has lived there one cannot know how many titanic battles are being fought, how the heroes of Ketman are falling, what this warfare is being waged over.' (Cited in Zagoria, op. cit.)

7. Unnamed persons in the offices of the Headquarters of the PLA General Staff, 'Basic Differences Between the Proletarian and Bourgeois Military Lines', *Peking Review* No. 48, 24 November 1967, 14; the 'guerrilla' line was codified and promulgated in Lin Piao's well-known, 'Long Live the Victory of the People's War!' dated 3 September 1965, appearing in *Peking Review* No. 32, 4 August 1967.

8. Lo Jui-ch'ing, 'Commemorate the Victory Over German Fascism! Carry the Struggle Against US Imperialism Through to the End', *Peking Review* No. 20, 14 May 1965, 10.

9. Ibid., emphasis added.

10. See Larry H. Addington, *The Blitzkrieg Era and the German General Staff 1865-1941* (New Brunswick 1971), 203, 206-210.

11. 'Basic Differences', 15.

12. Lo Jui-ch'ing, op. cit., 10.

13. 'Basic Differences', 13, emphasis added.

14. Lo Jui-ch'ing, op. cit., 11.

15. Li Tso-p'eng, 'Strategically Pitting One Against Ten, Tactically Pitting Ten Against One: An Exposition of Comrade Mao Tse-tung's Thinking on the Strategy and Tactics of the People's War', *Peking Review* No. 15, 9 April 1965, 16. Significantly, Li's article was reprinted from *Hung-ch'i* (Hongqi — *Red Flag*), the main party theoretical journal of 22 December 1964. Emphasis added.

16. 'Basic Differences', 15, emphasis added. The accusation that Lo had advocated 'blocking the water' is intriguing in light of a passage in Sun Tzu's classic work on strategy, *The Art of War,* in which a commentator observes: 'The nature of water is that it avoids heights and hastens to the lowlands . . . Now the shape of an army resembles water. Take advantage of the enemy's unpreparedness . . . avoid his strength and strike his emptiness . . .' The metaphor of flowing water is very similar to Liddell Hart's 'line of least resistance', which is the essence of both the *Blitzkrieg* and Soviet armour doctrine, i.e. bypassing, or flowing around centres of stiff resistance in order to maintain momentum and carry the advance into the enemy's depth so as to sever his laterial LOCs, preventing him from regrouping to meet the penetration. As Chief of the PLA General Staff, it is reasonable to assume that Lo was familiar with Sun Tzu. If this is not reading too much into the reference, the phrase 'blocking the water' may refer to blocking attempts to bypass strong point defences ('avoid the heights and hasten to the lowlands'), as with additional strongpoints — that is, a defence-in-depth (Sun Tzu, *The Art of War* trans. and ed. by Samuel B. Griffith, foreword by B. H. Liddell Hart, Oxford 1980, 89.)

17. Li Tso-p'eng, op. cit., 23, emphasis added.

18. *Jen-min jih-pao* (*People's Daily*) editorial, 'Unrivalled Power of the People's Revolutionary War', *Peking Review,* 14 May 1965, 24, emphasis added.

19. Lo Jui-ch'ing, op. cit., 10, emphasis added.

20. Ibid., emphasis added.

21. Ibid., 11.

22. 'Basic Differences', 15.

23. Lo Jui-ch'ing, op. cit., 11, emphasis added.

24. Song Shilun, 'Mao Zedong's Military Thinking Is the Guide to Our Army's Victories', *Junshi Xueshu (Military Science)* No. 7, 1981; reprinted in *Hongqi,* No. 16, 16 August 1981; translation in Foreign Broadcast Information Service (FBIS)-CHI-81-180, 17 September 1981, K 22. That Song's article was reprinted in *Hongqi,* the main party theoretical journal, suggests that the views expressed in the article have received the party leadership's *imprimatur,* and that they wish to communicate this to the *cognoscenti.*

25. David Bonavia, 'The Balance Tips Towards China', *Far Eastern Economic Review* (Hong Kong), 2 February 1979, 15.

26. Quoted in ibid.

27. Song Shilun, op. cit., K 16.

28. Ibid., 21.

29. Beijing XINHUA in English, 0751 GMT 18 January 1982; FBIS-CHI-82, 19 January 1982, emphasis added.

30. Song Shilun, op. cit., K23.

31. Beijing XINHUA Domestic Service in Chinese 0315 GMT 9 September 1979; FBIS-CHI-79-176, 10 September 1979, L 15, emphasis added.

32. Nihon Keizai Shimbun, cited in Beijing XINHUA in English 1510 GMT 13 June 1981; FBIS-CHI-81-118, 19 June 1981, D2.

33. Map, 'Where the Soviet Union Deploys its Divisions', accompanying article, 'Soviet Armed Forces Show Weaknesses in Many Key Areas', *The New York Times,* 9 December 1980, A 10.

34. D. Vernet, 'Sur La Frontière Sino-Soviétique: Un dimanche comme les autres à Khabarovsk . . .', *Le Monde,* 27 February 1979, 3; Japan Defence White Paper cited in Tokyo KYODO in English 0259 GMT 5 August 1980; FBIS-APA-80-152, 5 August 1980, C 4; See also David R. Jones, *Soviet Armed Forces Review Annual,* Academic International Press, Vol. 4, 1980, 79-82.

35. Song Shilun, op. cit., K 21.

36. June Teufel Dreyer, Prepared Statement in *The Implications of U.S.-China Military Cooperation,* Workshop sponsored by the Committee on Foreign Relations, United States Senate and the Congressional Research Service, Library of Congress, US Government Printing Office, 1982, 7.

37. Song Shilun, op. cit., K 21, emphasis added.

38. 'Basic Differences', 15.

39. Song Shilun, op. cit., K 21, emphasis added.

40. See especially the Soviet literature on the Manchurian Campaign, e.g. Lilita Dzirkals, *'Lightning War' in Manchuria: Soviet Military Analysis of the 1945 Far East Campaign* (The Rand Corporation 1976).

41. *The Military Balance 1980-1981,* International Institute For Strategic Studies (London), 62-64; see also *Handbook of the Chinese Armed Forces,* US Defence Intelligence Agency, 1976, A 3-4, A 7-8; the latter source should be used with caution: it is highly imaginative in much of its discussion, to put the matter delicately. (This is probably understandable, since for approximately twenty years no Western analysts were able to observe the PLA firsthand.)

42. *Voyenno-Istoricheskiy Zhurnal* (Military-Historical Journal), (Moscow, Voyenizdat — Military Publishing House), No. 3, March 1979, 63.

43. Bonavia, op. cit., 15.

44. See n. 29, emphasis added.

45. Yan Wu, et al., 'Penetrating the Heavy Smoke of Gunpowder — Sketch of a Military Training Ground in the North', *Tianjin Ribao,* 6 November 1981, 3; Joint Publications Research Service (JPRS) 79765, 30 December 1981, emphasis added.

46. Kan Wei, 'The PLA Enters Three-Dimensional Warfare Training — China's Military Affairs Take a New Step Toward Modernization', *Ta Kung Pao* (Hong Kong) 1 August 1981, 2; FBIS-CHI-81-154, 11 August 1981, W 3.

47. *Jiefangjun Pao* editorial, 'Hold High the Great Red Banner of Mao Tse Tung's Thought, Thoroughly Criticize and Repudiate the Bourgeois Military Line', *Peking Review,* 4 August 1967, 44.

48. 'Basic Differences', 12.

49. Xiao Ke, op. cit., L 14.

50. Song Shilun, op. cit., K 20.

51. 'Basic Differences', 13.

52. Lo Jui-ch'ing, op. cit., 11, emphasis added.

53. Ho Lung, 'The Democratic Tradition of the Chinese PLA', *Peking Review,* 6 August 1965, 14.

54. Song Shilun, op. cit., K 23.

55. Xiao Ke, op. cit., L 15.

Mira Beth Lansky
is currently Fact Finding Director for the
Civil Rights Department of the Anti-
Defamation League in Washington, DC,
engaged in monitoring extremist and
terrorist groups. She is at present writing a
dissertation entitled 'Imperial Insecurity:
The Military Dimension of Soviet-Chinese
Relations'.

CLIO AND THE BITCH GODDESS

Quantification in American Political History

Allan G Bogue *Past President, Social Science History Association*

Contains a set of essays concerned with the development of social science history, written by one of its most distinguished practitioners. Bogue draws on his substantial knowledge and experience to provide a fascinating examination of the evolution of American political history over recent decades. With its blend of historiography, methodology, and historical analysis, this volume deals with a set of issues which are central to the concerns of all historians and social scientist.

New Approaches to Social Science History Volume 3
December 1983 ● approx 280 pages
Cloth (8039-2089-X) ● Paper (8039-2090-3)

 SAGE Publications ● 28 Banner Street
London EC1Y 8QE ● Telephone: (01) 253-1516

Amnon Sella

Khalkhin-Gol:
The Forgotten War

. . . Russia is an extremely cold and remote country. If I send an expedition
[there] it will doubtless end in a complete fiasco . . .

Emperor K'ang-hsi in a message to Peter the Great

On 11 May 1939, a tiny detachment from a Manchukuo-Japanese
force clashed with guards manning a remote outpost on the
Mongolian-Soviet border. This minor encounter eventually
escalated into a full-scale political and military conflict engulfing
thousands of men and vast quantities of war machines and
equipment. The War of the Khalkhin-Gol River, as it has gone
down in the annals of Soviet history, or the Nomonhan Incident, as
it is known to the Japanese, officially ended on 16 September 1939
with the conclusion of a truce between the belligerent parties. It had
cost the Japanese 25,000 and the Soviets 10,000 dead, with many
more maimed and wounded on each side.[1] When, at dawn on 20
August, the Soviets launched the victorious offensive that was to
end the war, the Molotov-Ribbentrop negotiations were nearing
their climax; when the truce was signed, Germany's drive into
Europe had already lasted a fortnight and Poland was in her death
agony. Yet once the blood of their respective champions had been
spilled, Japan and the USSR, following the custom of ancient
times, found it expedient to disengage their troops for several
years: to be precise, until 1945, when the world of Versailles lay in
ruins and new horizons were in prospect for both countries.

The present paper attempts to analyse various aspects of this
little-publicized and well-nigh forgotten war. Looking at it from a
historical standpoint it poses the question of why it took place at
all, and why at that particular moment of history. From the
military standpoint what immediately strikes the scholar is the

Journal of Contemporary History (SAGE, London, Beverly Hills and New Delhi),
Vol. 18 (1983), 651-687

remote and desolate character of the battlefield, entailing huge
problems for both combatants. The paper will examine the location
and terrain of the battlefield, the logistical problems posed by these
and the solutions to them sought by the Red Army; it will seek to
analyse how war heroes are born, or made; and last but not least it
will ask why, so soon after a brilliant victory had been achieved, the
lessons of that victory should have been disregarded and forgotten.

A few months after the War of Khalkhin-Gol had ended, the
Russians and the Japanese tried once again to reach agreement over
the border between Manchukuo and Outer Mongolia.[2] Their
representatives met in December 1939 in Chita and the following
month in Kharbin, and although their territorial claims were based
on different maps, they were able to reach some kind of general
compromise, though it was far from conclusive. The Japanese, for
their part, were in the midst of a painful reappraisal, both political
and military, of the Soviet Union, whilst the Kremlin, now
preoccupied with the first and most disastrous phase of the Winter
War in Finland, had never wanted to get involved with Japan in the
first place.

Yet despite the many reasons both sides had for exercising
caution, hundreds of major and minor incidents took place along
the borders delimiting the sovereign territory of the USSR: proof of
the ambitions still nurtured by Imperial Japan.[3]

It was certainly not for want of time that the borders between
China, Outer Mongolia and Russia had still not been agreed,
properly defined and laid down in mutually approved maps. The
first the Russians heard of China was in 1567, when two Cossacks
returned from their travels to tell Ivan the Terrible about the great
country they had discovered there.[4] After that date, informal
contacts between the two lands developed into a relationship which
from 1689 on received formal recognition in numerous diplomatic
documents.[5] Over the several decades required to consolidate this
process, both Russia and China were exposed to domestic turmoil
and repeated threats from without. In the case of both countries,
the regions where the frontiers separating them were eventually
defined lay far from their respective capitals; for both, the
development of these remote areas ranked low on their scale of
priorities. After Ivan the Terrible's reign, the Russian side of the
shared border with China was wide open to adventurers, hunters

and marauders of every kind. During the two brief episodes when, in 1669,[6] the Cossacks founded a township there, they obviously saw the place as a convenient base from which their unruly followers might launch further attacks in a region almost untouched by government. Although Albazin did not last long, the very fact of its establishment was seen by Emperor K'ang-Hsi as so great a menace that on two occasions he mobilised 30,000 troops against its population of fewer than one thousand, and this influenced the nature of the relationship between Russia and China for centuries to come.[7]

The border that took shape over the years was thus the result of a clash of opposing wills and of numerous armed encounters. Viewed in historical perspective, it is seen to reflect the declining power of the Chinese, and the ascendant power of the Russian Empire. Whereas during the late sixteenth and much of the seventeenth centuries, contacts between Russia and China testified to the former's subordinate position, by the eighteenth century Russia had acquired the status of a sovereign nation, and in the nineteenth and early twentieth centuries she became much the stronger power of the two — a change to which reciprocal treaties signed in the late nineteenth century bear witness.[8] Between 1689 and 1915 no fewer than forty-one treaties were concluded which set out to define the border or regulate trade relations between Russia, China and Mongolia, whilst several more were signed between 1917 and 1939. Yet in spite of that no agreement was ever reached as to the precise geographical demarcation of the frontier. The language of the first agreement concluded between the two countries (at Nerchinsk in 1689) is so vague as to make it difficult to determine where the geographic divide really lay. The text runs as follows:

> The river known as the Gorbitza, which flows into and runs below the River Shilka on its left side, close to the River Chernoi, shall be designated as the border between the two countries.[9]

Even in subsequent years, however, when neither terminology nor modern demarcation methods could any longer be seen as a problem, the obscurity persists.[10] In other words, even though linguistic impediments certainly arose in the early years, in the final analysis it was not language that obscured the issue but rather the fact that each of the parties — and Russia in particular — had a vested interest in fostering the obscurity until such time as each was in a position to decide contentious points in its own favour.

Before signing the treaties of Nerchinsk and later (1728) Kiakhta, the Emperors of China (K'ang-Hsi and Yung-Cheng respectively), had good political and military reasons for placating the Russians.[11] But in later years, when Russia was in the process of consolidating her Far Eastern policy, other interests came to the fore. In the course of the nineteenth century, she discovered the advantages of establishing a land bridge through Russian territory to link Europe with the Far East. The project was thought of not merely as beneficial in itself but as able to compete with the British sea route to China. The turnover of goods imported through Manchuria in fact increased during the nineteenth century: goods imported from China outweighing those exported from Russia, however.[12] Sino-Russian relations in the latter half of the nineteenth century had other unexpected repercussions on Manchuria. Despite their interest in developing their Far Eastern territories, the Russians had proved none too successful in promoting population growth there. The Chinese, on the other hand, who until the middle of the century had actively discouraged the population of Manchuria from increasing, now, wary of Russian expansionism, changed their tack. The result was that from a mere three million in mid-century, between the years 1895 and 1900, the population trebled, to nine million.[13]

The ascendancy of Imperial Russia as a great power, and the decline of the Chinese Empire, both left their mark on the diplomatic exchanges between the two powers as well as on the geographical frontiers dividing them. As China grew weaker and Russia stronger, so the Chinese were forced into making concessions in every field, whether territorial, commercial or diplomatic. Whilst Russia played the role of an expanding power, China struggled to maintain the status quo. This situation in the Far East began to change at the beginning of the twentieth century and accelerated in the first decade after the October Revolution in Russia.

At the beginning of the twentieth century and immediately after the Bolshevik Revolution, Russia was concerned mainly with her European territories, the Far Eastern regions of the country being relegated to second place in the scale of priorities. But these years witnessed the rise of a dynamic new power in the Far East in the shape of Japan. Japan's claim to territorial rights in China rested on the 'Boxer Protocol' of 7 September 1901 and on the 'Great Powers' decision at Versailles to make over to Japan Germany's concessionary rights in Shantung.[14]

However, it was Japanese military might and industrial potential which combined with Chinese instability to create the necessary preconditions for the formation in 1932 of Manchukuo. In the previous year, Japan had occupied the north-eastern provinces of China after encountering only desultory and ineffectual resistance.

The answer to the first question which this paper set out to solve is that the Soviet Far East (or if we look at it from the Chinese point of view, northern China) is an area prone to confrontation because far removed from densely populated areas and important administrative nerve centres where decisions can be reached with promptitude and authority. The social and political forces which had been linked together for centuries, but at the same time were mutually antagonistic, branched off in different directions and developed independently. The interests of each, whilst not always incompatible with those of the other, were invariably viewed by the latter with a great deal of suspicion. Over the years it has never seemed to matter what name was given to the political entity aspiring to power in this area: it has always managed to arouse the suspicion of either China or Russia. Given that the region was so remote, so climatically inhospitable and so rugged in places, it was hardly surprising that the primitive cartographic instruments in use gave inaccurate recordings, and the resulting technical obscurities led to political complications. If we bear in mind how volatile this part of Manchuria and Inner Mongolia has always been, and how unsuccessful both Chinese and Japanese were in pacifying it,[15] it becomes clear why it was the scene of so many conflicts.

The twin problems of European and Asiatic Russia, with all their implications in the sphere of politics, economics, demography and communications, have exercised the minds of several generations of Russian strategists, scholars, statesmen and men of letters.[16] When the crisis of the first world war was over, a relative calm returned to the world: the horrors of the Civil War, exacerbated by the Intervention, finally subsided as the 'twenties wore on, and there were no further attacks on the 'first Socialist country in the world'. Germany had emerged from the Great War defeated, and

Poland was put out of the running in 1920. Consequently up to the early 'thirties, Soviet strategy did not envisage a war waged simultaneously on both western and eastern fronts. The strategic ideas which had until then been accepted as the conventional wisdom, and which surfaced once again after Tukhachevskii's execution, were based on the premise that the USSR was so vast that it could fall back on internal secondary lines of defence to hold one front while pursuing a more aggressive policy on the other.

At the beginning of the 'thirties, the USSR once again found itself in difficulties all round. (The term USSR is used here to denote the geographical entity which included large parts of the former Russian Empire, at any rate in the Far East.) On the home front, the enforcement of the first Five-Year Plan and the collectivization of agriculture were in full swing, bringing in their train untold upheaval and human suffering. Abroad Moscow was presented at one and the same time with increasing threats in the West and in the Far East.

The problem of the Far East was possibly the most complex on the Soviet horizon. At the end of 1935, alarm began to grow in Soviet intelligence circles as the first rumours circulated of the existence of an Anti-Comintern Pact, and an urgent need was felt to reassess strategic policy. Soviet strategists started to think in terms of a war on two fronts, i.e. one which would deal with Germany and Japan not singly but at the same time.[17] By 1936 this shift in Soviet strategy was no longer a secret. The Japanese were able to trace the process in the steady growth of Soviet forces confronting them in the Far East — evidence corroborated by reports from Captain Kotoni Etsuo, their Assistant Military Attaché in Moscow.[18] Whether it was a result of the painstaking work of this diligent officer, who read the Soviet press with assiduity and duly informed Tokyo of what the Soviet generals had to say — or whether there was a deliberate leak from Soviet sources, can only be a matter for conjecture: in any case an influential school of thought within the Japanese High Command was confirmed in the view that the USSR was the 'natural enemy' of Japan, and that sooner or later Japan would be forced to take up arms against it. Moreover, Japanese strategic thinking was hardly poles apart from that of the Soviet High Command:

. . . the capture of Far Eastern Russia would not prove fatal to the Soviet Union if the main body of its army remained intact and the heart of the Soviet Union remained unimpaired.[19]

The logic of this argument led its advocates to believe that it would be in the interests of Japan to enter into a military alliance with Germany and prepare for war against the Soviet Union. It was Tukhachevskii who used the authority of his rank as a Marshal of the USSR to give voice to the new Soviet strategy in public for the first time. He said in a speech before the Central Executive Committee of the Communist Party (TsIK): 'Under certain circumstances the need may arise to defend our two fronts, situated some 10,000 km. from each other, simultaneously and independently'. It was quite obvious to Tukhachevskii how such a state of affairs could come about: 'It goes without saying that under present conditions, when between Germany and ourselves there are certain countries that maintain special relationships with Germany the German army will be only too delighted to take advantage of this fact to attack our territory'. Such an attack would furthermore come as a surprise, since the German army trained especially for this type of warfare. 'The position on our Far Eastern border is also a serious one,' Tukhachevskii pursued, 'and there the problem is of even longer standing.' An official of the Japanese War Ministry, Sigetomi, had recently published an article in which he said that 'the Japanese army must prepare itself for a long war, and it is especially necessary to train the Japanese soldier to eat Mongolian and Siberian products seeing that he is unaccustomed to such food'.[20] Even if this pronouncement were taken as the standard boast of a military man, the article was nevertheless well provided with facts and figures, contained few slogans, and was couched in impartial language.

The spectre of a war waged on two fronts haunted the minds of all those concerned in the final stages of the Soviet/Anglo-French and Soviet/German negotiations which had started in April 1939.[21] As the war in Khalkhin-Gol went on and the talks in Moscow drew to a close, the parallel between events on the battlefield and progress round the green table impressed itself even more strongly on the Soviet negotiators, for a spectacular victory in the East would obviously strengthen the hand of the Soviet delegation in its dealings with the West. Similarly, the Germans for their part were eager to act as mediators between the USSR and Japan. Had they been able to do so, it would have given them some leverage in influencing Japanese policy; they could also have clinched their negotiations with the Russians under the very noses of the British and the French. For its part, the Soviet government was keen to secure British and French agreement to a general settlement also embracing the Far East. In the event of its reaching agreement with Germany, the danger of a war on two fronts would be reduced; whilst an agreement with the British and French would mean that if a war on two fronts could not be averted, the USSR at least would not stand alone.[22]

Developments in the Soviet Far East lagged far behind the immediate needs of the nation, let alone its long-term needs. The steadily increasing threat from Japan triggered off the natural response of military reinforcement and organizational modifications both in the command structure and the deployment of forces. Transport and communications matters, however, although not disregarded, were not accorded the preferential treatment they deserved.

The Soviet Union as a whole and the Far East in particular have never had the benefit of an adequate network of roads and railways. Not only have such means of transport been scarce: they have also usually been in poor repair. Moreover, the mere fact of a town being situated at the junction of two such means of transport (say of a railway and waterway system, or of two railway lines) would not turn it into a centre of economic or administrative significance.[23] In 1955 there were still in Eastern Siberia only 0.7 km. of track to every 1,000 square kilometres (about eight times less than the proportion for the rest of the country);[24] yet in that year 37.6 per cent of all freight in Eastern Siberia was conveyed by rail.[25] The Soviet government made a considerable effort to improve the rail network. In February 1930, for example, a 34-member delegation arrived in the USA as guests of the State of Pennsylvania, and an American delegation returned the visit later on in the year. Many American recommendations were put into effect between 1935 and 1945, and as a result there was a marked improvement. Loads were increased, faster average speeds were attained and turn-around times were improved.[26] Some years after the Revolution were in fact marked by considerable progress. However, an analysis by region of the number of kilometres of track completed in the Russian railway system during the periods 1918-27 and 1928-37 reveals only a slight alteration in the ratio between Western and Eastern Siberia/Far East and the rest of the USSR. Between 1918 and 1927, 6,800 km. of track were laid in the whole country, 1,700 km. of which (25 per cent) were in Western and Eastern Siberia and the Far East; whilst between 1928 and 1937, 8,100 km. were laid in the whole country, 2,100 km. of which (25.9 per cent) were in Western and Eastern Siberia and the Far East.[27]

By 1937 the Japanese threat seemed very ominous; it was also close, perhaps immediate, so that the inadequacy of the railway network stood out even more than it had before. Despite the great efforts made to remedy the situation and the marked progress that was achieved, the Soviet Far East still depended on European Russia for such staple commodities as grain, oil, iron ore and steel. From the specifically military point of view the ordnance industry, beset with technical obstacles and problems of adjustment even in European Russia, was in still poorer shape in the Far East.[28] In July-August 1939, when the war of Khalkhin-Gol was at its climax, the transport of supplies to the region was still wholly dependent on the Trans-Siberian Railway.

Alongside the general trend towards opening up the Far East, and the increasing Soviet unease in the face of the mounting threat from Japan, some advances were now achieved in the region in the field of logistics, a line of development that was naturally geared to serving the needs of the military machine. This in turn was seen by the Japanese as a provocation and exploited by certain interested circles within their High Command to foment a mood of belligerency towards the USSR.

At the height of the Mukden Incident, the Soviet government offered to sign a non-aggression pact with Japan, but in December 1931, Tokyo rejected this move. As a result the Committee of Defence, newly set up by the Council of People's Commissars, decided on 13 January 1932 to strengthen the Soviet forces in the Far East and increase their technical capacity.[29] In the same year, it was also decided to establish a naval force for the Far East commanded by M.V. Viktorov and represented on the Military Council by Bulyshkin; and also to initiate the construction of a whole network of fortified areas [UR], airfields, fuel dumps and military stores. In March 1932, the three northerly regions of China were declared autonomous, a fortnight later the entity thus created was given the name of Manchukuo, and in September as the sequel to a joint protocol signed by Japan and the 'government' of Manchukuo, Japan committed herself to defend the new state. The USSR had meanwhile resumed work on the section of railway track linking Karimskoe with Khabarovsk, a task left unfinished by the former Imperial government.[30]

The 17th Congress of the Communist Party took place in January 1934; a resolution adopted in May as a corollary to it decided to develop the railway system in the Far East with the aim of expanding the economy and reinforcing the defence capability of the entire region. It was also resolved to establish the BAMTRANSPROEKT, and to post military engineering detachments and military railway construction units to the East,[31] measures given force by the allocation of extra funds and manpower and by a degree of administrative reorganization. The work now progressed fairly rapidly, if to the occasional detriment of the resultant service available. Between the years 1934 and 1940 a number of major projects reached completion: the Karimskoe-Khabarovsk line was finished in 1937, the Borzya-Tamsag line (started in 1936) in 1939, and the last section of track linking Khabarovsk with Vladivostock was laid in 1940.[32] As some of the work was carried out negligently and in great haste, without benefit of a proper geological survey, the haulage capacity, speed and safety of the rolling-stock plying along the track left much to be desired.[33]

According to Japanese estimates the capacity of the Trans-Siberian Railway in 1945 was as shown in Table 1.[34]

Also according to these estimates, the haulage capacity of one train in summertime was 750 tons, dropping in winter, however, to 600 tons. A simple calculation reveals that whilst the annual capacity of (for example) the Vladivostok-Khabarovsk section of the line was 10,402,500 tons, the average annual capacity of the entire stretch of line between Omsk and Vladivostok was only 11,402,500 tons. Moreover, as the intelligence officer attached to the Japanese High Command remarked, 'operations vary according to the state of the locomotives, the degree of skill of the railway engineers, the availability, in these vast expanses, of coal and water, and other factors'.[35] Theoretical capacity, however — and here it must be stressed that the above refers to 1945 and not 1939, when capacity was even less — was, it seems, not to be equated with operational capacity; and in fact when the crucial time arrived of intensive

TABLE 1

Railway Section	Peace-time			War-time		
	Track capacity (Daily trains)	Maximum number of trains capable of operation		Track capacity (Daily trains)	Maximum number of trains capable of operation	
		Summer	Winter		Summer	Winter
Vladivostok-Khabarovsk	43	38	36	49	44	41
Khabarovsk-Kuibyshevka	41	36	34	49	44	41
Kuibyshevka-Karimskoe	49	44	41	51	45	43
Karimskoe-Ulan-Ude	51	45	43	60	54	51
Ulan-Ude-Taishet	45	40	38	60	54	51
Taishet-Novosibirsk	60	54	51	60	54	51
Novosibirsk-Omsk	100	80	80	100	80	80

preparation for the decisive battle of Khalkhin-Gol, an enormous amount of reorganization and redeployment was needed to keep the huge military machine rolling.[36]

When the skirmish on the Khalkhin-Gol River began to take on the aspect of an international crisis, it was found that several constraints hampered the use of the existing system of transport. In the first place, problems arose from the necessity to transfer rolling-stock from the standard wide gauge of the Soviet railroad system as a whole to the narrow-gauge, single-track branch lines hastily constructed while the conflict was still in progress. In the second place, there was the matter of dealing with civilian trains in transit which had nothing to do with the developing military situation. This involved a great deal of manoeuvring and shunting of locomotives and trains. The lines leading to Chita, Borzia, Khailar and Kharbin continued to function as they normally did in peace-time, and military freight arrived at the branching-off points together with a variety of other commodities. Last but not least, there was the problem of assigning the cargoes to different trains, and especially of unloading and reloading liquid freight. As a result of difficulties of this kind, in August, when 2,937 wagons arrived on the wide-gauge track, only 1,409 (some 47 per cent) could be transferred onto the narrow-gauge line, and 1,528 had to be left behind.[37]

Not until some time had elapsed after the first shots were exchanged near Kalkhin-Gol did it dawn on the Soviet government that unless extraordinary measures were taken they would lose control. The degree of alarm generated by this discovery can be deduced from the different levels of investment in the crisis. Up until mid-July, it was sufficient in order to supply and feed the troops which had arrived in the area, to send in 103 tons of solids and 54 tons of liquids per day. But once 57 Corps and the remainder of the forces in Mongolia were reorganized into the 1st Army under the command of Zhukov (from 19 July), no less than 1,450 tons of solid matter and 500 tons of liquid fuel were required per day.[38]

When supplies arrived in such massive quantity, the distribution system hitherto in existence was no longer able to cope. Until mid-July, the supply system was organized into two chains. One consisted of the troops stationed in Mongolia (as from 19 July, the 1st Army), whose support services in the rear (*tyl*) lay at a distance of some 175 km. from the front line on the Khalkhin-Gol River. Behind that rear lay the rearward lines of Zabaikal Military District (which on 5 July had become a front, commanded by Army Commander G.M. Shtern). Before the war, the supply system for the area had been conveniently based on the railways, which meant in practice the Trans-Siberian and the narrow-gauge branch line No. 79. At the end of this branch line was a station under the command of Commissary of the 2nd Rank I.P. Osinenko; the adminstration consisted also of his deputy, a senior clerk and two junior clerks. This station was also supposed to administer another line leading to Solovievsk, some 110 km. away, and to deal with a volume of freight amounting to 800-1,000 tons a day. But the difficulty of effecting a transfer from a wide- onto a narrow-gauge track meant that only 300-400 tons a day actually went through. This was quite inadequate to the task in hand.

The reorganization of the railway and supply systems involved two other stations, No. 78 in Kadabulak and No. 80 in Borzia, and a more rational allocation of supplies. Thus station No. 78 concerned itself only with unloading and reloading, station No. 79 only with artillery, aircraft and engineering parts and station No. 80 only with armoured vehicles coming from the direction of Ulan-Ude. Another station far in the rear of the 1st Army in Solovievsk dealt with fuel, lubricating agents and miscellaneous freight; Bain-Tumen station handled food supplies, Tamtsak station chemicals, clothing, signals equipment and heating materials. Also to the rear of the 1st Army were a hospital, a bakery, a bathhouse, a laundry and a workshop, whilst in Burdo-Nor there was another hospital and a slaughter-house.[39]

The area of operations at Khalkhin-Gol was only 200 km. removed from Japanese supply depots, but 700 km. away from their Soviet counterparts. Thus the railway was obviously unequal to coping with all the demands of the battlefield. From the terminal sited on the perimeter of the Front's rear to the Army's depots — i.e. its divisions, brigades, battalions and airfields — an elaborate system of truck transport operated. Two roads led to the operational rear lines of the 1st Army: the southern road running from Ulan-Ude to Naushki (the furthest removed from the battlefield) and the road running eastward from Solovievsk to Bain-Tumen. The majority of the arsenals, services and means of supply were concentrated along the southern road, the command post of which (*shtab nachal'nika gruntovogo uchatka (NGU)*) was in Solovievsk, having under its jurisdiction 500 companies (*dorozhno komendantskie roty (DKR)*) strung out along 600 km. of road. Each of these companies could service from three to four stations (*dorozhno komendantskie punkty (DKP)*), and each station in turn could provide one meal a day for 3-4,000 troops and 200-400 beds a night. Spaced out along another 240-km. section of the road were 500 more companies. As from 13 August, 1,181 lorries and buses, travelling day and night, passed along the road. The whole journey from Solovievsk to Bain-Tumen took four days. The system was organized as shown in Figures 1 and 2.

FIGURE 1

A scheme of the supply system (TYL)[40]
of the Front-Line Group, 5 July
1939-21 June 1940

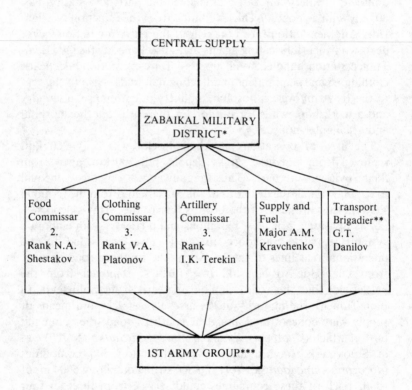

*From 5 July 1939 the Military District was turned into a Front-Line Group under
the command of Commander of the Army 2. rank G. M. Shtern. HQ in Chita.

**A section for transport was added to the existing 4 sections after the reorganization
of 19 July 1939.

***The 57th Corps was turned into the 1st Army Group under the command of
Divisional Commander G. K. Zhukov.

FIGURE 2

A scheme of the 1st Army Group[41]
supply by lorry

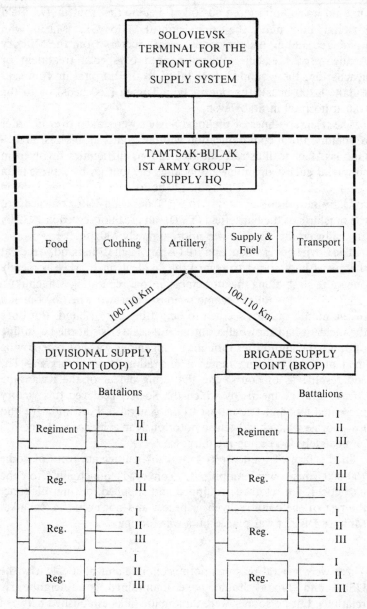

Medical aid formed an important part of the services provided in the rear. The Red Army attached great importance to organizing medical treatment as close as possible to the front line. Surgical first aid was administered 40-50 km. behind the front, in two field hospitals built under the supervision of Major G.V. Mazin, who numbered among his personnel several doctors from the Military Academy of Medicine. When in need of special treatment or evacuation, the wounded were taken to the hospital in Tamtsak-Bulak (1,100 beds), the one in Bain-Tumen (200 beds) or to the transit hospital in Solovievsk.

The telegraph lines of the local Soviets were taken over in order to maintain oral communication with all points in this vast area.[42] One last fact to illustrate the tremendous difficulties involved in supplying such a gigantic war machine: the journey by express train from Moscow to Ulan-Ude took 120 hours, that from Ulan-Ude on to Ulan-Bator another twenty-four,[43] from Ulan-Bator onwards, to the outskirts of the battlefield (TVD), an area not served in 1939 by any railway, the distance was approximately 700 km.

The Soviet government and Red Army High Command, which at the outset had tended to regard the incident on 11 May as merely one more clash along the intractable border separating Manchukuo from Inner Mongolia, became seriously alarmed when by the end of the month matters seemed to be getting out of hand. But once the incident had snowballed into a full-scale crisis at the beginning of June, the authorities thought up ingenious ways of redeploying men and reorganizing material and administrative organs. The end result was of course the shattering defeat of the Kwantung Army; and the means by which the Soviets achieved this victory presented a complete contrast to the general lack of initiative and low morale which had been so notoriously in evidence in the period immediately succeeding the purges.

In the face of immense practical difficulties an army of some 100,000 men was mobilized, conveyed punctually to the battlefield, fed, clothed, equipped and supplied; during this time, the rest of the country lived in peace, and not even the Zabaikal Military District was placed on a war footing.

There were several reasons, both economic and political, why the USSR and Japan should have maintained good-neighbourly relations; but no sooner were diplomatic links established between them in 1925 than the two countries found themselves at loggerheads. It may be useful here to remind the reader of the historical argument set forth in the first section of this paper and to place it in perspective. There was a growing feeling in Japan, particularly in military circles, that their country was stronger than the USSR, reeling as it was under the multiple blows inflicted by collectivization and its economic aftermath, show trials and purges (mainly of military men). It is always difficult for a government in power to maintain a just balance between image and reality, and to keep its perception of itself sensibly in proportion with its perception of a potential adversary. Japan's setbacks during the 'thirties actually appeared to certain elements among the Japanese military as eminently reasonable, acceptable and even indeed opportune, as though they were purposefully leading up to the 'real' national goal: a strong Japan in control of the Far East (the precise area in question was not defined). Simultaneously, such elements regarded collectivization, the purges and the Terror as senseless, pointless policies — which they were — bound to sap the energies of the Soviet Union and bleed her white — which they were not. Influenced by this dual perception, local Japanese military commanders envisaged the Soviet Far East, with its inadequate communications, relatively small armed forces and disputed border area as even more vulnerable than heretofore.

Even though the Japanese government could hardly have been happy to sacrifice its oil and fisheries concessions on Sakhalin, and even though the Soviet government for its part was by no means anxious to add to its military contingent in the Far East, nevertheless the Japanese government determined to make war on China, and to set up its own régime in Manchukuo. But in practice many of the decisions that bore the official seal of Japan were conceived, worked out and executed by the military: the government was torn apart by dissension and incapable of pulling its weight. In October 1934 the army published a pamphlet entitled 'The essence of national defence, with proposals to strengthen it'.[44] This summed up the ideas circulating among the military (in particular the ground forces) after the incident in Manchuria. Its conclusion was that both domestic and foreign policy should be geared to preparing the country for a general war. The paper foresaw a crisis looming in 1936 or 1937 as a result of disruption of the existing global order, US naval competition and the completion of the Soviet Five-Year Plan. When Ishiwara Kanji took up his post as Chief of the Operations Section of the General Staff in August 1935, he set about strengthening the army in Manchukuo in anticipation of what he saw as the Soviet challenge.[45] Partly in order to counter this challenge and partly because they had not thus far managed to subdue Manchukuo's rural areas, the Japanese put a great deal of money and effort into expanding its railway network,[46] a fact which did not escape observation on the Soviet side of the border.

After the establishment of Manchukuo, Soviet concern with the Far East had seemed to grow steadily, and it now increased to such a point that strong words were uttered and forceful decisions taken; by the end of 1935 indeed some Soviet leaders were actually contemplating the possibility of a war on two fronts. If any doubts as to Japanese intentions still lingered, they must have been severely tested on 12 January 1936, when the Japanese Foreign Minister, Hirota, laid down the three cornerstones of his country's policy towards China. These were:

1. [That] the [Chinese] Nationalist government be prohibited from condoning any anti-Japanese activities, and be encouraged to promote Sino-Japanese cooperation;

2. [That] the Nationalist government recognise the existence of Manchukuo and promote cooperation between China and Manchukuo in the region of Northern China;

33. [That] Japan and China continue to oppose Communism in Outer Mongolia.[47]

To this the Soviet government responded by signing a pact of mutual assistance with Mongolia, reinforcing this move by making frequent promises to aid and defend her, and uttering frequent warnings to Japan to cease from meddling in her affairs.[48] On 23 October 1936, Japan acceded to the Anti-Comintern Pact. This event not only represented a milestone along the road which led from Versailles, with its lofty aspirations, to the harsh realities of the second world war; it also marked a watershed in diplomatic relations between the USSR and Japan. An official of the Japanese Foreign Ministry's Research Division, Nimiya Takeo (an adherent of the 'Renewal Movement' in Japanese diplomacy), argued in a paper he published in December 1936 under the title 'The unique principles which guide Japan's diplomacy' that China and the Soviet Union were the two most formidable challenges to that diplomacy. The USSR, he insisted, must be driven out of China, for her propagation there of 'Red ideas' threatened to rend asunder the whole fabric of Asia.[49]

On 7 July 1937, Japan launched her war on China. She aimed at a quick killing, intending to crush the numerous Chinese armies and subjugate the land within months rather than years. The Soviet Union responded at once, signing a non-aggression treaty with China on 21 August 1937 and ratifying it on the spot in contravention of established protocol.[50] In the years 1937/38 certain circles in Japan were convinced, perhaps more strongly than at any other time, that the moment had come for war with the USSR. Their convictions were shared by Japanese field commanders in, for example, Korea and Manchukuo, as well as by proponents of the notion that such a war was not merely imminent but positively necessary.[51] The incident at Lake Khasan, [Chenkufeng], may be seen as in many ways the forerunner of Khalkhin-Gol, albeit smaller in scale, less costly in time and blood and fraught with far less menacing consequences.[52]

The beginning of 1939 saw the start of an international game of prodigious complexity played out in a vast arena. The war at Khalkhin-Gol seemed so utterly remote from every world centre of diplomatic activity that it hardly rated a mention in the press — even the Soviet and Japanese press. Skirmishes had begun to take place along the border at the beginning of the year,[53] but diplomatic attention was chiefly focused on events further east such as the protracted negotiations over Japanese fishing rights in Soviet territorial waters and fish-canning and oil concessions on Sakhalin.[54] The USSR was of course deeply involved in and worried about developments in both Europe and the Far East (i.e. Japan, China and other interested nations). Every single diplomatic move had to take into account the possible reactions of Britain, France, Germany, Japan and the USA: the diplomatic, political and military alternatives that presented themselves were too many to enumerate. In Japan's case, even at the best of times the army did not see eye to eye with the navy, nor did it take much heed of the Foreign Ministry. The global situation was worsening week by week, but the coalitions which eventually went to war (in 1939 and 1941) had still not been properly cemented. Japan was not yet fully committed to a military alliance with Germany, and Germany, although interested in such an alliance, did not want to see a military confrontation between Japan and the USSR lest the latter be propelled into the arms of Britain and France. Britain was not very happy about the war in China and developments in Europe, but she was militarily too weak and diplomatically too compromised to carry any weight internationally. Even before he went to Munich, Chamberlain was warned by his military advisers not to run any risks. The USA for its part had stayed seemingly aloof from the course of events in Europe, and by slow, well-nigh imperceptible degrees was turning against Japan. The USSR, even by objective and certainly by subjective standards a vital thread in the web of international diplomacy, was almost left out. A prey to its inherently suspicious nature, it was regularly primed with expert advice[55] and often excellent intelligence reports which from time to time it misinterpreted. Diplomatic deliberations, speculation and intrigue formed the accompaniment to the din of battle on the Khalkhin-Gol River until the Soviet government had satisfied itself that the danger of war on two fronts had been averted; indeed the timing and tempo of its last offensive were tailored to fit the pace of the Russo-German negotiations in Moscow.[56] That the armistice in the Far East and the Molotov-Ribbentrop Pact were not signed on the selfsame day was due merely to the customary lack of coordination between soldiers and diplomats. At the very last minute, with the Anglo-French delegation still lingering in Moscow, both Germans and Italians tried to mediate between the USSR and Japan. It had by then been brought home to the government in Tokyo that the Kwantung Army had been severely mauled, and it made independent efforts to obtain a cease-fire through German mediation, a fact not unknown to Soviet intelligence.[57] At the time of these events, and while the intricate negotiations were under way between Soviet and Anglo-French representatives on one side and Germans on the other, there was an atmosphere of mutual suspicion. After the Grand Alliance had ended and the Cold War had begun, the Soviet historical attitude to its former allies changed. In later years Soviet historians have freely used British and US official documents in dealing with this period.[58]

It is a moot point whether or not the Soviet government could have fulfilled the Second Five-Year Plan with the sums envisaged for investment in the Far East. The military in any case had no bearing on the matter; whereas in China and Manchuria it was only by force of arms that the Japanese government was able to achieve its goal. At the time of the Manchurian incident in 1931, Soviet forces east of the Urals numbered some 100,000, a figure which rose steadily as the Japanese threat intensified and world stability deteriorated.[59] According to estimates compiled by the Japanese High Command, the Soviet military presence in the Far East grew between 1932 and 1939 as illustrated in Table 2.[60]

TABLE 2

	Soviet Far Eastern Armies			Kwantung Army			
Year	Infantry divisions	Number of aircraft	Total manpower	Infantry divisions	Air regiments (gps.)	No. of aircraft	Total manpower
1932	8	200		4	1	30	
1933	8	350		3	3	100	60,000
1934	11	500	230,000	3	3	100	60,000
1935	14	950	240,000	3	3	100	
1936	16-20	1,200	340,000	3	5	180	80,000
1937	20	1,560	370,000	6	5		
1938	24	2,000	450,000	8	12		
1939	30	2,500	570,000	9	18		

Even if allowance is made for the fact that most intelligence assessments habitually underestimate one's own strength and exaggerate that of one's adversary, Japanese estimates of Soviet military strength are quite accurate. According to Soviet sources, on 1 September 1939, 30 per cent of all Soviet (that is, Red Army) personnel was concentrated in the Far East.[61] If foreign sources correctly gauged Red Army strength at this time, we get a figure of about 2,000,000 men. This means that there would have been some 600,000 in the Far East, not all of them, of course, stationed in the immediate vicinity of Khalkhin-Gol. The same sources also put the number of Japanese divisions in Manchukuo at nineteen. There were 20,000 men to a division.[62]

All through the 'thirties the USSR and Japan augmented their forces; not only did their respective armies increase in size overall, but their Far Eastern contingents also increased. The main contention of the present paper is that Japan was the chief instigator of tension in an area traditionally regarded, whether by Imperial Russia or the Soviet Union, as prone to attack. Some Japanese sources argue that the Kwantung Army exceeded its brief and acted in contravention of Imperial orders. The reasons, so they maintain, were the proud traditions of the Army, the dispute then current in Tokyo over the signing of a military alliance with Germany and the wish of the Army Command to encourage such a move by defeating the Red Army whenever and wherever it was most vulnerable. Naturally, a prolonged series of clashes between two powerful armies in a disputed area far from home is bound to lead to a crisis. Once the two countries began to exhibit the 'attack-retaliation-counterattack-reinforcement-attack' syndrome, it was difficult to break the vicious circle without forcing a confrontation. In this situation G.K. Zhukov was the very man that was required.

Soviet intelligence reports indicated as early as January 1939[63] that the Japanese Army had embarked on a series of provocative strikes in the Nomonhan district. In the months which followed, as diplomatic wrangles at either end of the globe intensified by the day, the Kwantung Army, the commanders of which apparently had influential backing in Tokyo in the shape of certain generals in the War Ministry,[64] struggled to gain a free hand to deal with any emergency arising on the border with the USSR. Until after the armistice was signed, on 16 September 1939, nobody was prepared to assume responsibility for issuing a definite order, such as 'go ahead' or 'stop', where border incidents were concerned. So the orders issued were ambiguous. In April, as the negotiations in Berlin and Moscow gathered momentum, the Kwantung Army command put out a new operational order, 'Guidelines for the settlement of Soviet-Manchurian border disputes'. This order enjoined on the one hand: 'Do not attack even if attacked by the enemy', which represented a middle-of-the-road approach and conformed with the Imperial wish; but on the other, it stated that 'the frequency and escalation of incidents can only be prevented by the resolute application of just punishment, the basic principle being neither to invade nor to permit invasion . . . in areas where the lines of demarcation are unclear, the officer responsible for defending the border shall himself determine the demarcation line'.[65] That was the root of all the trouble: the borders were not precisely delineated, and the order gave commanders at local level *carte blanche* to decide whether or not to provoke an international crisis.

It may be that the local Japanese commanders were inspired by the rumours they had heard of the enfeebled state of the Red Army as a whole; or perhaps they encountered only token resistance from their opposite numbers on the Soviet side of the border. Either way, as we have already indicated, the first serious action which sparked off the war on the Khalkhin-Gol River started on 11 May 1939 with a minor Manchurian incursion against a Mongolian border outpost. The skirmish intensified rapidly, and by early July, both sides having reinforced their troops, the Japanese were in control of an important high point, Bain-Tsagan, allowing them to command a wide stretch of the river. At the top was a Dalai temple which provided a certain amount of cover.

On 1 June the Minister of Defence, Voroshilov, summoned Zhukov and ordered him to leave post-haste for Mongolia, at first, ostensibly, to report back on the situation. Several competent accounts of the war are extant, and we need not go into detail about it here.[66] However, some points still remain deplorably vague, and would repay investigation.

It has already been stated that one of the chief problems in the Soviet Far East was that its borders were not properly demarcated. We went into the historical reasons for this at some length. In addition, however, reports from the battlefield show that no topographical survey of the region was ever carried out, or at least if one was, its end-product in the form of maps never reached the troops, nor yet their officers.[67] The conclusion which may be drawn from this episode is that a great deal of misunderstanding between China and the USSR might have been avoided if topographical and cartographical skills had been more highly developed. It was not simply a case of some authoritative State body making a conscious decision not to survey a particular area; nor can we lay the blame at the door of Stalin, under whom, for fear of espionage, maps were later to be classified as a state secret. What was at fault was rather the poorly developed state in both Tsarist Russia and the Soviet Union of geographical science.

Several scholars have drawn attention to difficulties in connection with the Soviet munitions industry during the Great Patriotic War of 1941-45, but it seems that a marked discrepancy between the quality of Soviet war machines and that of the ammunition was already discernible at Khalkhin-Gol. The Japanese could hardly fail to notice that the Soviet artillery was superior to their own, yet many of the shells proved to be duds, and on examination were found to be ill-designed and amateurishly produced. The same held good of machine-guns.[68] It should be noted that both at Khalkhin-Gol and during the Russo-German war, artillery played a crucial role in defeating, respectively, the Japanese and the Germans. At Khalkhin-Gol the army experimented for the first time with the use of artillery fire over open sights (*pryamaya navodka*), a device later used to good effect against the Germans. On meeting Stalin, Zhukov made a point of praising N.N. Voronov, who had commanded the artillery units at Khalkhin-Gol. But the question still remains as to why the guns should have proved so far superior to the ammunition.

The War of Khalkhin-Gol was the first in history to use aircraft on any large scale. The first air battles were in fact very minor affairs involving a few fighters and reconnaissance planes on either side, but from 28 May onwards the numbers multiplied until at last 150-200 or more aircraft were engaged in a single battle. The mere presence of large numbers of bombers and escort planes in such close proximity to sensitive areas affected the balance of forces in both an operational and a political sense. Soviet bomber pilots were involved as 'volunteers' in the Chinese war against Japan, and their aircraft influenced the course of hostilities even before Khalkhin-Gol.[69] In those days, however, sorties of this kind brought to light the inherent weaknesses of the aircraft. Because of difficulties in maintaining the correct cabin pressure and in regulating the flow of oxygen, the bombers were obliged to fly at a height of 4,500-5,800 metres.[70] The Japanese planes were poorly equipped when it came to radio receivers/transmitters. Only two or three machines in every squadron boasted a radio, and the transmitters were unreliable. When a Japanese bomber eventually arrived over its target, it could never be very effective because its bombs only weighed 15 kg. (33 lb.), 50 kg. (110 lb.) or at most 100 kg. (220 lb.). Even these rather small bombs had to be dropped from a great height, because the Soviet anti-aircraft batteries were highly effective.[71]

The Japanese apparently managed to maintain air superiority, or at least hold their own against mounting odds, until the beginning of August. Then their air force started to disintegrate under the pressure of a variety of factors. For one thing the VVS (Red Air Force) enjoyed a growing numerical advantage; for another, the Japanese were unable to replace their pilots, who were desperately needed for the war in China. Their bombers suffered the same defects as those of their Soviet opponents when it came to the oxygen supply, but in spite of that they had to fly very high to avoid anti-aircraft fire. When the Soviet pilots had gained more experience and were placed under more competent command, discipline tightened up and they could no longer be lured into sporadic dogfights.[72] As a result their air formations became better organized and their losses fell.

By the time of the great offensive of 20 August, Soviet air force equipment and tactics showed considerable improvement. The I-16, TYPE-17 fighter, in addition to its 7.62 mm. machine-gun, also carried two 20 mm. cannon or 12.7 mm. machine-guns. The cockpit was reinforced with 8-mm. armour-plating, and the fuel tanks were likewise protected.[73] As regards tactics, the SB-2 bombers used to fly at a height of 6,000 m. (20,000 feet), drop their bomb load and return to base before the Japanese fighters could climb up to meet them. This obliged the Japanese to maintain round-the-clock air patrols, which placed a strain on both men and machines. The Russians also displayed tactical flexibility in air battles, and developed a tactic of flying in three 'layers'. Three separate groups of fighters would fly at different levels, each maintaining a constant height, thus affording protection to other groups and engaging in battle when the opportune moment presented itself.

The greatest technical innovation introduced into air warfare at Khalkhin-Gol was indubitably the aerial rocket, which made its début there, though to what effect it is difficult to establish.[74] In July 1939, when the Khalkhin-Gol incident was being given high priority, several pilots were sent on a special instruction course near Moscow where they were trained to operate the RS-82 (air-to-air rocket powered by solid fuel). Those achieving the best results were posted to Mongolia, where five I-16s had been adapted to carry the rockets in racks under their wings. The planes originally went into operation on 5 August, flying in formations which did not carry rockets. The existence of these projectiles, a great innovation, was kept secret until 20 August, when they went into action for the first time.[75]

During the war and after it, both sides boasted of scoring great victories in the air;[76] indeed, the number of enemy aircraft claimed to have been destroyed occasionally exceeded the total number known to have been deployed by the opposing side at any given moment. Presented with such an abundance of dubious statistics, the historian finds it well-nigh impossible to establish the true figures or assess in real terms the amount of damage inflicted by the rival air forces; on the Soviet side, however,[77] there was certainly some effect on morale.

Japanese intelligence, as has already been stated, relied on the Red Army being enfeebled as a result of the purges. It seems appropriate therefore to take a look at the human aspect of the war — first and foremost the question of leadership. It is a well-known fact that Zhukov was placed in command of the 1st Army set up for the express purpose of conducting the war at Khalkhin-Gol. This army comprised all available front-line personnel, both Soviet and Mongolian. The date when this army was brought into being is, however, problematical. Soviet and Japanese sources report that one major organizational re-shuffle took place just before the outbreak of the war, and was followed just after the outbreak by another one.[78]

According to official Soviet data, the reorganization of the forces in the Far East took place in three distinct stages. On 5 July 1939 the Supreme Military Council of the Red Army (*Glavnyi Voennyi Soviet RKKA*) decided to establish a Front-Line Group of forces comprising the 1st and 2nd Armies of the Red Banner, the Zabaikal Military District and the 57th Special Corps. Its headquarters was to be in Chita, its commander Army Commander (2nd Rank) G.M. Shtern. The field of jurisdiction, functions and authority of the new Front-Line Group's command were defined on 9 July. Its first order was signed by the People's Commissar for Defence, Marshal K. Voroshilov, its second by the Red Army Chief of Staff, Army Commander (1st Rank) B. Shaposhnikov. A third order, again signed by Voroshilov, was issued on 19 July and authorized the reorganization of the 57th Corps[79] into the 1st Army Group under the divisional command of G.K. Zhukov. Zhukov arrived in Chita during the first week in June while the 57th Corps was still under the command of H.V. Feklenko. However, Major Grigorenko, who arrived in Chita only a few days after him (i.e. in the middle of June at the very latest) maintains that Chita was already the Headquarters of the Front-Line Group by that date and that Zhukov and Shtern were already in command respectively of the front and the 1st Army Group. Although it may be inferred that in his rather impressionistic volume of memoirs Grigorenko may have got his dates mixed up, it does certainly seem that the process of reorganization was a painful and protracted one and that several heads rolled in the course of it. No source has described in any detail why or how Zhukov came to be appointed to the command of the fighting forces in Mongolia. O.P. Chaney says in his biography of him: '. . . by order of General Headquarters and with the blessing of Stalin himself he was sent to China with a Soviet military mission to observe Japanese strategy and tactics'.[80] If Stalin did indeed bless Zhukov, he must have done it without meeting him, since according to Zhukov's own memoirs he met Stalin for the first time only several months after the end of the war in Khalkhin-Gol. That war established Zhukov's reputation well and truly as a great soldier, and a tough one. One reason for his assignment to the post in Mongolia was probably his experience of China, where he was sent in 1938 together with V.I. Chuikov and P.F. Batitsky, among others. But perhaps the most immediate reason was his conduct in the summer exercise that terminated at the end of May, from which Voroshilov summoned him in the middle of a debriefing session.

It is true that at that moment the command of the 57th Special Corps left much to be desired; but then again, it was certainly in Zhukov's interests to show up how bad things had been before his arrival, and how greatly they had improved thereafter. In more general terms, Zhukov's leadership at Khalkhin-Gol, as elsewhere, spurred officers and men alike to action (Grigorenko says: '*Lyudei zhalet' ne umel'* [Zhukov] . . . 'was insensitive to human feelings'). It would seem, then, that Japanese intelligence was wrong as to the effect on Red Army morale and initiative of the purges. It is true that they had a paralysing effect on the officer corps, but other factors also came into play. Not all those officers who fell victim to the purges were of uniformly high quality, nor were all those appointed after their demise necessarily inferior. The armed forces at Khalkhin-Gol represented a cross-section of the whole army. Far away from Moscow, in a dynamic war situation and under determined leadership, for these men it was the task in hand that counted, not the grievances of the past nor yet the menace of the future. For every officer dead or exiled there were several young, eager men waiting to step into their shoes, convinced of the rightness of what they were doing.

The might of the Red Army combined with the shock of the Molotov-Ribbentrop Pact to throw the Japanese government into confusion.[81] And to make confusion worse confounded rumours probably leaked by the Germans were in circulation suggesting that the Russians were ready to conclude a similar pact with the Japanese.[82] The result was that the Hiranuma government was forced to resign, and a new one came into being headed by General Nobuyuki as Prime Minister. The military was permeated by a sense of defeat. Several officers at Supreme Headquarters were obliged to step down, officers of the First (Operational) Section of the Kwantung Army were removed to other jobs and a number of officers preferred to commit suicide sooner than return home at the head of a vanquished army.[83] The Nomonhan Incident led the Japanese to the general conclusion that they too ought to sign a treaty of non-aggression with the USSR — a train of thought which eventually resulted in the Russo-Japanese Neutrality Pact of April 1941.

When the time came to negotiate an armistice, the Soviet government, which had never wanted to become involved in the incident in the first place, was very careful to humour Japanese susceptibilities. Moscow's interests were indirectly served all the better because they happened to coincide with Zhukov's own in his capacity as senior officer on the battlefield. Zhukov's deputy at Khalkhin-Gol was Col. M.I. Potapov, who commanded the Southern Group of forces during the offensive of 20 August. When the Japanese sent over a delegation headed by Maj-Gen. T. Fujimoto to negotiate armistice terms, Zhukov cabled a suggestion to Voroshilov that to spare his adversaries humiliation, Potapov be upgraded to the rank of *Kombrig* (equivalent to the rank of General).[84] When the armistice had been duly signed, the Japanese Foreign Minister, Ugaki, reflected happily that you could sometimes achieve more through diplomacy than you might suppose.[85]

After decorating the gallant victors of the War of Khalkhin-Gol, the Soviet government put the lessons of the war into cold storage until after the German attack on the USSR in 1941.[86] The explanation for this is to be sought in the famous controversy then raging among military theoreticians and Red Army field commanders regarding the properties of the tank as an independent factor in warfare. The conclusion reached in November 1939 was that the tank cannot and should not operate as an independent weapon. Yet at Khalkhin-Gol, Zhukov had just proved precisely the opposite by demonstrating that the tank was an agile weapon capable, if well handled as an independent factor, of tilting the balance of a battle in favour of the user.

Another reason why the lessons of Khalkhin-Gol were shelved was that on 1 September 1939 war broke out in Europe and everything else was forgotten.[87]

Grigorenko advances one further explanation. When the Khalkhin-Gol war was over, a large group of officers from 1st Army Group prepared a detailed report on it. After Zhukov was appointed Chief of Staff, however, in February 1941, he ordered that this document be filed away, because (according to Grigorenko) although no overt accusations were levelled in it against him, and no overt praise was bestowed on Shtern, anyone reading it would understand what really happened at Khalkhin-Gol. Still, at least until there is a great deal more evidence to go on, Zhukov must have the last word. 'But they weren't there,' he says of the authors of the report. 'They haven't understood a thing!'

War broke out at Khalkhin-Gol because the existing world order was crumbling and the various powers — the USSR, Germany, Britain, France, Japan and the USA — were all either locked in conflict, deep in negotiations or busily deploying their forces in anticipation of the coming crisis. The old order introduced at Versailles had disintegrated and the old alliances were giving place to new; governments were mustering their diplomatic and economic resources and flexing their military muscle in the hope, preferably, of latching on to a victorious grouping or — at the very least — of not being left as odd man out. An atmosphere of tension gradually crept into international relations. The reason was that from about 1930 in the East and 1933 in the West, restless and dynamic forces were entering upon the world scene which cared nothing for the status quo. The rest of the globe meanwhile, failing to comprehend the nature of the peril, could do nothing to defend the existing order.

In 1939 a situation of near crisis arose because Germany and Japan, who led the nations in their armaments programmes and had already forged an alliance, carefully fostered a series of misconceptions. Germany, in comparing her current military strength with that of her possible adversaries and finding the latter wanting, proceeded to underestimate their economic potential and political resilience. Similarly, the Japanese military establishment tended to underestimate the military potential of the Soviet Union, and since the government in Tokyo was apparently incapable of dealing resolutely with the powerful army groups outside its reach, the bellicosity of the military carried the day.

Once the Kwantung Army had been given a vague free hand in this way, it chose to attack the USSR at the point where, other things being equal, it was most vulnerable. The regions of Manchuria, Mongolia and the Maritime Territories, the rivers Amur, Ussuri, Argun and Khalkhin-Gol, all these were controversial areas which Russia and China had bickered over for centuries. The Kwantung Army command could easily convince the sceptics at home and abroad that the Soviet claim to Khalkhin-Gol was at least as contentious as these. If their gamble had come off, because the USSR either decided not to take up the challenge or else was defeated in battle, they would have won a great strategic and political victory. They had carefully chosen the theatre of operations so as to present the Red Army, then (so they thought) at its lowest ebb, with insurmountable problems of logistics. But as it turned out, the Red Army was better equipped than ever before, and quite prepared to improvise ingenious solutions to unaccustomed difficulties. Benefiting from Zhukov's forceful leadership and Shtern's organizational skill, it seemed not directly affected by the purges at all.

The outcome of the battle had far-reaching consequences. It entered into the calculations of the Soviet diplomats as they negotiated with Germany and with the Anglo-French delegation in August 1939. As for Japan, the defeat of the Kwantung Army caused her to reassess her future policies towards the USSR and Germany. In the USSR, it turned an extremely talented commander into a mature general whose influence was to make itself felt in the Great Patriotic War.

Notes

1. Several different accounts have been given of the number of Japanese casualties. See, e.g.: Introduction by Alvin D. Coox to Hata Ikuhiko, 'The Japanese-Soviet confrontation 1935-1939', in J. W. Morley, *Deterrent Diplomacy* (New York 1976), 116, in which he quotes the official Japanese announcement of 17,000 deaths; D. Ortenberg, *Vremya ne vlastno* (Moscow 1979), 37.

2. Katsu H. Young, 'The Nomonhan Incident, Imperial Japan and the Soviet Union', *Monumenta Nipponica*, vol. 22, 1967, 89; Hata Ikuhiko, op. cit., 175.

3. J.W. Morley, op. cit., 133.

4. *Entsiklopedicheskii slover*, S.-Petersburg, 1895, vol. XV, 208 (henceforward *ES* — 1895).

5. P.E. Skachenko and V.C. Myasnikov, *Russko-kitaiskie otnosheniya 1689-1916* (Moscow 1958); *ES*, vol. XV, 208; *Bol'shaya sovetskaya entsiklopediya, 1973*, 210 (henceforward *BSE* — 1973); *Sbornik dogovorov Rossii s drugimi gosudarstvami* (Moscow 1952); V. H. Aleksandrenko, *Sobranie traktatov 1774-1906* (S.-Petersburg 1906) (henceforward *ST* — 1906).

6. Immanuel C.Y. Hsii, 'Russia's special position in China during the early Ch'ing period', *Slavic Review*, vol. XXIII, 1964, 689. See p. 689 NS for a controversy regarding the date when Albazin was established; also *ES* — 1895, 208.

7. Ibid., 689-90 for the reasons and location of the two sieges of Albazin, especially the end of the second siege, a landmark in the art of 'power diplomacy' and a model for many future encounters between China and Russia.

8. Cf. *ES* — 1895, 208; *BSE* — 1973, 210; *The Cambridge Encyclopedia of China* (Cambridge 1982), 231, with *ST* — 1906, 130-131; *The Cambridge Encyclopedia*, 239-40. For the treaty of Nerchinsk (1689) see also M. T. Florinsky, *Russia, A History and an Interpretation* 9th pr. (New York 1964), 265.

9. P. E. Skachenko and V. S. Myasnikov, op.cit., 9.

10. Harriet L. Moore, *Soviet Far Eastern Policy 1931-1945* (Princeton 1945).

11. Immanuel C. Y. Hsii, op.cit., 689-90, 695.

12. *The Cambridge Encyclopedia*, 239-40.

13. Ibid., the population of Manchukuo in 1937 was about 30 millions. See T. A. Bisson, *Japan in China* (Westport, Conn., first reprinting 1973), 373.

14. T. A. Bisson, op. cit., 12-15.

15. Ibid., 391-405.

16. A. Sella, *Soviet Political and Military Conduct in the Middle East* (London 1981), Ch.I.

17. *Japanese Special Studies on Manchuria*. Study of Strategical and Tactical Peculiarities of Far Eastern Russia and Soviet Far Eastern Forces, vol. XIII, ch.IV, 52. (Henceforward *JSSM*).

18. Hata Ikuhiko, in J.W. Morley, op.cit., 132.

19. *JSSM*, vol. XIII, ch.I. 13.

20. Marshal Tukhachevskii, *Krasnaya Zvezda*, 16 January 1936, 1.

21. David J. Dallin, *Soviet Russia and the Far East* (London 1949), 41-42.

22. Ibid., 43; *SSSR v bor'ba za mir nakanune vtoroi mirovoi voiny* (Moscow 1971).

23. *Vostochnaya Sibir'* (Moscow 1963), 376.

24. Ibid., 377.

25. Ibid., 372. 37.6% — 88 million tons — by rail, 5.9% — 14 million tons — along the waterways, 56.5% — 133 million tons — by lorry (but this was freight which had previously reached a certain point by other modes of transport).

26. Antony C. Sutton, *Western Technology and Soviet Economic Development 1930-1945,* Stanford University, 1971, 195-206.

27. Edward Ames, 'A Century of Russian Railroad Construction 1837-1936', *The American Slavic and East European Review,* vol. VI, 1947, Nos. 18-19, 57, 60.

28. *JSSM,* vol. XII, ch.I, 23.

29. *Voenno-istoricheskii zhurnal,* 9, 1981, 64 (henceforward *VIZ*); *JSSM,* vol. XIII, 77.

30. Ibid., 77.

31. *VIZ,* 9, 1981, 64; A.I. Alekseyev, '*Po marshrutam Baikalo-Amurskoi Magistrali' Voprosy Istorii,* 9, September 1976, 118.

32. *JSSM,* vol. XIII, 78; also Ch.I, 32.

33. *JSSM,* vol. XIII, 79; *Voprosy Istorii,* op. cit.

34. *JSSM,* vol. XIII, ch.I, 25.

35. Ibid.

36. For Japanese strategic construction in Manchukuo from 1935 onwards, see *JSSM,* vol. I, 54; T. A. Bisson, op.cit., 391-9. For other roads leading from the USSR to Mongolia, see Harriet Moore, op.cit., 95.

37. Polkovnik V. Odintsov and Polkovnik V. Ovsyannikov, '*Nekotorie osobennosti tylovogo obespecheniya sovetsko-mongol'skikh voisk v boyakh na Khalkhin-Gole',* *VIZ,* 9, 1980, 55.

38. The breakdown was as follows: 600 tons artillery shells, 220 tons aircraft ammunition, 130 tons food, 240 tons firewood, 260 tons miscellaneous supplies, 500 tons fuel and lubricating agents. See *VIZ,* 9, 1980, 56; G. K. Zhukov, who gives the following breakdown: 18,000 tons artillery ammunition, 6,500 air force ammunition, 15,000 tons fuel and lubricating agents, 4,000 tons food, 7,500 tons firewood, 4,000 tons miscellaneous, total: 56,450 tons. Zhukov probably had in mind all the supplies ordered between 19 July and 30 August.

39. *VIZ,* 9, 1980, 55-59.

40. The scheme of a supply system for the Front-Line Group, and the one which succeeds it, for the Army Group, was compiled on the basis of the following material: *Organy upravleniya sovetskimi voiskami v period voennykh deistvii na Khalkhin-Gole (1939 g.) VIZ,* 8, 1979, 47-50; *ZIV,* 9, 1980, 55-60; S. Isaev, *Meropriyatiya KPSS po ukrepleniyu Dalnestochnykh rubezhei v 1931-1941 gg',* *VIZ,* 9, 1981, 64-69.

41. Ibid.

42. D. Ortenberg, op. cit., 8.

43. *VIZ,* 9, 1980, 57.

44. J.W. Morley, op. cit., 12; R.P. Browder, *The Origins of Soviet-American Diplomacy* (Princeton 1953), 200-201. It seems that the Japanese and the Russians shared the same fears in reverse, and even had a similar timetable in mind.

45. Ohata Tokushiro, 'The Anti-Comintern Pact', in J. W. Morley, op.cit., 16-17.

46. *JSSM,* vol. I, 54; *Istoriya Velikoi Otechestvennoi Voiny* (henceforward *IVOV*) *Sovetskogo Soyuza,* vol. I, 236.

47. Ohata Tokushiro, op. cit., 18.

48. *Foreign Relations of the US, 1933-1941.* Soviet Union, 767-768.

49. Ibid., 16-17.

50. *JSSM,* vol. XIII, ch.IV, 54, 81; Max Beloff, *The Foreign Policy of Soviet Russia 1929-41,* (Oxford 1949), vol. II, 175.

51. Katsu H. Young, op. cit., 83.

52. J. Erickson, *The Soviet High Command,* 494-499.

53. Polkovnik K. Yakovlev, '*Eto bylo na Khalkhin-Gole',* *Voennyi Vestnik,* 2, 1978, 47.

54. *New York Times,* 17 February 1939, C, 13, 15 March 1939, 12; Jane Degras, *Soviet Documents on Foreign Policy,* vol. III, 1939-41, 354-356; *SSR v bor'be za mir,* 664-665.

55. L.M. Kutakov, *Istoriya sovetsko-yaponskikh diplomaticheskikh otnoshenii,* (Moscow 1962), 227; Z.M. Zhukov, *Mezhdunarodnye otnosheniya Dal'nem Vostoke* (Moscow 1973), vol. 2, ch.4, 144; *IVOV,* vol. I, 239-40.

56. *VIZ,* 9, 1980, 60. The timetable for the final offensive ran from 20 to 23 August. Ammunition was shared out to the units accordingly.

57. Hata Ikuhiko, op. cit., 177.

58. Compare *IVOV,* vol. I, 240 to *Documents on British Foreign Policy 1919-1939,* Third Series, vol. II, (London 1955), 279, dispatches 325, 326, 327, 328. Cf. also Z. M. Zhukov, op. cit., 144 with *Documents on American Foreign Relations 1939-40,* 242, 244; also *The Foreign Relations of the US,* Soviet Union, 1933-1941, 775-779.

59. Hata Ikuhiko, op. cit., 131.

60. *JSSM,* vol. XIII, ch.IV, table facing p.43; J.W. Morley, op. cit., 158, based on the same sources as preceding reference.

61. *VIZ,* 9, 1981, 66.

62. *New York Times,* 23, 24 April 1939 for estimates of the Japanese Army. Ibid., 2 July for estimates of the Red Army. See also *League of Nations* C.206. M.112. 1938 IX, 824, 825, N.1, 549-550.

63. S.N. Shishkin, *Khalkhin Gol* (Moscow 1954), 12. *New York Times,* 5 February 1939, 1 gives the Japanese version of events along the border.

64. Katsu H. Young, op. cit., 88-89.

65. Hata Ikuhiko, op. cit., 159.

66. S.N. Shishkin, op. cit; *IVOV,* vol. I; D. Ortenberg, op.cit; G. K. Zhukov, *Razmyshlenie i vospominanie,* M. 1969; *VIZ,* 8, 1979, 8, 1980, 9, 1981; *Voennyi Vestnik,* 2, 1978; *JSSM;* J. Erickson, op. cit; Katsu H. Young; Gen. Grigorenko. All references to Gen. Grigorenko are derived from the Russian MSS of his memoirs, recently published in the USA in English translation.

67. S.N. Shishkin, op. cit., 15 Shishkin says that the Japanese had good maps on the scale of 1:100,000. The following maps may be consulted: A.M.S. 5301 Non-Chiang (Mergen); first edition (AMSI) 1943; N 4800 — E. 12000/400-600; prepared under the direction of the Chief of Engineers US Army by the Army Map Service (AMPT) US Army, Washington D.C. 1943; NM51, NL51, NL49, NL50, NM49, NM50. Cf. also *The Times World Atlas* 1976. Gen. Grigorenko (op. cit.) says that after some Japanese maps were captured, they were hastily copied.

68. *JSSM,* vol. XI, Part 3, Book C, 475, 477; A. Sutton, op. cit., 245.

69. F.P. Polynin, *Boevye marshruty* (Moscow 1981), 60-70; Hata Ikuhiko, op. cit., 131.

70. Polynin, op. cit.

71. Eiichiru Sekigawa, 'The Undeclared Air War', *Air Enthusiast* June 1973, 47, 294.

72. After the disastrous air encounters of 26 and 28 May, Corps Commander Yakov V. Smushkevich was sent to the Far East on 29 May in order to take command.

73. Eiichiro Sekigawa, op. cit., 247-8, 296.

74. M.T. Florinsky, *Encyclopedia of Russia and the Soviet Union* (New York 1961), 479-482 for a short history of Soviet rocketry dating bak to 1607; A. B. Belyakov, *V polet skvoz gody* (Moscow 1981), 294; Roy Wagner (ed.), *The Soviet Air Force in WWII* (New York 1973), 10.

75. Eiichiro Sakigawa, op. cit., 26-27. Roy Wagner, op.cit., 10.

76. *IVOV,* vol. I, 244 claims 660 Japanese planes destroyed, and admits the loss of 207 Soviet planes; Eiichiro Sekigawa, op. cit., 29.

77. D. Ortenberg, op. cit., 9; G. K. Zhukov, op. cit., 158; A. B. Belyakov, op.cit., 294. It is safe to assume that night attacks of the Soviet Air Force had an impact on Japanese morale.

78. For the reorganization which followed the incident at Changkufeng see *JSSM,* vol. XIII, Ch.IV, 56; J. Erickson, op. cit., 517. In 1940 the command in the Far East was once again reorganized; *JSSM,* vol. XIII, Ch.IV, 59.

79. *VIZ,* 8, 1979, 48-49; Katsu H. Young, op. cit. On 10 August the Japanese also reorganized their forces in the area, presumably for the great offensive they planned for 24 August.

80. O.P. Chaney, *Zhukov* (Newton Abbot 1972), 35.

81. *Documents on British Foreign Policy 1919-1939,* vol. V. series III, 167-168; *SSSR v bor'be za mir,* 637.

82. *Foreign Relations of the US,* 1939, 53, 54.

83. Alvin D. Coox, introduction to Hata Ikuhiko, op. cit., 123; Katsu H. Young, op. cit., 97 N46.

84. D. Ortenberg, op. cit., 35.

85. Hata Ikuhiko, op. cit., 156. For the conditions of the armistice, see Jane Degras (ed.), *Soviet Documents on Foreign Policy,* vol. III, 373-74.

86. *Krasnaya Zvezda,* 30 August 1939; *VIZ,* 8, 1979, 72.

87. J. Erickson, op. cit., 536-537. There is some irony in the fact that one of the people whom Zhukov praised when he met Stalin and discussed the war at Khalkhin-Gol with him, was Pavlov. He lauded him for the great experience he had gained in the Spanish Civil War; however, it was this same experience which swayed the opinion of the committee that decided to disperse the Red Army's tank formations. Pavlov was a member of the committee. See Zhukov, op. cit., 182-183.

Мар 1

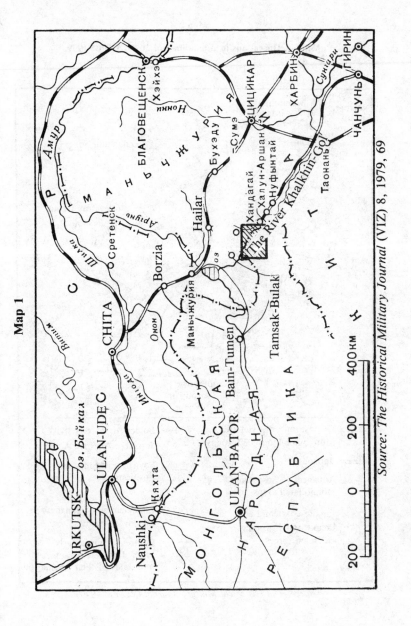

Source: The Historical Military Journal (VIZ) 8, 1979, 69

Map 2

Military Operations in Khalkhin-Gol 20-31 August 1939

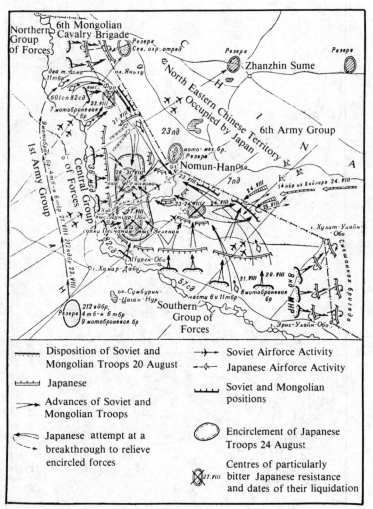

Source: *The Historical Military Journal* (VIZ) 8, 1979, 71

Amnon Sella
is a Senior Lecturer at the Hebrew
University of Jerusalem. He is the author
of *Soviet Political and Military Conduct in
the Middle East* (Macmillan 1981), and is
currently involved in research into the
Israel-Egypt peace process.

EICHMANN INTERROGATED

Edited by Jochen von Lang
Translated by Ralph Manheim

Transcripts of Eichmann's pre-trial testimony from the archives of the Israeli police

According to Hannah Arendt these transcripts formed one of the two most important documents in the Eichmann case. 'For those who wish to understand the Nazi mass murders of World War II, this book is indispensable.'

SAUL BELLOW

£8.95
BODLEY HEAD

The Bodley Head (S6759)   2nd 28.7   SF11983   057064

David Thomas

The Importance of Commando Operations in Modern Warfare 1939-82

Commando operations in the sense of self-contained acts of war mounted by self-sufficient forces operating within enemy territory are as old as warfare itself.[1] However, before the second world war, the types of missions that later would become known as 'commando operations', for instance, assault raids, intelligence collection, reconnaissance, sabotage, pre-emptive seizure, and covert diversionary action, were regarded in western military thought as belonging to the separate phenomenon of irregular warfare, that is, to partisan and guerrilla activity.[2] Clausewitz, for example, acknowledged the efficacy of partisan warfare behind an enemy's lines in support of a regular army. However, he assumed that this form of warfare would be waged by irregular forces, not by regular military units. Moreover, Clausewitz seems to have distrusted irregular warfare per se.[3]

Nevertheless, in the nineteenth century, and later, in the first world war, European armies sanctioned the conduct of irregular warfare.[4] However, the attitude of Clausewitz almost certainly encouraged the opposition of general staff officers to irregular forces and unorthodox forms of warfare. As late as the beginning of the second world war, irregular warfare was still regarded by most regular officers as exotic and fundamentally unimportant, if they had any conception of this form of warfare at all, and it was commonly held to be incompatible with the military code of honour which career officers associated with their profession.[5] Thus, until the second world war, no major army deliberately developed and systematically deployed specialized forces designed to execute the types of missions mentioned above, or methodically employed such forces in conjunction with the operations of regular units. Nor was there any idea that regular troops with special training might be used to conduct such missions. For this reason, commando operations may be fairly seen as an innovation of the

Journal of Contemporary History (SAGE, London, Beverly Hills and New Delhi), Vol. 18 (1983), 689–717

second world war, and this discussion may usefully begin in 1939.

In this interpretative essay, an attempt is made to evaluate, in brief compass, and in a non-technical manner, the military value of commando operations in modern warfare. The discussion is of necessity a *tour d'horizon*. It must omit the analysis of particular operations and the treatment of commando-type operations conducted by indigenous forces under the control of intelligence organizations in the context of resistance and guerrilla warfare.[6] Moreover, space precludes the consideration of problems of generic organization, command and control, military doctrine, and so forth, as these are related to the role of commando operations in the national style of warfare followed by this or that army. In a theoretical sense, the value of commando operations in any army, including those discussed below, is affirmed by four essential criteria: the existence of a formal military command structure authorised to conduct commando operations, include the functions of these operations in war planning, and ensure the adequate capability for their execution in the formulation of strategy and doctrine; the acceptance of commando operations as an important form of warfare; the presence of a coherent doctrine for the employment of commando forces; the recognition of the value of integrating commando operations with the mission of regular forces. Here, the approach is historical, and the emphasis is upon the importance of commando operations in those armies which have conducted them or are equipped to do so, and upon those armies which have played a formative role in the development of commando warfare. There is no theoretical examination of the value of commando operations, and thus no abstract judgment of their importance in the operational art of war is attempted.[7]

During the second world war, every major army involved in the fighting formed specialised forces and employed them to execute commando-type missions behind enemy lines.[8] However, the historical record discloses that only the British, German, and Soviet armies attached particular importance to commando warfare per se, established commando units on an important scale, and conducted what may be properly described as commando operations, *strictu sensu*. It is only in these armies that we find a coherent, if practical and improvisational, concept of commando operations informing the operational deployment of commando forces. Since the bulk of all commando operations in the second world war was in fact carried out by the British, German, and Russian armed forces, the discussion may be profitably restricted to these armies.[9]

In a general sense, the particular organization of commando units, the type of command structure to which they were subordinated, and the kinds of missions for which commando forces were utilised, differed in the case of each army. The peculiar concept of commando operations that was developed more or less separately by these three armies evolved from previous national military experience. However, in the main it was derived from earlier tactical experimentation with irregular warfare of some kind, and from the requirements of military doctrine, dire necessity and simple expediency after the war had begun. The national style of warfare adhered to by each army also conduced to the development of commando warfare.[10] It is no coincidence that armies which adopted a relational and manoeuvre-style of warfare, that is, a style designed to avoid an enemy's strengths and exploit his weaknesses using agility, deception, and imagination, readily became adept at commando operations, but that armies which followed a doctrine of attritive and logistical warfare, the American Army, for example, never grasped the concept of commando operations, or attached any value to commando forces in the second world war.

The German army (*Wehrmacht*) was the first army to develop a systematic concept of the military value of commando operations and to employ commando units on a large scale. From the beginning, the German understanding of the function of commando operations was connected with the operational requirements of the new *Blitzkrieg*-style of offensive.[11] Thus, the *Wehrmacht* was the first modern army to integrate commando operations with the mission of regular units instead of treating these operations as a separate, insulated phenomenon. The value of high-risk, but high-payoff, surprise operations at the beginning of a theatre offensive was recognized in the context of the developing German conception of manoeuvre-warfare, which of necessity emphasized the circumvention of the enemy's strength in order that his weaknesses might be attacked with a minimum expenditure of Germany's inferior military resources. The *Wehrmacht* developed a capability for commando operations in a premeditated manner, and the purpose of the forces which were established to conduct these operations was soon defined in German strategy and doctrine. Until 1943, German commando operations were designed almost exclusively to support the armoured spearheads that opened the great offensives. These operations were planned to take advantage of two specific situations created by the German style of war: first, the fluid conditions at the front engendered by the *Blitzkrieg*-form of attack; and secondly, the psychological weaknesses of the enemy's army and his civilian population owing to pre-existing instability among national ethnic minority groups exacerbated by German propaganda and subversion. Thus, the military value attached to commando operations in the *Wehrmacht* was in direct relation to the practical ability of these missions to support the German style of offensive warfare.[12] However, the tactical and strategic application of commando operations was not developed all at once; rather, it evolved in three stages.

The first German commando force was formed by the *Abwehr* on the orders of the General Staff in preparation for the invasion of Poland in 1939. The purpose for which the General Staff wanted to employ the *Kampftruppen,* as these units were called, was sabotage-prevention and pre-emptive seizure in respect of vital industrial installations and transportation facilities in Polish Silesia. The operations planned to accomplish these tasks were in general not co-ordinated with the tactical movements of the armoured divisions, and a number of the targets assigned to the *Kampftruppen* were of no immediate military value with regard to the advance of the *Wehrmacht*. Nevertheless, the idea of seizing vital objectives in advance of the *Panzer* and motorized divisions was appreciated, and it was decided to retain units of this kind in the *Wehrmacht* despite the limited success of these formations in Poland.[13]

For invasion of the Low Countries, Belgium, and France in 1940, the original, limited conception of the mission of the *K-Trupps* was expanded to embrace the pre-emptive seizure of all communications and transportation facilities and military fortifications of immediate military importance to the advance of the *Panzer* divisions. New commando units were established, the most important of which was the so-called Brandenburg Battalion zbV 800. In the actual invasion, over sixty commando operations were carried out with the strategic purpose of ensuring and expediting the rapid and unimpeded advance of the armoured divisions along the multiple, selected axes of penetration by seizing pre-emptively and holding temporarily vital road and railroad bridges, tunnels, sluicegates, and fortifications (the most famous of which was Fort Eben Emael). These operations were most successful, and German military records obtrude no doubt as to their importance.[14] The Armed Forces Operational Staff and the General Staff henceforth assumed a detailed interest in the development of the Brandenburg unit and in the planning of commando operations for Operation Barbarossa. The Brandenburg Battalion was expanded into a regiment, and its capabilities were refined and improved to facilitate the complete integration of its operations with the requirements of the Army High Command in Russia.

For the invasion of Russia in 1941, and during the great offensives in the Ukraine and the Caucasus in 1942, Brandenburg units (and special formations of ethnic volunteers) were assigned to each of the three army groups (North, Centre, South, B) and entrusted with a five-fold strategic mission of unprecedented scope in the history of commando operations.[15] The tasks of the commandos now included the following: pre-emptive seizure of vital objectives (over 100 on 22 June 1941); sabotage of military targets in the Soviet rear; deep scouting and intelligence collection ahead of the *Panzer* divisions; diversionary and undermining actions among Red Army units and behind Soviet lines; instigation of rebellion among ethnic minorities in the Baltic States, the Ukraine, and the Caucasus. The bulk of these manifold operations were coordinated with the movements or requirements of the *Wehrmacht,* and many of them enjoyed success.[16] However, the German concept of commando operations was suited essentially only to offensive warfare. After the *Wehrmacht* was forced onto the defensive in Russia and elsewhere, there was no further need for commando operations to assist the armoured divisions. The Brandenburg Regiment was expanded into a regular division, and the operations of its successor unit in Russia, the Regiment Kurfurst, were restricted to self-contained missions involving intelligence, reconnaissance, and subversion, otherwise unrelated to the operational requirements of the *Wehrmacht*. The direct successor of the Brandenburg Regiment as a whole, the special SS formation under Otto Skorzeny, was used almost exclusively to carry out *coup de main* operations and minor sabotage and diversionary missions behind enemy lines independently of the *Wehrmacht*.[17]

German military records and the memoirs of certain leading *Wehrmacht* field commanders leave no doubt as to the value attached to commando operations in the great armoured offensives in France and Russia. On other fronts, the importance of commando operations appears to have been negligible. On balance, commando operations were of definite and measurable value to the German Army, precisely because these operations were normally conducted in the light of specific, well-defined mission-functions and for narrow objectives of direct importance to the army.

Perhaps in a general historical sense, the British concept of commando operations derived from the English tradition of maritime raiding and seaborne assaults, and from the experience of irregular warfare in the Peninsular War and the Boer War. However, before Dunkirk, there was no coherent appreciation in the British army at the command level of the tactical or strategic value of special forces and commando operations and almost no systematic development of specialised units for any purpose. From 1940, it transpired that commando forces were established in each major theatre of the war, northwest Europe, the Mediterranean, and the Far East, in response to the operational requirements of the theatre command, but in general without any reference to pre-existing doctrine or a systematic plan formulated by the General Staff in Britain. Every British military commando force was essentially an inspired improvisation or invention in the face of necessity or expediency. The several forces which came into existence between 1940 and 1942 owed their formation not to British army strategy and doctrine, nor to any far-reaching conception of commando warfare, but to the fertile imagination of Prime Minister Churchill and a number of gifted officers.[18]

The first commando force, the Army Commandos, was an *ad hoc* unit, for which the regular military establishment originally could foresee no useful or permanent function beyond the one assigned to it by the Prime Minister at the time of formation, namely, to serve as a reserve, mobile strike-force in the defence of Britain against the expected invasion. Thus, when the threat of invasion passed, the Commandos at first had no well-defined military function.[19] However, they were shortly re-deployed as amphibious raiding forces for operations against occupied Europe designed to bolster military and civilian morale and regain a measure of the tactical initiative at a time when the army was confined to the strategic defensive. The numerous pin-prick missions conducted in 1940 and 1941 otherwise had no serious military value. In terms of the resources expended upon them, the amount of training and rehearsal, and the casualties suffered, the costs of these coastal raids were quite out of proportion to the minimal results achieved. However, these operations represented a form of psychological warfare, and they were less important for what they attained in terms of losses inflicted on the Germans and information obtained, than for their effect upon the psychology of the British and German armies.

Between 1942 and 1944, additional commando units were formed within the Commandos, including the Special Boat Section and the Small Scale Raiding Force. These units conducted specialised missions which embraced assisting indigenous resistance groups in Europe, beach reconnaissance, and intelligence tasks in preparation for the Normandy landings. In this phase of commando operations in northwest Europe, the essential value of the missions carried out lay with the collection of intelligence, and in some spectacular instances, sabotage. Unfortunately, the lessons imbibed from the numerous operations in northwest Europe between 1940 and 1944 about the development of new techniques of assault and the military value of commando operations in direct support of regular forces were limited in imagination. True, the importance of commando operations for the purpose of deep reconnaissance, intelligence, sabotage, and the mobilization of resistance was acknowledged. However, the commando phenomenon was mostly regarded as something separate from the regular operations of the army. Thus, the British army in northwest Europe did not avail itself of the full capabilities of the commando units at its disposal before, or after, the Normandy landings. For example, there apparently was no thought given to parachute sabotage operations in France against German airfields. After the successful sabotage operations of the Special Air Service in the North African theatre had demonstrated the tactical versatility of mobile commando forces in the enemy rear in conjunction with regular units, the commando units deployed in northwest Europe continued to be thought of, and employed as, elite spearhead formations, to be used once in an amphibious landing or river assault crossing, and then withdrawn or left in the line as an ordinary infantry formation. With the exception of the SAS diversionary missions in France in the summer of 1944, British commando units were employed almost exclusively against relatively insignificant, static objectives, under specialised conditions of terrain or time, in attacks otherwise appropriate for assault engineer troops, but inappropriate for a war of manoeuvre.[20] The use of commando units for self-contained missions behind enemy lines was rarely contemplated, and the need to organize these units in accordance with the purposes of specific conventional operations was often unappreciated. The result was a mechanical application of standardized operational repertoires (e.g. the amphibious assault landing) to different circumstances.

Thus, until the end of the war in Europe, there persisted a disparity between the sophistication of commando training and the high quality of commando units, on the one hand, and the insignificance of the objectives assigned to these units and the limited tactical employment of commando forces in general, on the other. It was precisely this disparity, combined with the fact that regular army units also were used successfully in a number of coastal assault operations and river crossings, which conduced to persuade several senior British (and American) commanders that commando units had no special function.[21] In the event, it can be said that the commando operations in northwest Europe between 1944 and 1945 were never indispensable to the success of the conventional operations with which they were associated.

In the Mediterranean theatre, a plethora of small-scale commando forces were formed, usually at local initiative, and with specific operational requirements in mind.[22] Again, no pre-existing British doctrine underpinned the creation of these formations. As with the commando units established in England in 1940, the most important formations in the Mediterranean, the Long Range Desert Group (LRDG) and the Special Air Service (SAS), were the inspiration of unorthodox officers, who were supported by enlightened senior commanders of the British Eighth Army in an hour of need. The mission of the LRDG and the SAS evolved in accordance with the needs of Eighth Army, in a pragmatic manner, and after some trial and error. The LRDG was used primarily for intelligence collection and deep scouting in the German rear and on the southern flank of Eighth Army. The other mission of the LRDG was the delivery of agents and other raiding units to their objectives. While the British army in North Africa was on the defensive, the intelligence collection missions of the LRDG were of considerable value. However, after the battle of El Alamein, the usefulness of the LRDG was essentially over. The primary mission of the SAS soon became the sabotage of enemy aircraft and attacks on supply depots beyond the tactical zone of the Eighth Army. The operations of the SAS certainly weakened the German Air Force in North Africa and obliged General Rommel to commit substantial forces to prevent raids against the logistical system of the *Afrika Korps*. But the final value of the SAS should not be overestimated.[23] While the Eighth Army was on the defensive, SAS operations provided useful assistance. However, it cannot be said that the various raiding forces in the Middle East, including the SAS, made a decisive contribution to British victory in the desert. At El Alamein, neither the SAS nor the LRDG played any important role. As for the various amphibious assault raids carried out in the Aegean and along the Dalmatian coast, again, it would be impossible to argue that these operations constituted anything more than a nuisance to the Germans or that they influenced the outcome of the war in the Mediterranean.

In the Sicilian and Italian campaigns, the SAS and other commando units conducted a useful series of operations, including the standard amphibious assaults against fortified beach objectives, but also involving overland infiltration missions, pre-emptive seizures of tactical targets, and deep scouting and resistance organization. The tactical versatility of commando units was well utilised in Italy.[24] Yet, it would be difficult to select a single commando operation that was of strategic importance to the regular forces. In general, the proliferation of competitive special units in the same area of operations, but under different commands and organizations, resulted in a lack of coordination in planning and in the conduct of operations, in duplication of function, and in needless competition for scarce resources in manpower and equipment.

The British Far Eastern theatre of war was well-suited to the employment of small-scale raiding and reconnaissance forces. However, the regular army was disorganized by the rapid withdrawal from Malaya and Burma and could not undertake offensive operations for some time. An organization for the employment of commando-type forces had to be built from scratch, and it was not until 1944 that commando units were used on any useful scale. The first operations were carried out on the sea flank of the British forces in the Arakan. They consisted of conventional amphibious assaults on the flank of an army and were of no great importance in ensuring the success of the regular forces.

The main commando forces in the Far Eastern theatre were the Small Operational Group (SOG), which conducted long-range strategic and short-range tactical missions by land, river, and sea, primarily for reconnaissance and intelligence-collection, and the Long Range Penetration Group (LRPG), a large, independent raiding force, which operated on a self-contained basis behind Japanese lines. The results achieved by the LRPG were not in fact very impressive, nor can this force be regarded as a commando unit in the strict sense. Columns of the LRPG executed a few sabotage missions and collected some valuable intelligence. However, the first operation of the LRPG in 1943 was not coordinated with the movements of the regular army. A second major operation in 1944 involving three brigade-size forces, which was designed to sever Japanese communications and disrupt Japanese supply routes, was successful and did contribute directly to the advance of the Fourteenth British Army into Burma. But this operation was not a commando operation in the proper form.[25]

Summing up the importance of British commando forces in general in the second world war, it must be said that the contribution of commando operations has perhaps been over-estimated with the passage of time. One commando unit, the SAS, did achieve results out of all proportion to its size and the resources expended upon it. However, no commando operation in any theatre of war can be said to have made an indispensable contribution to the tactical or strategic success of the regular army in any battle. Except in the case of intelligence and reconnaissance missions, which may have been the most valuable types of operations undertaken by the various commando units, commando operations provided the British armed forces with a welcome, though not essential, bonus, whether as the result of successful sabotage and diversion or of the capture of fortified objectives that otherwise might have delayed the advance of the infantry inland after a landing. The German army certainly took notice of commando operations, and Hitler became obsessed with British commando warfare,[26] as witness the infamous Commando Order. Yet, no commando operation had a decisive effect upon any German military operation in the war.

The origin of Soviet commando operations, or 'diversionary actions', as they are commonly described in Soviet military writing, is not well-documented. For the second world war, Soviet sources of all kinds are chary of precise detail about the organization and the operations of the various special forces which are known to have been employed by the Red Army and the intelligence and security services. Historically, both Tsarist Russia and the Soviet state devoted substantial resources to special operations involving sabotage, intelligence, and diversion behind enemy lines. Yet, Lenin was opposed to all forms of irregular warfare connected with partisans. In the Civil War, the Bolsheviks refused to encourage partisan warfare. And it was insisted that all military units should be formed into orthodox camps, regiments and divisions and directed by a centralized command structure that in turn was obedient to the political leadership in Moscow.[27]

At the beginning of the Great Patriotic War, Stalin was compelled to tolerate the existence of partisan units as a tactical necessity, though these forces often had come into existence spontaneously. However, Stalin refused to allow them to mix with regular units, and partisan operations were centrally directed from a separate partisan headquarters under the control of the NKVD. Yet, partisan units were allowed to operate in conjunction with the offensives of the Red Army. Perhaps for this reason the Partisan Movement has obscured the importance of commando operations in the Soviet Army on the Eastern Front.[28] The diverse formations of the partisans were used by the army, the NKVD and the GRU to perform the tasks of commando units behind German lines. But it is clear that considerations of secrecy and security, the unavailability of partisan forces in particular areas, and specialized operational requirements resulted in the establishment of commando units as early as the summer of 1941.

These units consisted of the special designation units (*spetsnaznacheniya*) under the control of the NKVD and the GRU, and the Special Guards Sabotage Battalions (*Ossobi gardjeski batalljon minjorev*) and parachute assault and reconnaissance units (*desantniki* and *reidoviki*) under the Red Army. In broad outline, the employment of these commando forces embraced two phases. While the Red Army was on the defensive during most of 1941 and the summer of 1942, Soviet commando operations were of a strategic nature and were not designed as the rule to complement the mission of the army. The commando operations launched in this period were self-contained missions concerned with deep reconnaissance before German offensives, intelligence collection, assassination, sabotage, and raids against German field headquarters and signals intelligence facilities. These operations appear to have yielded quantities of valuable intelligence. But it is evident that they did not in any way influence the outcome of any major engagement or retard the offensives of the *Wehrmacht*.

In the offensive phase from late 1942, the special Red Army commando units were used in direct conjunction with the *Fronts* and the mobile armoured operational groups for tactical-level sabotage and infiltration operations. The airborne assault detachments were employed on clandestine reconnaissance missions in the deployment areas of the German reserve forces in connection with all large-scale Soviet offensives. Both types of unit also executed pre-emptive seizure operations and assault raids, which were integrated with the penetrations of the newly developed mobile groups into the middle and deep rear of the *Wehrmacht*.[29] These operations were often conducted in such a way as to make them blend with the more numerous, but less skilful missions carried out by the partisans. Soviet sources credit these operations with providing invaluable tactical support for the armoured forces. But it is clear from German military records that it was the sheer number of Soviet rear-area operations, not the success of any particular mission, that caused so much difficulty for the German security forces and the *Wehrmacht*. These Soviet commando operations apparently had no serious effect upon the morale of the front-line *Wehrmacht* divisions. However, the record discloses that Soviet operations in the rear often enkindled panic and confusion among the support troops and headquarters' staffs.

From 1943, the various commando units were used methodically for two main purposes: strategic missions in direct support of specific Soviet *Fronts*; and tactical-level operations in the shallow rear in connection with major offensives. For the Red Army, the value of commando operations was now understood to reside in the usefulness of these missions in continually weakening the offensive military capabilities of the *Wehrmacht* at the front by disrupting communications, assassinating key officers, and sabotaging vital facilities in the rear. In the Soviet view, the destruction of supply depots, airfields, headquarters, and communications installations, even more than the pre-emptive seizure of bridges and fortifications, was of greater assistance to the main offensives. The *Wehrmacht* often found it more difficult to organize its defences and plan effective counter-attacks in the face of disruption and chaos in the rear areas than to mop up individual assault units holding key objectives in the tactical zone directly in front of the spearheads of the Red Army. Furthermore, the *Wehrmacht's* effective use of fortified defences in depth and of mobile armoured defence in both instances reduced the number of targets that could be, or needed to be, seized to assist the rapid advance of the first echelon of a Soviet offensive. In sum, commando operations, in the Soviet view, were best harnessed to the tasks of furnishing real-time intelligence during large offensives and collapsing resistance in the deep and middle rear with a view to undermining entire stretches of a front.

Soviet commando forces on the Eastern Front constituted an integral component of the Soviet style of warfare. From the beginning, it would appear that commando operations in the Soviet sense were given a well-defined role and a clear purpose in Soviet strategy and doctrine. The available evidence, such as it is, discloses no spectacular Soviet commando operation to compare with the raids against St. Nazaire, Tobruk, and Bruneval. As a rule, Soviet commando operations were on a smaller scale, and they were coordinated with the intelligence or operational requirements of the Red Army and of specific Soviet *Fronts* and Armies. In this respect, commando operations in the Red Army were as important as were the missions of the Brandenburg Regiment in the *Wehrmacht*.[30]

In retrospect, the second world war emerges as the decisive period in the history of commando operations, if only because of the sheer number of operations carried out and the multiplicity of special forces established to conduct these missions. Unless another conventional war in Europe should occur, it is doubtful that commando forces will ever be employed on the lavish scale that they were in the second world war. Thus, to judge the value of commando operations in the second world war is no small responsibility. Still, with the wisdom of hindsight, it is possible to draw certain conclusions.

The military (as distinct from the political or psychological) value of commando operations in the war was minimal, at least as long as this form of warfare represented an essentially defensive measure in the strategic sense — even if, in the tactical sense, it was compelled to be offensive to be effective. This judgment would apply to the British Army in northwest Europe until 1944, to the Red Army until late 1942, and to the *Wehrmacht* from 1943. The numerous British operations from 1940 along the Channel coast and in Norway exercised a certain effect upon Hitler and the coastal garrisons. But of themselves these operations prompted no serious strategic redeployment of German forces in Europe before 1944. Soviet commando operations before 1942 did not hamper the *Wehrmacht* in any important sense when the Germans were winning.[31] The great offensives of 1941 and 1942 would have succeeded in any case, regardless of the Soviet operations behind German lines. After the *Wehrmacht* itself was forced upon the defensive in Russia and on all other fronts, the manifold commando operations mounted by the *Abwehr* and the SS were quite irrelevant in terms of affecting Allied offensives or assisting the German army on the defensive. For an army on the defensive, the real value of commando operations was connected with their psychological effect upon morale and the collection of intelligence.

In the offensive phase of the war, the value of commando operations consisted in their usefulness in assisting conventional armoured attacks and naval assault landings, whose ultimate success was in any case already assured. In this context, it is true that commando operations sometimes achieved results out of proportion to the resources expended upon them, especially when commando forces were organized and deployed in accordance with the purposes of specific conventional operations. Nevertheless, on balance, the numerous, successful German, Soviet, and British commando operations that smoothed the way for conventional attacks and hastened armoured offensives cannot be said to have changed materially the outcome of a single battle or campaign in the strategic sense. On the tactical level, it is of course true that commando operations often helped to sustain the tempo of an advance, save lives, and demoralize the enemy and his civilian population. Commando operations in the rear certainly tied down enemy resources and in some cases these operations palpably weakened the resistance of enemy forces in a particular sector of the front.[32] Yet, in the final analysis, commando operations contributed little to the great military victories of the armies discussed here.

No conflict since 1945 has afforded any army a comparable opportunity for the employment of new forces such as the commando units of the second world war, or imposed upon orthodox military establishments a similar necessity for innovation in conducting military operations. If it is difficult to assess the value of commando operations in warfare after the second world war, the reason is first that there have been fewer commando operations in general, and the bulk of the most important operations has been carried out in 'peacetime', not in conventional war. Secondly, although the military strategy and doctrine of certain major armies attaches great importance to commando operations in any future war, there has been only the slightest opportunity to observe the practical application of theoretical prescriptions and the demonstration of actual capabilities in war. Indeed, it is something of a paradox that commando operations have become more important in peacetime than in conventional war. In this respect, it should not be forgotten that the western armies, with the exception of the Israeli Defence Force (IDF), have been engaged primarily in fighting so-called wars of national liberation or colonial conflicts.[33] Anti-guerrilla, or 'counter-insurgency' warfare has proven to be ill-suited to the comprehensive use of commando operations on the classical world war two model, and the western armies that have been obliged to fight wars of this kind seem to have had few opportunities to use commando forces on a self-contained basis against enemies capable of waging irregular warfare themselves.[34] Of course, the use of commando-type forces in resistance warfare in an anti-guerrilla role is another matter. But this employment of commando forces cannot be described as commando warfare in the proper sense.

In the event, after the second world war, almost every major army retained, or established commando units. The importance attached to commando operations in formal military doctrine or in the national style of war varied with every army, according to previous experience, or not, with commando warfare. As a generalization, it can be said that the value of commando operations was least understood in the armies which adopted, or remained committed to attrition and logistical warfare. Thus, the American army, whose doctrine after the second world war persisted in stipulating a logistical style of warfare dependent upon superior firepower as distinct from manoeuvre, failed totally to grasp the concept of commando warfare as exampled in the war, distilled no coherent lessons from the history of commando operations, and for long did not establish any useful capability to conduct commando operations in conventional war. In contrast, Britain and the Soviet Union, by virtue of their deep experience with commando operations and all forms of subversive and irregular warfare, not only imbibed the essential lessons of commando warfare in the second world war, but also adopted commando operations as a permanent element of national strategy and doctrine. Moreover, a new army, the Israeli Defence Force, built upon the Jewish experience with irregular warfare and understood the efficacy of commando operations in the context of the style of manoeuvre warfare for which it was preparing itself. Thus, three armies, each of which in its own way was committed to a style of relational and manoeuvre warfare after 1945, accepted the phenomenon of commando warfare as a full-fledged element of the operational art of war. For this reason, the discussion of commando operations after 1945 may focus primarily upon these armies.

The manifold use of commando operations in the second world war endeared the concept of 'diversionary actions' to the Soviet General Staff and the intelligence and security services.[35] The high-speed operations involving KGB, GRU, and special airborne units, which issued in the seizures of Prague in 1968 and Kabul in 1979, show that the lessons of the history of commando operations have not been lost upon the Russians.[36] Indeed, in respect of doctrine and strategy, no modern army, including the IDF, attaches a greater value to commando operations at every operational level in offensive warfare than the Soviet army. The Soviet armed forces, and the KGB and the GRU, maintain between themselves the largest commando forces of any nation. The role assigned to these forces in Soviet strategy and doctrine now reflects not only the Soviets' own experience with commando operations in the second world war and their experience at the hands of the Germans, but also the specific requirements of the evolving Soviet concept of combined arms warfare.[37] Yet, in contrast with the IDF and the British and American armies, the Soviet Army has had only a modicum of practical experience in conducting commando operations since 1945. Thus, the value of commando operations, and indeed, the validity of the Soviet concept of commando warfare, can be evaluated only on the basis of doctrine and present capabilities.

Be that as it may, Soviet doctrine stands at the far end of the manoeuvre spectrum: that is, it is purely an offensive doctrine, which is designed to take advantage of the weaknesses of the enemy's forces and neutralize his strengths. In accordance with this doctrine, commando operations are divided into three basic categories: strategic, operational, and tactical. The purpose of the division is to harness all commando forces to the task of achieving the primary strategic objective of Soviet strategy in a surprise theatre offensive against western Europe or the Peoples' Republic of China: the rapid advance of ground forces to destroy both the military and the political-economic systems of the NATO countries or China. The essential conditions for the success of such an attack, apart from surprise, are shock and pre-emption. To ensure surprise, increase the initial shock, and prevent or hinder the mobilization and deployment of NATO forces, Soviet doctrine stipulates the conduct of manifold operations in the rear areas. Under this scheme, commando operations are not treated as a separate, insulated phenomenon, of no direct value to the mission of the regular forces, rather, as an integral element of the Soviet offensive design with a specific function to fulfil. It is certain that this Soviet concept of the utility role of commando operations has been derived both from the Soviets' experience with similar operations in the second world war, and from a thoroughgoing appraisal of the vulnerabilities and weaknesses of every NATO army in respect of deployment, morale, and rear area security.[38]

On the strategic level, commando operations would be conducted by KGB units in the deep rear. The purpose would be to demoralize the civilian population, create chaos, and undermine resistance. Strategic missions also would be carried out by special airborne reconnaissance and sabotage units. The function of these operations would be to destroy enemy nuclear delivery systems and storage sites, command and control centres and headquarters complexes, and communications facilities.[39] Commando operations would be executed on the operational level to support the particular Soviet Front and the subordinate field armies. These operations would be conducted by airborne assault forces, GRU special designation (*spetsnaz*) units and army sabotage and reconnaissance units. The primary objective of these missions would be the destruction of the enemy's tactical nuclear delivery systems within the Front's area of operations, to a depth of 350 to 1,000 kilometres.[40]

Tactical commando operations would be conducted in support of divisions and would be similar to the operational-level missions, except that they also would attempt to take advantage of the fluid conditions at the front created by the Soviet *Blitzkrieg*, in the style of the German Brandenburg Regiment in Russia. Thus, on the evidence of doctrine and capability, it appears that the Soviet armed forces attach the greatest value to commando operations in support of a main offensive. Soviet commando forces are designed to assist a surprise attack and ensure that Soviet armoured forces seize and sustain the initiative.[41]

Final evidence of the importance of commando operations in the Soviet style of war is the fact that these operations are controlled at the highest level of authority. The most important special designation units are commanded directly by the KGB and the GRU: these authorities are responsible for planning and conducting all missions on the strategic and operational level in war or in peacetime. In addition, the Soviet armed forces maintain élite naval and airborne commando units, including underwater demolition units and maritime assault and raiding forces, reconnaissance and sabotage units, and long-range reconnaissance detachments. The Airborne Troops, the cream of the Soviet Army, are under the direct control of the Soviet General Staff.

In Britain, the value of commando forces was debated after the second world war. The army Commandos and the numerous specialised raiding forces were disbanded. However, the SAS, the Royal Marine Commandos, and the Special Boat Section, were retained.[42] Each commando force retained the mission which it had been assigned in the war, but the capabilities of these units were intelligently and progressively adapted to the strategic and tactical requirements of Britain's small, well-trained post-war army, which was called upon to fight several small-scale wars against subversive movements in former or existing British colonial possessions. Neither the SAS nor the Royal Marines always played out their planned operational repertoires in the several colonial conflicts waged by the British army.[43] For example, most of the world war two-style naval assault and sabotage operations carried out by the Royal Marine Commandos attach to the Korean War or the landing at Suez in 1956. Many of the operations carried out by these forces were not commando operations in the proper sense. But the value of the versatile capabilities of the SAS and the Marines was confirmed and used in amphibious, airborne, and overland assaults and raids of a self-contained nature or in conjunction with the many battalion-size actions of the regular army and anti-guerrilla campaigns in Malaya, Borneo, Aden, Cyprus, and Oman.

The mature British concept of commando warfare in conjunction with the operations of regular forces, whether in war or in 'peacetime', has been on show in Northern Ireland, where the SAS has been used for a wide range of sensitive, small-scale missions relating to intelligence-collection, reconnaissance, assassination, and anti-terrorist activity. The importance of commando warfare in the British style of war has been demonstrated most clearly in the recent Falklands Campaign, where the fighting was staged in the manner of a commando operation writ large, and the full range of the missions of the SAS, the Marines, and the SBS comes on record: sabotage raids against airfields behind enemy lines; amphibious assault landings; diversionary attacks; and clandestine reconnaissance and intelligence-collection in real time. Again, on the basis of capability in place and actual operations, the value of commando operations to the British army is certain.

The genesis of the Israeli concept of commando operations may be sought, in part, in the experience of Orde Wingate's raiding units, the Special Identification Group (under British command in North Africa in 1942), and the Palmach units. But in the last analysis, the formation of the first commando units from the Paratroop Forces in the IDF in the 1950s represents another example of gifted improvisation in response to a particular operational requirement, in this case, reprisal raids against Arab terrorists. The IDF has deployed commando forces as standing units since 1953, and these forces have been employed continuously in every Arab-Israeli war since 1956, and also in 'peacetime', most noticeably in the so-called War of Attrition between 1969 and 1970. [44] From the Six-Day War of 1967 through the end of the 1970s, Israeli commando forces have conducted the largest and most successful series of operations of any modern army after the second world war.

Prima facie evidence of the importance of commando operations in the IDF is the fact that commando units receive the best officers and occupy an important place in the force-structure of the IDF. As witness the use of commando operations after 1967, commando units have a well-defined strategic and tactical purpose in Israeli military doctrine. Since 1956, the fundamental importance of commando operations has been connected with the integration of these missions with Israeli military strategy and the use of commando forces for two essential purposes: counter-terrorist activity, and deep-rear attacks in support of the IDF. In peacetime, the proven ability of Israeli commando forces serves as a deterrent; in war, commando units would have an offensive role.

The bulk of Israeli commando operations have in fact been carried out in 'peacetime', between 1967 and 1982, in particular, during the aforementioned War of Attrition, and in the first half of the 1970s. Most of these operations served no tactical function. Instead, they were conducted for strategic or psychological purposes. For example, the numerous commando operations executed inside Egypt during the War of Attrition were related to the 'counter-attrition' strategy of the IDF, which was designed to deprive Egypt of the initiative on the Suez Front. In the 1967 War, Israeli commando units did not conduct traditional commando operations. Commando units were used for conventional, but independent assault missions related to the armoured attacks in the Sinai and on the Golan Heights. In the Yom Kippur War, the tempo of the fighting precluded the planning and conduct of commando operations in the enemy rear to support the IDF, with the exception of a major strategic mission in northeast Syria.[45]

For the IDF, commando operations have proven to be of the greatest value in 'peacetime', precisely as an instrument against terrorist organizations. Numerous operations have been conducted against terrorist bases in Lebanon for purposes of sabotage, intelligence, reconnaissance, and assassination, and Israeli commando units have been used for hostage-rescue missions. The IDF has a standing commando force possessed of its own headquarters, integrated with the operational elements of the intelligence services, and ready for immediate deployment. The establishment of such a command structure is the result of the recognition by the IDF of the essential function of commando operations in war and in peacetime, and of the importance of integrating commando operations with the mission of the IDF. The commando phenomenon has not been separated in the IDF; rather, it has been deliberately exploited as a deterrent element, as a morale-generating factor for the IDF as a whole, and as a school for the Israeli art of war.[46]

The American Armed Forces, in particular the US Army, have never understood fully the nature or the role of commando operations in modern warfare — notwithstanding the American tradition of irregular warfare which dates from the colonial era. In the second world war the US army formed Ranger units and the US Marine Corps established Raider Battalions.[47] But the operations of these forces were never regarded as important in connection with conventional military offensives. Despite the British example, which in fact inspired the creation of the Rangers, the US Army did not accept commando operations as an integral part of conventional warfare in the American style. As a result, the US Army emerged from the second world war with no useful experience in commando operations, and without a coherent understanding of the value of commando forces. The suspicion of élite units, and the aversion to any form of irregular warfare which informed the military art of most senior American commanders in the second world war, persisted after 1945 and ensured that American military doctrine remained unaffected by the lessons of commando warfare in the second world war.[48]

Indeed, after 1945, the US Army Rangers were disbanded, the OSS was dissolved, and no systematic attention was paid to commando warfare. In the Korean War, the Rangers were reactivated, but only in response to the particular operational and topographical requirements in this theatre, specifically, the need for reconnaissance and raiding units. However, in practice, the opportunity at the tactical level for commando operations proved to be small, and the Rangers in Korea performed no useful tasks.[49] In 1952, the US Army Special Forces were established for the purpose of waging what the army defined as 'unconventional warfare' in the rear. Under the definition set down in the US army doctrine, this form of warfare encompassed guerrilla warfare, escape and evasion, psychological warfare, and subversion. Thus, it had essentially nothing to do with commando operations in the proper sense. The organization, mission, and relationship of the Special Forces to the regular force-structure of the US army reflected the concept and the experience of resistance, guerrilla, and psychological warfare developed by the OSS in the second world war under the tutelage of the British Special Operations Executive.

When the US Army Special Forces were deployed to Laos and South Vietnam in 1960 to conduct counter-insurgency warfare, it was soon found that the nature of the war in these areas required that the Special Forces adapt their capabilities and the American concept of unconventional warfare to conditions quite different from those for which they had been prepared, and from those in which commando units had operated in the second world war. The Special Forces and the other US specialized units subsequently sent to Indochina were organized and trained to wage unconventional war under the conditions of conventional warfare. In the Vietnam

War, these forces were obliged to conduct commando-type operations against an unconventional enemy in guerrilla war. The Special Forces in Vietnam were the first American units to carry out operations which can be described as commando operations in the proper sense. However, after the large-scale deployment of ground combat troops in South Vietnam in 1965, the missions of the Special Forces were relegated to the status of a sideshow by the US high command in Saigon. Special Forces units became the object of suspicion and intense mistrust on the part of many senior American field commanders. The operations of the Special Forces were rarely integrated at the tactical level with the missions of the regular American and South Vietnamese ground forces. US Army Ranger units also were used in Vietnam, but only on the divisional level as tactical forces for reconnaissance and ambush-patrols.

The many successful operations conducted by the Special Forces in Indochina in enemy territory ought to have affirmed the military value of commando warfare. Instead, after the Vietnam War, the Special Forces were run down and they became a backwater in the force-structure and doctrine of the US Army. The Rangers were de-activated and re-formed as airborne and helicopter-borne ranger battalions, to be used in war for tactical-level missions in enemy territory. The value of commando operations in a conventional war, as distinct from guerrilla warfare in enemy-controlled territory, was simply ignored in US army doctrine after the Vietnam War. No importance was attached to the retention of a permanent, standing commando force on the British or Israeli model, capable of conducting self-contained missions on short notice in any theatre of war with a minimum of adaptation. No thought has been given to redefining the purpose of the Special Forces, the Rangers, and the other US special units to include the conduct of operations behind enemy lines without the use of indigenous personnel. The operational content of the specialized units presently included in the US force-structure, and their relationship to the regular military command system, precludes any role for commando operations in US strategy that would be more than marginal. Doctrine and capability — as demonstrated by the abortive rescue mission in Iran — combine to suggest that commando operations are still regarded as exotic and fundamentally unimportant in the US style of warfare, except perhaps for purposes of resistance warfare and anti-terrorist activity.[50]

To register a comprehensive judgement about the value of commando operations in modern warfare would be difficult, if not incautious. Such a judgement would not necessarily apply with equal validity to every army that has conducted these operations. Moreover, as we have seen, the experience of the armies that have employed commando forces has been different. Yet, certain patterns emerge from the history of commando operations, and they should be briefly mentioned.

As a generalization, commando operations have had the greatest military value when they have been used against high-value targets, whose capture or destruction has required absolute surprise and specialized training and operational capabilities. In conventional war, commando operations have been most useful as an instrument of the offensive rather than as a defensive measure. When commando operations have been integrated with the tactical movements of armoured forces in large offensives and utilized for specific well-defined purposes, they have contributed directly to the success of conventional offensives. In anti-guerrilla warfare, against enemies with no fixed assets, who themselves practise irregular methods of combat, commando operations have been less helpful, indeed, in many cases, the importance of commando missions has been negligible, except on the tactical level for purposes of intelligence and reconnaissance in difficult terrain. After the second world war, commando operations have assumed more importance in peacetime than in war, owing to the use of commando units against terrorist organizations and the deterrent effect of a standing commando force capable of undertaking sensitive operations beyond national boundaries, in an international crisis or in response to an act of international terrorism.

For the future, it is possible that commando operations will be of great military and political value either in toppling governments in peacetime by means of the *coup de main,* or in preserving regimes after they have been weakened by this form of threat. Unless the Soviet Union should invade western Europe, it is quite unlikely that commando operations will ever be employed on the same scale as they were in the second world war. Yet, the theoretical importance of commando operations at the beginning of a conventional war would seem beyond question, and it is certain that the British and Israeli armies, and the armies of the Warsaw Pact, including the Soviet Union, have reached this conclusion. For in these armies, doctrine and capability demonstrate that commando units are regarded as an essential, not as a supplementary or sometime, instrument for the conduct of offensive operations.

If there persists a certain tendency in western military thinking to categorize commando operations as an auxiliary form of warfare, or even as a separate, and exotic, phenomenon of war, the reason in some cases is secrecy related to the fact that actual military strategy and war planning belie published doctrine. On the other hand, for example, in the case of the American military establishment, the reason is that the lessons of the history of commando operations have escaped the understanding and the attention of senior commanders and strategists. A final reason would seem to be that the domination of western military strategy and doctrine by technology has imposed a new orthodoxy upon the operational art of war, which has in turn obscured the necessity of maintaining old-fashioned units capable of inflicting the unexpected and the unorthodox upon the enemy in the fog of war. Commando operations properly conducted have always been able to do this, and it is unlikely that complicated battlefield technology, including radars and sensors, and command and control and intelligence systems, will be successful in protecting orthodox-minded armies from the unexpected.

Notes

All citations from captured documents in the United States National Archives (NAR) are noted as follows: NAR, the microfilm publication number (e.g. T-77), microfilm roll number, the first frame or frames containing the document(s) in question: e.g. T-78/462/6439670ff.

1. Here, such operations are termed 'commando operations', rather than 'special operations', or 'unconventional operations', for reasons of uniformity. This is an arbitrary categorization: for the term, 'commando operation', was a late British coinage based on British experience in the Boer War. Other contemporary armies already had their own official designations for operations of this kind: e.g. 'diversionary action', and *desant* (Soviet Army); *Sonderunternehmen,* and *Handstreich (Wehrmacht).*

2. See M.R.D. Foot, 'Special Operations/1', in *The Fourth Dimension of Warfare,* ed. Michael Elliot-Bateman (Manchester 1970), v. 2, 19-34, for an excellent overview. See also Liddell Hart, *Strategy* (New York 1974), chap. 23.

3. General Carl von Clausewitz, *Vom Kriege* (Berlin 1832), Part II, v. 6, chap. 26, 374ff. See also Liddell Hart, *Defence of the West* (London 1961), chap. 7.

4. E.g., the *francs-tireurs* in the Franco-Prussian War, on which Michael Howard, *The Franco-Prussian War* (London 1961), 249-250. See also General Denis Davidov, *Essai sur la guerre de partisans* (Paris 1841), for the Cossack units operating against the French in Russia. Wellington in the Peninsular War coordinated the activities of the Spanish guerrillas with the operations of the British Army. See Charles Oman, *A History of the Peninsular War* (Oxford 1914), vol. 5, 551ff. See also T.E. Lawrence, *Seven Pillars of Wisdom* (New York 1962), chap. 33, 190-200. The Zeebrugge Raid in 1918 is the best-known 'commando operation' of the first world war. See Phillip Warner, *The Zeebrugge Raid* (London 1978); Alexander Fullerton, *Sixty Minutes for St. George* (London 1977). Raiding operations were conducted by German-led African irregulars in East Africa.

5. See Heinz Hoehne, *Canaris* (New York 1979), 376-377, for Canaris' initial objection to the formation of a combat unit to wage psychological warfare behind the lines as a 'Bolshevist' technique. See Harris Smith, *OSS. The Secret History of America's First Central Intelligence Agency* (Los Angeles 1972), 243-244, for General Stilwell's prejudice against irregular warfare and guerrilla tactics as 'illegal action', and 'shadow boxing'.

6. See M.R.D. Foot, 'Special Operations/2', in *The Fourth Dimension of Warfare,* v. 2, 35ff., for this facet. Also Otto Heilbrunn, *Warfare in the Enemy's Rear* (New York 1963), chap. 1; Kenneth Macksey, *The Partisans of Europe in World War II* (London 1975), has a useful overview. See also M.R.D. Foot, 'Was SOE any Good?' in *The Second World War,* ed. Walter Laqueur (London 1982), 239-253.

7. See, for example, R. Beaumont, *Military Elites. Special Fighting Units in the Modern World* (Indianapolis 1974); Eliot Cohen, *Commandos and Politicians. Elite Military Units in Modern Democracies* (Cambridge 1978). See also Robert Thompson, *War in Peace: Coventional and Guerrilla Warfare since 1945* (New York 1982); Lt. Col. Peter Kelly, 'Raids and National Command: Mutually Exclusive', *Military Review* (April 1980).

8. See Myron Smith, *The Secret Wars. A Guide to the Sources in English* (Santa Barbara 1980), vol. I, for a comprehensive bibliography.

9. See Heilbrunn, *Warfare in the Enemy's Rear,* chap. 2.

10. Heilbrunn, ibid., chap. 3, for a conspectus of forces.

11. See in general, Paul Leverkuehn, *Der geheime Nachrichtendienst der deutschen Wehrmacht im Kriege* (Frankfurt a.M. 1957), chap. 2; Wilhelm Brockdorf, *Geheimkommandos des zweiten Weltkrieges* (Munich 1967); Hoehne, *Canaris,* 334-341; 376-379.

12. See Leverkuehn, ibid., esp. 22-25; Liddell Hart, *Strategy,* 218-220. See the *Gesamtanweisung,* or 'General Directive', for the Brandenburg Regiment, cited in Helmut Spaeter, *Die Brandenburger zbV 800. Eine Deutsche Kommandotruppe* (Munich 1978), 189-190:

> 'Aufgabe des Lehr-Rgt. 'Brandenburg' zbV 800 ist der kampfmässige, getarnte Einsatz gegen taktisch, operativ oder kriegswirtschaftlich wichtige Objekte. Er erfolgt dort, wo andere Einheiten der kampfenden Truppe noch

nicht mehr kampfen können. Im Hinblick auf die Bedeutung rascher Bewegungen im modernen Krieg steht die Inbesitznahme von Verkehrsanlagen . . . im Vordergrund.

13. See Hoehne, *Canaris,* 336-338. For operational reports of missions in Poland in 1939, see NAR T-77/1505/1118ff., *Abwehrabteilung II, Tagebuch General Lahousen,* 1-129; T-77/1501/652-1202, for reports on *K-Trupps* and sabotage missions in Poland.

14. See Spaeter, *Die Brandenburger,* 32-42, for a good summary of operations in 1940; also Werner Melzer, *Albert Kanal und Eben Emael* (Frankfurt a.M. 1957). For official reports, NAR T-314/478/1188-1195; T-315/1010/436ff.

15. See in general Oscar Reile, *Geheimfront Ost* (Munich 1967); John Erickson, *The Road to Stalingrad* (London 1975), 82; 97; 109; Nikolai Tolstoy, *The Secret Betrayal* (New York 1977), 28-30; for detailed discussion, Spaeter, *Die Brandenburger,* 140-266. See NAR T-78/482/6466472-640, for target lists for 22 June 1941, and operational orders.

16. See NAR T-313/333/8614495ff., (4 *Panzer* Army), 'Erfahrungsbericht über z.b.V. Einsätze in Sowjet Russland'; (June 1941); 'Erfahrungsbericht über Einsatz des Lehr-Rgt. ''Brandenburg'' z.b.V. 800 in der UdSSR im Bereich der Heeresgruppe Nord vom 16.5-30.6.41'. For 1942, see NAR T-77/1499/727-892, 'Abwehrabteilung II, Arbeit Ost, S-Einsatz, Einsatz und Erfahrungsberichte'; T-77/1500/1-96, 'Abwehrabteilung II, Arbeit Ost, Z-Einsatz'; *Tagebuch Lahousen,* 130-261.

17. See NAR T-77/1499/893-1086, 'Abwehrabteilung II, Arbeit Ost, K-Einsatz, Einsatz-und Erfahrungsberichte'; T-77/1502/1-67, 'Abwehrabteilung II, Arbeit Ost, R-Aktionen, Einsatz-und Erfahrungsberichte'. On the SS formation, Otto Skorzeny, *Meine Kommandounternehmen. Krieg ohne Front* (Wiesbaden and Munich 1978); idem., *Geheimkommando Skorzeny* (Hamburg 1950); NAR, *European Theater Historical Studies,* 'Ardennes Offensive: Role of Commandos of 150th Panzer Brigade'.

18. See Winston Churchill, *The Second World War* (London 1950), 217; 251-252; 413. See also C. Buckley, *Norway. The Commandos, Dieppe* (London 1951), 160-162; B. Fergusson, *The Watery Maze* (London 1951), 15-16; Brig. Gen. Dudley Clark, *Seven Assignments* (London 1948).

19. For opposition to the Commandos, see, for example, Fergusson, ibid., 76-77; 121-123.

20. See M. McDougall, *Swiftly They Struck* (London 1954), 30ff.; 72-74; 93ff; Heilbrunn, *Warfare,* 47-50. For appraisals of operations, see Major-General R.E. Laycock, 'Raids in the Late War and their Lessons', *Royal United Services Institute* v. 92 (1947), 528-538; Lt. Gen. John Hackett, 'The Employment of Special Forces', *RUSI* v. 97 (1952), 34ff.

21. For sources, see Heilbrunn, ibid., 43-44; also T.B. Churchill, 'The Value of Commandos', *RUSI* v. 95 (1950), 87ff. J.P. O'Brien Twohig, 'Are Commandos Really Necessary?' *Army Quarterly* (1948).

22. For standard sources, Virginia Cowles, *The Phantom Major* (London 1958); W. Kennedy Shaw, *Long Range Desert Group* (London 1945); Lt. Col. David Lloyd-Owen, *The Desert. My Dwelling Place* (London 1957); Lt. Col. V. Peniakoff, *Popski's Private Army* (London 1950); see also Barrie Pitt, *The Crucible of War* (London 1980), vol. 1, 349-352; vol. 2, 19-25; 253-262.

23. For German reactions, see NAR T-77/1434/1136ff., *Abwehr* report on

British commando sabotage missions. See Barrie, ibid., vol. 1, 317-318; vol. 2, 27; 261-262, for a clear judgement of these operations.

24. See for example, D. Harrison, *These Men are Dangerous* (London 1957); Major Roy Farran, *Winged Dagger* (London 1956); idem., *Operation Tombola* (London 1960).

25. See Colonel P.A. Tobin, 'Bertrand Stewart Prize Essay, 1952', *Army Quarterly* 65 (1953), 170-174, for a summary of operations.

26. See for example NAR T-314/844/1-325, *Wehrmacht* report and after-action critique of Dieppe and Vaagso Landing; T-77/1443/904ff., commando order; NAR H 2/704 (2.1943), Foreign Armies West report, 'Special Service Truppen', on British commando troops, missions, organization, equipment and officers. Cf., M.R.D. Foot, 'Was SOE any Good', 248-249. See also NAR T-77/1454/76-80, 'Kommandounternehmen', on Führer Order of 18 October 1942; T-77/1428/744-1089, 'Behandlung von Sabotagetrupps und englischer Kommando-Angehöriger'.

27. See Heilbrunn, *Warfare*, 20-23, on the Soviet partisan tradition. See George Leggett, *The Cheka* (Oxford 1982), 331-335, for special operations of the Cheka against bandits and peasant revolts.

28. See Edgar Howell, *The Soviet Partisan Movement 1941-1944*, Department of the Army Pamphlet, N. 20-244 (Washington, D.C. 1956), 77-83; John Armstrong, *Soviet Partisans in World War Two* (Madison 1964), for case studies; John Erickson, *Road to Stalingrad*, 241-248.

29. See for example, NAR T-78/461/6439738ff., for *Abwehr* reports on Soviet 'Besondere Garde-Sprengbatallione'; T-78/461/6439896ff., on NKVD special designation units, *desant* units for special missions; T-78/461/6440127ff., report on parachute reconnaissance unit of 6th Red Army and Soviet *desant* units; T-315/1524/298ff., 'Überfall eines russischen Sonderbatallion 23-24.11.1941'; T-315/1100/388ff., report on *Sondertrupps* of Soviet 19th Assault Division; T-315/1524/288ff., 'Marine-Einsatzkommandos Schwarzes Meer'. For Soviet accounts, see Fedor Timofeyavich Ilyukhin, *Dvesti dvatsat dney v tylu vraga* (Simferopol 1967); Yuri Antonovich Kolesnikov, *Osoboye Zadaniye* (Kishenev 1968); *Razvedehiki v boyakh za rodinu* (Moscow, DOSAAF, 1967). See also C.N. Donnelly, 'The Soviet Operational Manoeuvre Group', *International Defence Review* v. 15, n.9 (1982), 1186.

30. See General G.K. Tsinev, 'Guard the Interests of the Armed Forces of the USSR. Soviet Military Counter-intelligence is Sixty Years Old', *Kommunist Vooruzhennykh Sil* n.24 (December 1978), 26-31.

31. See Howell, op. cit., 34-35, on the ineffectiveness of partisan sabotage missions.

32. See J.D. Ladd, *Commandos and Raiders of World War II* (New York 1978), chap. 14, for an evaluation.

33. See Michael Carver, *War Since 1945* (New York 1981), for a useful conspectus of these conflicts. The Royal Marines were used sporadically in Korea for sabotage operations. See Lt. Col. D.B. Drysdale, '41 Commando', *Marine Corps Gazette* v. 37 (August 1953), 28ff.; T. Saxon, 'Royal Marines: Soldiers from the Sea', *Marine Corps Gazette* v. 60 (October 1976), 35ff.

34. For example, the French *Commandos de Chasse* in the Indochina War, on which Jean Mabire, *Commando de Chasse* (Paris 1976); Bernard Fall, *Street Without Joy* (New York 1962), 267-279. See for Algeria, J. Talbot, 'The Myth and

Reality of the Paratrooper in the Algerian War', *Armed Forces and Society* v. 14 (November 1977), 69-81.

35. See, in general, H. Whittier, 'Soviet Special Operations/Partisan Warfare: Implications for Today', *Military Review* (January 1979), 48-58; C.N. Donnelly, 'The Soviet Concept of the Desant', *RUSI* (September 1971); idem., 'Operations in the Enemy Rear', *IDR* v. 13, n.1 (1980), 35-41.

36. Robert Littel, *The Czech Black Book* (New York 1969); John Collins, 'The Soviet Invasion of Afghanistan: Methods, Motives, and Ramifications', *Naval War College Review* v.33 (November-December 1980), 53-62.

37. John Dziak, 'Soviet Intelligence and Security Services in the 1980's: the Paramilitary Dimension', in *Intelligence Requirements for the 1980's*, v. 3, *Counterintelligence,* ed. Roy Godson (Washington, D.C. 1980), 95-112.

38. See Donnelly, 'Operations in the Enemy Rear', 35-36. The 'Lightning Campaign' in Manchuria in 1945 against the Kwantung Army is an obvious precedent for the use of *Spetsnaz* forces in a theatre offensive. See John Despres, et al., *Timely Lessons of History: The Manchurian Model for Soviet Strategy* RAND Report R-1825-NA (Santa Monica 1976), esp. 43-44; Lilita Dzirkals, *'Lightning War' in Manchuria: Soviet Military Analysis of the 1945 Far East Campaign* RAND Report P-5589 (Santa Monica 1976), 80-82.

39. See Aleksei Myagkov, 'Soviet Sabotage Training for World War III', *Soviet Analyst,* 20 December 1979, 2-6. Also A. Zuehlke, 'Unconventional Warfare Operations', Defense Intelligence Agency, *Review of the Soviet Ground Forces* (October 1981), 5-6.

40. See Peter Vigor, 'The Forward Reach of the Soviet Armed Forces', in *Soviet Military Power and Performance,* ed. John Erickson (Hamden 1970); Graham Turbeville, 'Soviet Airborne Troops', in *Soviet Naval Influence* ed. M. McGwire (New York 1977); Horst Tolmein, *Aufmarsch gegen die Bundesrepublik* (Landeshut 1976), esp. 98-112.

41. Lynn Hansen, 'Soviet Helicopter Operations', *IDR* v. 11, n.8 (1978), 1242-1246; G. Turbeville, 'Soviet Bloc Maneuvers: Recent Exercise Patterns and the Implications for European Security', *MR* v. 58 (1978), 19-35. Add now 'Viktor Suvorov', *Inside the Soviet Army* (New York 1983), 75-77; 95-97.

42. See Heilbrunn, *Warfare,* 43-44, for references. Also Brigadier T.B.L. Churchill, 'The Value of Commandos', *RUSI* v.95 (1950), 85-90.

43. See for example Phillip Warner, *The Special Air Service* (London 1971); Tony Jeapes, *SAS: Operation Oman* (London 1980); David Smiley, *Arabian Assignment* (London 1968); Tony Geraghty, *Who Dares Wins* (London 1980).

44. Edward Luttwak and Dan Horowitz, *The Israeli Army* (London 1975), 108-118; 178.

45. See Chaim Herzog, *The Arab-Israeli Wars* (New York 1982), 200-202; 209-213. See also Yaacov Bar-Siman-Tov, *The Israeli-Egyptian War of Attrition 1969-1970* (New York 1980), 99ff; Luttwak, ibid., 318-322.

46. See Herzog, ibid., 327-336.

47. The US Army Rangers were originally developed as a marine raiding force and accompanied the British Army Commandos and Royal Marines in Operation Torch in 1942. But the Rangers' role soon became that of spearheading amphibious landings. See William Darby and William Baumer, *We Led the Way: Darby's Rangers* (New York 1981). For the US Marine raiders, see Charles Updegraph, *U.S. Marine Corps Special Units of World War Two* (Washington, D.C. 1972).

48. See Alfred Paddock, Jr., *US Army Special Warfare. Its Origins. Psychological Unconventional Warfare, 1941-1952* (Washington, D.C. 1982), esp. 23-35; Charles Thayer, *Guerrilla* (New York 1963), xvii-xviii.

49. Colonel Walter Booth, 'The Pattern that Got Lost', *Army* (April 1981); Paddock, ibid., 124-126.

50. Paddock, ibid., 119-142. See also Klaus Buschmann, *United States Army Special Forces 1952-1974* (Frankfurt a.M. 1978). On the Vietnam War, see Colonel Francis Kelly, *U.S. Army Special Forces 1961-1971* (Department of the Army, Washington, D.C. 1973); Captain Shaun Darragh, 'Rangers and Special Forces: Two Edges of the Same Dagger', *Army* (December 1977), 14-19. On the Iran mission, R. Gabriel, 'A Commando Operation that was Wrong from the Start: the US Rescue Mission into Iran, April, 1980', *Canadian Defence Quarterly* v. 10 (Winter 1980-1981).

David Thomas
is a defence analyst in Washington, D.C.
He has published articles on military
history and intelligence, and is currently
working on a study of German intelligence
on the Eastern Front, 1941-45.

Manfred Messerschmidt

The Wehrmacht and the Volksgemeinschaft *

The role of the Wehrmacht in the National Socialist state cannot
be limited to the relations between the Wehrmacht leadership,
Hitler and the Nazi party organization, or the relationship between
Nazi *Weltanschauung* and 'military thinking'. To posit opposed
and quite independent entities, separate in both organization and
mentality, in order then to examine the strategies and policies of
each, makes it impossible to grasp the 'whole' history of the
German military in Hitler's one-party state.

There is only an apparent contradiction between this thesis and
recent research into the social psychology of national socialism and
the Hitler myth. At first sight it might seem that a 'movement'
which voiced the hopes and aspirations of the petty bourgeoisie[1]
could hardly be very attractive to generals, whose social background
was mostly quite different, or offer them much to identify with. In
socio-psychological terms, a better general picture, more
intelligible and plausible, can probably be constructed around the
younger ranks of officers and the mass of the troops. Yet by 1933
the Wehrmacht was already fascinated by the idea of the
Volksgemeinschaft and petty bourgeois anxieties about social status
hardly entered into it. The alluring political slogan of the cure-all
Volksgemeinschaft did not only appeal to the 'extremists of the
Centre' or those sections of the middle classes that felt themselves
unrepresented in the pre-1933 political system,[2] who either longed
for a real community (*Gemeinschaft*) with a charismatic leader, or
who had been manoeuvred into such longings or expectations by
völkisch propaganda. The slogan was also taken very seriously by
the top military leaders, albeit out of strategic considerations of
domestic and foreign policy.

Martin Broszat has rightly drawn attention to the link between
the idea of the *Volksgemeinschaft* and the *Burgfriede* of 1914.[3] The
phenomenon of a nation welded together by war intoxicated

*Translated from the German by Mr. Anthony Wells.
Journal of Contemporary History (SAGE, London, Beverly Hills and New Delhi),
Vol. 18 (1983), 719–744

nationalists of every social class. For the military, it meant they were relieved of the one shadow hanging over all their calculations, namely the question of whether the social democrats would support a nationalist war. Shortly before the outbreak of the war, von Falkenhayn, the Prussian war minister, found it necessary to point out that the social democrats would behave 'as befits every German in the present situation'.[4] A little earlier, the army had still been drawing up contingency plans for civil war against the social democratic party and its millions of supporters. To neutralize them, the military had enlisted the ex-servicemen's organizations, 'to be able to counter with force any attempts to endanger the state'.[5] They were to be 'bulwarks against social democracy',[6] a front-line weapon of secondary integration. In the first world war, the first to be understood as 'total war', Wilhelminian Germany had been unable to organize a *Volksgemeinschaft* which in time of war was transformed into a *Wehrgemeinschaft*. The *Burgfriede* lasted only a short time. It was broken by the right, because there the need for greater and greater national identification with increasingly extravagant war aims, with unrestricted U-boat warfare and with the denial of democratic rights demanded expression: demanded in effect a militarization of society that was unattainable.[7] Domestic propaganda very largely failed in its attempts to build up an ideology of *Gemeinschaft* because it was unconvincing and lacking in social credibility. Open statements of Germany's war aims failed to appeal to the nation as a whole, while the attempted mass mobilization for a victorious peace, to be achieved through the 'patriotic instruction' inaugurated by the high command of the army came to nothing, as did open propaganda support for the movement of national unity represented by the *Vaterlandspartei*.[8] The transformation of the *Volksgemeinschaft* into a *Wehrgemeinschaft* remained a dream of those groups who wanted to harness the nation as a whole to particular interests, interests which had nothing to do with the 'defensive war' which was the basis of the *Burgfriede*. German nationalism in its economic and military manifestations had lost touch with reality. Having failed to understand the general war-weariness and the fears and longings of those at home, it now, as in Ludendorff's case, tried to place the blame for the consequences of its own failures on the destructive activities of 'supra-national forces'. These 'supra-national forces' or whatever the 'enemy within' was called, were in the first place Marxism and Jewry. The preoccupation with these stereotypes in the military's conception of the *Volksgemeinschaft* dates from this period. It followed quite naturally from this that in any future 'total war' protective measures would have to be taken against such dangerously divisive elements: thus Ludendorff spoke of 'the necessity for a racial (*völkisch*) closing of ranks by the German people and the creation of the people on a *völkisch* basis'.[9] After his humiliating dismissal in 1938, General von Fritsch, commander-in-chief of the army revealed himself to be a model political disciple of Ludendorff. He stated that after the end of the first world war he had reached the view that three struggles remained to be fought, namely against the workers, against ultra-montanism and against the Jews — 'and the struggle against the Jews is the hardest'.[10] On certain crucial issues — the 'stab in the back', anti-Marxism, anti-parliamentarism and the demand for national 'cohesion' — the military's values and its reading of history were identical to those of the '*völkischen*', the DNVP and the National Socialists. They also agreed on the 'enemy': bolshevism and pacifism.[11]

As, in the period of the presidial cabinets, the Weimar republic began to crumble and a 'wave of war-books and films'[12] broke, devoted to the militarization of society, the Reichswehr leadership called on the government 'finally to put our people's defensive forces in readiness for the future'.[13] The intention was to draw 'the lessons' from the Great War. In the interests of the military preparedness of the entire nation, the 'social tensions within the German people' were to be resolved, in the time-honoured tradition of 'Prussian socialism', by the young being given back 'the right to state military service'.[14]

The foregoing is perhaps sufficient to indicate how significant was the convergence between the programmes of the national socialists and the military, even before Hitler's 'seizure of power'. Ludwig Beck, later chief of the general staff and a member of the resistance, was not just mouthing phrases when, in a letter to Julie von Gossler, he wrote apropos of the 30 January 1933 that the political change was something he 'had been hoping for for years and (I am) happy that my hopes have not been deceived; this is the first true glimpse of light since 1918'.[15]

Hitler delivered social 'pacification'. The army could now hope soon to have a united nation behind it. The views it had inherited from Prusso-German military history coincided perfectly as far as the *Volksgemeinschaft-Wehrgemeinschaft* equation went with

Hitler's own views.

The socio-psychological hopes and fears which are known to have existed among the NSDAP's supporters and recruits do not fit so happily into this picture and it was for this reason that Hitler avoided presenting himself to the military as the şuper-ego of the petty bourgeoisie. His speech to senior generals of 3 February 1933 could only have come out of an instinctive grasp of the closeness of his and their views of domestic and foreign policy. In the context, his announcement of re-armament was less notable than the methods he suggested for the bringing-about of the *Volksgemeinschaft*, namely the strengthening of military will (*Wehrwillen*) and the extirpation of Marxist-pacifist thinking: 'those who refuse to be converted must be humbled. Marxism must be torn out root and branch. The young, the entire *Volk*, must be adjusted to the idea that struggle alone can save us.'[16] Between the lines, Hitler also hinted at a conquest of living-space and a ruthless policy of Germanization in the east.

The prospect left with the military leaders after this meeting was that they could rely on a socio-political under-pinning of re-armament: there would be general military service and a national army, without the constant worry of socialist infiltration. There would be no parliament to pose awkward questions. The *Volksgemeinschaft* could be constituted as a *Wehrgemeinschaft* and the *Burgfriede* become a permanent state of affairs, albeit at the price of oppression and *Gleichschaltung*. As a necessary step, this condition scarcely bothered the army. On the contrary, practically from the very start of its politico-philosophical educational work, it had accepted that violence would be needed to foster the military spirit and to form 'the new German man'. Here the army consciously borrowed from the ideas of Ernst Krieck, an educationalist of considerable influence in the early days of Nazi rule, and it in fact used the title of Krieck's programmatic book *National-political Education* for its own educational programme.[17] Krieck, building on earlier *völkisch* thinking, had argued that the formation and breeding of the new man, which was his chief concern, could be realised only within the *Volksgemeinschaft*. This *Volksgemeinschaft*, however, was not to be merely an ideal community reduced to the experience of the German spirit but an expression of a unified national will on a racial basis, pledged to the Führer — a military unit forged for the purpose of gaining living-space. Will Germany, Krieck asked, 'ever gain the freedom to make its own decisions and with such a decision take on the leadership of one of the great spheres of power or will it for ever be another's vassal, a bridgehead for other world powers?'[18]

Whether or not the new Reichswehr leadership under Blomberg and Reichenau closely followed Krieck's ideas in the 'national-political lessons'[19] they introduced in the winter of 1933/34 is immaterial, since the educational concepts they adopted were clearly related to those of the national socialists. The new educational programme made prominent use of statements by Hitler, as it did of Krieck's ideas and a conscious effort was made to place Hitler, as the Führer figure, at the centre of their political instruction.

Under Weimar, the Reichswehr, like its predecessor under the monarchy, had seen itself as one arm of the state, above and apart from political parties, with a direct link originally to the monarch, then to the Field-Marshal President. The Wehrmacht now sought a comparable position within the Führer-state. Even in this militarized state it did not want to be put on a par with the various sections of the party or its associated organizations. As the 'Führer's' armed forces they wanted a monopoly of arms. In their view, the ideal organization of the national socialist state would be one restricted to the charismatic Führer and the armed forces, on the one hand, and the party, as organizer and guarantor of the *Volksgemeinschaft* on the other. The role of the Nazi party and Nazi *Weltanschauung* would thus have been one of serving the political and military leadership.

However, Hitler actually described the armed forces and the party as the two equal pillars of the national socialist state and in the early years both were recognized as such. The tasks of educating 'German Man' and of building the foundations of the *Volksgemeinschaft* were deputed to both. At the 1935 party rally, Hitler formulated the principle as follows: 'The young boy will become a member of the *"Jungvolk"*, and the *"Pimpf"* will become a member of the Hitler youth, then he will go into the SA, the SS and other units, and the SA- and the SS-men will one day go into the labour service (*Arbeitsdienst*) and from there into the army, and the soldier of the people will return to the party, the organized form of the Movement, return to the SA and the SS, and then our nation (*Volk*) will never go to ruin the way it was unfortunately once allowed to do.'[20] The Wehrmacht, ranged as it was alongside the armed party organization of the SA and, after

30 June 1934, the SS, was never able to enjoy in tranquillity that monopoly of arms which it was always being promised. Its educational work was thus always carried out in a competitive situation. One consequence of this was a tendency to concentrate on the figure of Hitler, on the basic principles of the Führer state and on the most important elements of Hitler's version of philosophy, as propounded by the Führer himself. The various party structures on the other hand, were presented in different degrees as either dangerous, or rivals, or occasionally bureaucratic big-wigs. By 1934, even before the elimination of Röhm, the Reichswehr leadership felt confident, after the setting-up of the 300,000-man army provided for in the second armament programme, of being the victor in the struggle for its position in the Führer state.[21] Blomberg had put his finger on the heart of the matter as early as 3 February 1933, 'to be brought down to the level of a party cohort — no, but rather, the Wehrmacht to be supported and strengthened by a militarization (*Wehrhaftmachung*) of the whole people'. He went on to place the responsibility for organizing the *Volksgemeinschaft* in the hands of the party. Hitler's long-term view was, however, that after the introduction of general military service, reserves of both officers and men would be drawn from national socialist organizations almost without exception. In this way, Röhm's earlier dream of a Nazi people's army would, by a roundabout route, become reality.

The competition between the Wehrmacht and the SA and SS drove the Wehrmacht leadership to make special efforts in the field of political philosophy (*Weltanschauung*). The Wehrmacht leaders wanted to show their 'Führer' just what model national socialists they were in their thinking and how conscientiously they were working to bring about the *Volks-* and *Wehrgemeinschaft*. Schleicher had once spoken of using 'military thinking' as the 'healing serum against the poisons of suicidal pacifism that are debilitating our people'.[22] 'Military studies', he said, ought to be made part of the university curriculum.[23] Behind these thoughts lay Schleicher's idea of a 'military dictatorship on a mass basis'[24] — an idea which before 1934 had come to grief not least because the mass base Schleicher had in mind had already been attracted and fascinated by an even more militant organization, the Nazi 'movement'. The Reichswehr leadership's étatist manipulative idea of the *Wehrgemeinschaft* found itself overtaken by the aggressively *völkisch* potential of the Hitler movement. The pull was exerted not, as Schleicher had hoped it would be, by the Reichswehr on the party units,[25] but rather by the new political and ideological centre of gravity — by Hitler, who, as 'Führer' and chancellor, now had the reins of state power in his hands, reins he proved to be adept at using.

Yet for some years, the Reichswehr leadership continued to believe it could play the leading role in the organization of an armed force embracing all society, that would be based on Nazi *Weltanschauung* and would utilize the authority of the Führer, thereby securing for the Reichswehr that position in the state which it had felt 'entitled to' since 1848. It is necessary to bear this strategy in mind in any consideration of the elements of Nazi *Weltanschauung* which the Wehrmacht chose to propagate.

This strategy accommodated without reservation Hitler's methods and aims in the construction of the *Volksgemeinschaft*, in other words, the violent *'Gleichschaltung'* of democratic, liberal, socialist, communist and racial dissidents. In 1933 such groups could not by any means be dismissed as minorities. This violence was in actual fact a direct attack on all those historical traditions and forces within German society and intellectual life which the 'right' had been deliberately disparaging and undermining since 1918. Hitler's measures went further than just guaranteeing a 'contractual' *Burgfriede*; they guaranteed a permanent state of affairs in which the identity of the *Volksgemeinschaft* with the *Wehrgemeinschaft* appeared to be vouchsafed even in peace-time. This objective received the Reichswehr's tacit approval. There would be no repetition of 1918. Only a few military figures expressed any doubts about this *tabularasa* policy — Helmuth Stieff, for example, killed after the July 1944 plot, who in 1934 spoke of the 'lunacy of one-party rule'.[26]

As long as Hindenburg, the Field-Marshal President and Commander-in-Chief of the armed forces, remained alive, there seemed to be a good hope of the army maintaining a special position in the Führer state. Even after Hindenburg's death, Hitler continued to invoke 'the continued survival and sacrosanct character of the Wehrmacht',[27] but the chances in a future war of the Wehrmacht being able to impose its leadership and policies on the *Volksgemeinschaft* diminished as Hitler's power was consolidated. Beck, Chief of the General Staff, realized intuitively after Hindenburg's death, that to safeguard military interests another military Führer figure, a *Feldherr* (general), would need to

be built up as a counterweight to Hitler. Beck's choice was
Ludendorff, who he thought should be made a Field Marshal.
Blomberg and Fritsch proposed this idea, Hitler agreed, but Beck
failed to get Ludendorff's agreement.[28] Ludendorff, the
personification of the idea of the *Feldherr's* leadership of the
nation in time of war, was at the same time a fanatical proponent
of the concept of the *Volksgemeinschaft,* of the eradication of
minorities and of the racial-*völkisch* organization of the armed
forces. His *Der totaler Krieg*[29] published in 1935, was a single
extended argument for these objectives. It was permeated by the
same hostile stereotypes that obsessed Hitler: Jews, Freemasons
and communists. 'Socialist-communist collectivizing doctrines'
were the antithesis of *Weltanschauung*, it stated. But it also set out
very clearly the position the military leader was to occupy in the
Volksgemeinschaft: 'The people only begins to deserve its *Feldherr*
at the point when it places itself in his service, i.e. in the service of
the leader of the total war waged for its survival. When this occurs,
the *Feldherr* and the people form one unit, if not — the *Feldherr* is
wasted on the people.'[30]

At this period, 1935, the military still assumed that it would be
they who would provide the *Feldherr* in a future war. This
assumption lay behind their attempt to build up Ludendorff. It was
in this same year that Beck demanded that the Commander-in-
Chief of the army's influence on the conduct of the war should be
complemented by influence on the 'political bases' of that war.[31]
Hence there were reasons why the military allowed itself to believe
that the construction of the *Volksgemeinschaft-Wehrgemeinschaft*
would ultimately, at the critical moment, serve their own interests.
In addition, they thought that the 'lessons' of the first world war
could be corrected on the domestic front, with the cooperation of
the party.

It is true that in 1942, Beck did make some strong criticisms of
Ludendorff's doctrine of 'total war'. The main point on which he
took this monomaniac of total war to task was the latter's
assumption that all future wars would be 'total' wars — by this
time, however, it was quite clear that the *Feldherr* was in fact Hitler
and it was Hitler, not any of the generals, who controlled the
Volksgemeinschaft.[32] The realization that preparations for such a
war would become 'an insatiable moloch' had come too late: in its
rearmament efforts before the war, the Wehrmacht had had barely
any reservations on this score.

The Wehrmacht's educational and propagandistic work also aimed to inculcate a total view of politics, the waging of war and the organization of society. In an unmistakable gesture to Hitler and the Nazi party, the idea of the *Volksgemeinschaft* was traced back to the experience of the front in the first world war. A direct link was drawn from this to the cult of the 'national' military organizations of the Weimar Republic; and ready use was made of the literary effusions of the Jünger brothers and others. Military educational theorists such as Friedrich Altrichter, the author of a number of military writings, some of them running to several reprints,[33] were recruited for the cause. One of Altrichter's main arguments was that a soldier's education had to be 'related to the racial foundations on which the community of the *Volk* is constructed'.[34] The Reichswehr ministry appointed another apologist of military communal education, retired General von Cochenhausen, head of the *Deutsche Gesellschaft für Wehrpolitik und Wehrwissenschaften*, founded in June 1933. Von Cochenhausen was asked to draw up a programme for the military education (*Wehrerziehung*) of the nation. No doubt recalling military propaganda work among the young during the first world war, the General dreamed of even introducing military education into the schools: 'Today, in the written word, in film, in military sport and in the work-camps, we can see how the struggle is being waged against the unheroic materialist conception of life'.[35]

In many respects, these ideas were an exaggerated version of something that had already been formulated or demanded during and after the first world war as an essential element of German political self-understanding. It might appear that this conscious organization of the strength and psychology of the nation was carried out 'for' the military and 'in its interests'. To this form of militarization of economic, social and intellectual life, recognized before him by Werner Sombart, Walther Rathenau, Friedrich Naumann and Nachum Goldmann, and also by socialist critics, Michael Geyer has given the name 'functional' militarism.[36]

After 1933, however, this militarization of the whole of society was itself functionalized and gradually eased out of its position of power into an increasingly subservient role. National Socialism, itself the heir of a military conception of politics, and the gathering-point of those social sub-strata that embraced it, first outdid the military in military energy and then dragged the military leaders along with it. For Hitler, the army was only one of a number of factors he had to take into account in achieving, for his own political ends, the rearmament of the German people. In his foreign policy, which the military still saw in the terms of the Wilhelminian Empire, and in his plans for the education and breeding of the *Volk* for future wars, Hitler left the military leaders far behind. Hitler introduced conscription, on his own admission, not just as a part of rearmament but as a way of making unstoppable the integration of the Reichswehr into National Socialism.[37] The fact that his take-over had been legitimate, Hitler recollected in 1942, had allowed him to restrict the Reichswehr to purely military concerns until, by the introduction of military service, the *Volk* as a whole and, with the *Volk,* the National Socialist spirit, had swamped the Reichswehr and so, with ever-growing force, had 'overwhelmed' all elements opposed to the National Socialist movement — the officer corps in particular.

The above analysis indicates where the core of the opposition referred to by Hitler lay, namely in the military's ambition to play a greater role in military and foreign policy — indeed, in time of war, to have the last word on these matters. The army cannot, because of its special interests, be considered as part of the 'opposition' to National Socialism. It was very much in favour of the 'Führer state' but preferably one with a 'Führer' who left it all it had traditionally possessed in the Prusso-German military state. However, the very components of National Socialism which the Wehrmacht made most play of in its educational work and internal propaganda — the Führer principle and the *Volksgemeinschaft* — proved to be the tools by which the military's special position was whittled down. It is therefore certainly correct to say of the Wehrmacht that the larger it became and the more it reflected the *Volksgemeinschaft,* the more homogeneously it fitted into Hitler's system of rule. This became very clear after the decisions of spring 1938. With the structural changes at that time, Hitler absorbed the armed forces into the increased pace of rearmament.

But the Reichswehr and Wehrmacht's ideological and material rearmament policy, based on a far-reaching identity of political outlook, was in fact founded on self-deception and an under-estimation of Hitler. Everything seemed to be going according to plan: the military was only elaborating, as far as the construction of the *Wehrgemeinschaft* was concerned, something it had always aimed to achieve. That in the early years this happened under the illusion, on the military's part, that it was acting as an institution 'above the parties' only emphasizes its fundamental error.

The twelve years of the Hitler-National Socialism-Wehrmacht relationship present actualizations of a number of core politico-philosophical doctrines, but the concepts of the *Volksgemeinschaft,* the 'Führer' principle and race dominate throughout. The same is true of the complementary negative concepts of Jewry, democracy, liberalism, Marxism, socialism and bolshevism. This identity of negative stereotypes derived from the common historical origins of the main political ideas of both the military and National Socialism, which were: antisemitism; a distorted picture of the causes of German defeat in 1918; an inability to accept the compromises of parliamentary democracy; and a tendency to blame others. It must be added, of course, that these ideas were also widespread amongst the political parties of the right, in some bourgeois circles, in the business world and among academics. The defeat of 1918, which the military revealed to the nation far too late, caused immense disillusionment. It was experienced by many contemporaries as a 'moral collapse'. Only 'faith in the *Volk*', Werner Picht wrote, offered the hope of a new future beyond the 'despicable present'.[38] Other educationalists sought to construct a 'spiritual *Volksgemeinschaft*'. Hitler, too, saw the 'educational work' to be done as a 'greater deed' than 'the most glorious wars of our present bourgeois age'.[39] The concept of the *Volksgemeinschaft* reflected the political and military disillusionments of the years 1918 to 1933, as well as the immaturity of German democracy and a decision to create a new form of political life different to that of the West. From 1933, the military allied itself to these ideas.

For the President of the *Deutsche Gesellschaft für Wehrpolitik und Wehrwissenschaften,* the Weimar political system epitomized 'complete spiritual confusion'.[40] The task of 'military education' (*Wehrerziehung*) was, in his eyes and therefore, indirectly, those of the Wehrmacht leadership, the 'harnessing of all the forces of the *Volk* for battle'. In the *Volks-* and *Wehrgemeinschaft* there was no room for 'the precious individual self'. Hermann Foertsch, who, as head of the home department of the Wehrmacht ministry played a central role in the Wehrmacht leadership's political educational activities, wrote in his *The Officer of the German Wehrmacht. An Outline of his Duties* (reprinted four times before 1940): anyone who as the teacher of his unit is unwilling to support the state and his Führer, 'should keep out'. To argue about the meaning of

National Socialism was a waste of time. The officer would know instinctively what it meant. In the idea and practice of the *Volksgemeinschaft*, the tension between the individual and society was resolved, the individual being merged into a supra-individual body which was to be felt as the German *Volk*'s natural method of organization. This essential German model of society was particularly adaptable to military principles of subordination. A community, a Gemeinschaft, meant not 'society' with its dangerous pluralism, but the 'unity' of the Leader and the led. This concept made possible a dismantling of the social barriers between officers and soldiers and the propagation and often the practice of a 'comradeship' felt as very modern. This 'comradeship' seemed to be an example of the *Volksgemeinschaft* in action.

Blomberg touched on these connections in a directive of April 1935. What youth expected in the army, the Reichswehr minister and commander-in-chief of the Wehrmacht wrote, was 'the last stage of education in the service of the *Volksgemeinschaft*'. Youth expected 'strictness but humanity, drill but also education, orders and commands to be obeyed unquestioningly but also openness, counsel and living comradeship', not 'standoffishness or officiousness based on outmoded ideas'.[41] In these and similar ways, the Wehrmacht made intense efforts to try to present the National Socialist *Volksgemeinschaft* as something modern and of the future, not least because such ideas could, they thought, have a positive effect on military morale — and so it proved. The impetus behind this educational programme of the Wehrmacht was very much, as it had been with rearmament, both forward-looking and supportive of the system. One only has to look at Blomberg's directive on the newly introduced 'current affairs curriculum' of 4 April 1934 — that is during the period of bitter conflict with the SA leadership — where he wrote that in this second year of the National Socialist administration priority must be given to the permeation of the nation's spiritual life with the central ideas of the National Socialist state. To achieve this, particular educational measures were required. This applied 'especially to the Wehrmacht, which is the protector and guardian of National Socialist Germany and its living-space'.[42] As early as 1933, General von Fritsch, still commander of the Third Division, had said that traditional forms would have to be overturned to make way for something new, for 'the unitary state of the German *Volk*'.[43] 'National Socialist thought' was already the 'sole vehicle of German intellectual life' and the Wehrmacht had to become 'one of the chief exponents and promoters of the national movement'.

In their assessment of the National Socialist *Volksgemeinschaft,* Hitler and the military were in essential agreement on one main point which was that it was grounded in the experiences at the front during the first world war. National Socialism, Blomberg stated on 24 May 1934, rested on the 'idea of a community of blood and destiny of all German people'. The 'thinking of both our troops and National Socialism springs from the same source, our experience of the Great War'.[44]

The grim practical consequences of this 'communal ethos' at home and abroad and for internal and external enemies were revealed with the war. Even before the war, however, those excluded from the community felt the brutal vehemence of the ideas embodied in it. As early as 18 August 1933, there appeared in the *Militär Wochenblatt* — that is, with the approval of the Wehrmacht leadership — an article entitled 'The soldier and the national revolution', which because of its appropriateness at the time was reprinted by the organ of the Naval Officers' Association.[45] The author spoke of the world of thought of the national revolution, 'which was not created, but awoken, by its leader Adolf Hitler'. The article went on to discuss the indissoluble links between the *Volk*, the race and the state, and of 'the necessity of human breeding and, therefore, the need to combat anything foreign or harmful to the race'. The 'total state', the officer readership of the article was informed, offered the hope of an organization binding together all those of similar race and similar *Weltanschauung.*

Although the 'Law on the Reconstruction of the Professional Civil Service' of 7 April 1933 was as yet quite inapplicable to the armed forces, the Wehrmacht rushed to adopt its 'underlying principles'. In June 1933, at a conference of commanding officers, Blomberg stated he was intending to alter the marital terms and conditions of acceptance to prevent new Jewish intake.[46] In February 1934, the army's personnel office proposed, with reference to Jewish soldiers in the Wehrmacht, a 'dismissal on grounds of disability' because the civil service law left no other alternative.[47] The essence of this proposal was incorporated in a directive of the Reichswehr minister of 28 February 1934. The statistics of the numbers involved were already with the home department of the ministry by June of that year. Because of the draft clause in the 7 April 1933 law relating to ex-combatants, the number of those dismissed remained, at seventy, relatively low. But the military leaders' compliance was already obvious.

Racial attitudes emerged not only in educational activity but also in such things as oath-taking ceremonies for junior officers. Occasionally the racial content was linked to a 'racially specific experience of God' (*arteigenes Gotterleben*) along the lines of Ludendorff. One such occasion was an address at an oath-taking ceremony in Eckernförde and Stralsund in 1936/7 by Vice-Admiral Schuster, second admiral of the Baltic: [48] 'We soldiers of the Reich make our oaths to God in the conviction that every racially and spiritually healthy people has its own specific experience of God, that through the spiritual struggles of our time we shall fight our way through and must fight our way through, to such a unified experience of God, because such spiritual cohesion of the *Volk* also provides the basis of the Wehrmacht's ability to act.' Protestantism's susceptibility to a national 'German' Christianity also subsequently coloured the idea of the *Volksgemeinschaft*. [49] A highly regarded educational work for navy officers by Siegfried Sorge, which earned special praise from Admiral Raeder, had this to say on the subject: 'It goes without saying that a soldier's religious attitude cannot and must not be at odds with the basic ideas of National Socialism or with the doctrine of the *Volk* and of blood and soil.' [50]

The question has often been asked what effect National Socialist education had on the Wehrmacht. The question cannot be put in isolation. From 1935 onwards, more and more of the soldiers and young officers recruited to the Wehrmacht had already undergone 'education' in other organizations and politically already thought in terms of the *Gemeinschaft*. The effects of Wehrmacht education cannot therefore be assessed in isolation from other factors. At the same time, there are a few cases where one can pinpoint some actual effects of the national-political lessons which were introduced, after Blomberg's important directive of 30 January 1936, in all military and airforce colleges, the naval college, the naval and military academy, the airforce academy and the aeronautical academy. [51] In January 1937, the staff of these establishments gathered for a major conference at the Reich War Ministry, with senior party members present. The various colleges' replies to requests for agenda items provide a graphic insight into the ideological question-marks amongst the officers taking part.

They also show how doubtful they still were about some of the main features of National Socialist education and training. Here is a selection of the subjects suggested for discussion:[52]

- the spiritual foundations of National Socialism with special reference to the racial problem;
- how can the two concepts of class-consciousness (*Standesbewusstsein*) and *Volksgemeinschaft* best be reconciled?
- to what extent has National Socialism always been rooted in the Prussian soldiery in peace and war?
- on the Church: how does the racial idea fit in with the mission and the universal aims of the Christian Church?
- what powers does the Führer have?

Due to the political and military developments of spring 1938 and 1939 this conference was never followed up. However, it is clear, not least from this conference, that for the Wehrmacht the key ideas of military thinking in these fields were now the *Volksgemeinschaft*, including its racial justification, and the authority of the 'Führer' as the charismatic arbiter over the needs and aims of the *Volksgemeinschaft*. Courses at the War Academy included:

- bolshevism, Freemasonry, world Jewry, the political Church, the fight against enemies of the state, the principles of National Socialist racial policy, the Wehrmacht's place in the National Socialist educational system.

The commander of the academy, General Liebmann, wrote to the home department with reference to the ideas of Beck, the chief of the General Staff: 'the lectures will present National Socialist *Weltanschauung* as the main pillar of the German State and its Armed Forces'.[53]

There is one aspect which, because of its direct connection with the first world war and its direct consequences for the soldiers of the *Volksgemeinschaft,* deserves special attention and that is the military judicial system. Here, too, the instruments for a radical change of practice were to hand before the outbreak of the war. As early as 1933, one military lawyer was demanding that military justice should be altered in such a way as to protect the 'community of blood, sacrifice and destiny' and to ensure the 'unity of the state, *Volk* and Wehrmacht'. For him, this meant that the military courts should, if necessary, be made into a 'powerful arm' of the state. 'Pettiness, corrosive doubt and destructive unbelief' of the first world war kind were to be rooted out.[54] Another commentator, who still spoke of the 'military lawyer class (*Stand*)', demanded that military judges 'conduct a purging process' against the accused 'in which the principles of the *Gemeinschaft* are applied'.[55] With these as with many other military figures — army commander-in-chief von Fritsch for example — the ideal of the *'Stand'* merged into that of the community or *Gemeinschaft*.

The resulting ideological mixture attracted a very broad social substratum, officers and lower ranks from various social backgrounds. A prominent commentator on the military penal code called for a new concept of guilt to be applied in judicial proceedings. The law, he wrote, ought to 'review its entire attitude to make sure it conforms to the new ethos of our people'.[56] Military lawyers in the high commands drafted the notorious Special War Penal Code (*Kriegssonderstrafrechtsverordnung*). Paragraph 5 dealt with the 'undermining of military potential' (*Wehrkraftzersetzung*), a charge defined as follows by the Reich military Prosecutor's Office: 'Undermining of military potential is the disruption or impairment of the total *"völkisch"* combat-readiness required to win the final victory in this war.'[57] Under this heading large numbers of soldiers were sentenced to death as 'enemies of the armed forces' — a special category of 'enemies of the people'. Indeed, the military courts, by carrying out well over 10,000 death sentences, excelled themselves in the application of 'communal' principles.[58] At the 'Greater German Lawyers' Conference' in Leipzig shortly before the war, Rudolf Lehmann, the senior Wehrmacht lawyer, told Wehrmacht lawyers and judges that offences against the spirit of the *'Gemeinschaft'* should be more severely punished. It was not the job of the courts to try to discover an abstract 'truth' that did not exist in reality. 'It is the task of the courts, within the framework of the community in which they are placed, to use the means of the law to protect that community.'[59] The courts acted accordingly, with the results referred to above. Thus, at one point, the senior military judge requested statistics of the death sentences that had been passed, in order to show 'that the death sentences passed under the jurisdiction of the Army courts have been a work of purgation, undertaken with the highest sense of responsibility, not only of those that have undermined the military spirit but also of asocial elements in general'.[60]

Thus, in the Wehrmacht as well, the idea of the *Volksgemeinschaft*, in the form of socio-biological defence-mechanisms against outsiders, became the evil force behind politico-juridical sanctions.

The war against the Soviet Union, where the target was the long-standing hostile stereotype of the Jew-bolshevik, revealed the idea of the *Volksgemeinschaft* at its most aggressive. A number of recent works and studies have dealt with this subject in some detail.[61] What is significant in this context is that the idea of the vital needs of the German *Volksgemeinschaft* provided the Wehrmacht with something like a 'clear conscience' in its brutal conduct of the war in the East. It is hard to find any other explanation for such unequivocal orders issued by high-ranking officers as those, to name but two, of Reichenau of 10 October 1941 and Manstein of 20 November 1941. Reichenau's order, which spoke of 'rightful vengeance on the Jewish sub-humans', met, it is known, with Hitler's full approval. It was then forwarded in writing through Brauchitsch and Quarter-Master General Wagner to all army groups, armies and tank groups. Manstein, in his version, appended to this passage an appeal to preserve 'the honour of the soldier'. The two ideas could now, it seems, co-exist, in the name of the German 'struggle for existence'.

In the Wehrmacht's educational work after the first Russian winter and then, in its final manifestation, after the end of 1943, this destructive drive took on a fanatical character. The NSFO (*Nationalsozialistische Führungsoffiziere*) became a symbol of this fanaticism. Addressing an NSFO conference for officers and generals at the Ordensburg Sonthofen shortly before the assassination attempt on Hitler, General Ritter v. Hengl, head of the National Socialist *'Führungsstab'* at the OKH, said that an officer's duty was to train his soldiers in 'hate and the uncontrollable urge to destroy'.[62] The Commander-in-Chief of the Army Reserve, Fromm, Hengl went on, Specht, General of the Training Schools, and Zeitzler, Chief of the General Staff, would support him in his work. Dönitz said it was an officer's task to 'guard the unity of the *Volk*'.[63] Those who were a danger to this unity would have to be broken by him. The naval courts did their best to enforce this idea.

Ultimately, then, it was the idea of the *Volksgemeinschaft* which brought the final harshness and grimness into the struggle. Anyone failing to grasp why he should go on fighting what was a lost war was eliminated as a '*Schädling*'. The *Volksgemeinschaft* and its Führer had to tread the path of catastrophe to the bitter end. The generals knew how pointless it was to continue but only rarely were able to free themselves from their *Führer*, as Kesselring's behaviour over the armistice negotiations in northern Italy at the end of April 1945 shows.[64] An even more instructive case is Field Marshal Model's order of 29 March 1945 to his army group, which by then was already surrounded in the Ruhr basin.[65] The pressures of war revealed, this order stated, 'that wide sections of the German people, and therefore also of the troops, are infested with the Jewish democratic mentality of materialist thought. The victory of the national socialist idea is beyond doubt and the decision rests in our hands.'

Even in the rubble of the Ruhr, Field Marshal Model still clung to this most German of political philosophies, the chief assumption of which was that the 'German spirit' had to be something quite different to that of Western Europe. The significant question to be answered, however, is why this mania remained impervious to the visible signs of catastrophe and the experience of the war against 'bolshevism'. Many soldiers and officers knew what was being done in the East. Only a few individuals honourably admitted as much. One was General Röttiger, the first army inspector of the Bundeswehr and the chief of the general staff of the 4th Army from 1942 to 1943. In an early statement (probably November 1945), later withdrawn, he said he had become aware 'that the ultimate purpose of the fight we were waging against the partisans was that the army could then be used in the ruthless liquidation of the Jews and other undesirable elements'.[66]

A similar expression of shock is to be found in the memoirs of General von Gersdorff when he discusses Himmler's speech at an NSFO conference in Posen in January 1944.

It was there that the Reichsführer SS, in front of 300 officers and generals, had spoken of the 'total solution' of the Jewish question.[67] Two days later, these officers appeared at Hitler's headquarters in the company of the commanders of the Eastern Front. At this meeting Hitler demanded: 'If the worst should come to the worst, then what really ought to happen is that the field marshals and generals should defend the flag to the last'. Manstein took offence at this. 'That is what will happen, my Führer,' he replied.[68] Even in 1955 this field marshal continued to see 'lost victories' in the Wehrmacht's feats of arms. After the war, Hitler's penultimate general chief-of-staff, General Zeitzler, wrote some notes entitled 'Some thoughts about the attitude German generals should adopt to a German rearmament at the West's request'. They included the following:[69]

— we are not permitted indefinitely to relinquish our responsibility to Europe and the Western World for the preservation of Western culture and civilisation;

— we are in the happy position of it being recognised in the West that as the result of our close contact with bolshevism we probably still have, or again have, the best fighting morale of all the European peoples . . .

In academic discussion, National Socialism and its concept of the *Gemeinschaft* are labelled either 'modern' or 'antiprogressive', according to which definition of fascism is being followed.[70] As far as the German military is concerned, both terms apply. They, like Hitler, wanted to create for the *Volksgemeinschaft* the most modern of instruments of war. Their concept of the *Gemeinschaft* was neither romantic or utopian, nor steeped in the Middle Ages or Germanic prehistory. Interested in preserving an effective *Wehrgemeinschaft*, they readily accepted the consequences of National Socialist *'Gleichschaltung'* and were themselves ruthless in their administration of justice and their conduct of war, particularly in the East. With barbaric methods they sought to protect 'the West' from the 'Asiatic hordes' and Jewish world domination. At the same time, however, they were interested in an expansion of power in the old strategic and military sense, in military victory for its own sake and in a share of domestic power. The latter was to be handed them in time of war by the welded mass of the *Volksgemeinschaft* for strategic and other purposes. Their adoption of 'modern' methods of leadership went back to their experiences in the first world war and the revolution of 1918 — this was the extent of their interest in social change. Their ideal of the *Volksgemeinschaft* could, without the complementary enemy stereotypes that formed part of it, be summarized as a dream of unlimited power over a disciplined mass of men all pursuing the same end. *Gemeinschaft* meant, firstly, discipline and secondly, the struggle for 'living space'. Other ingredients of *Weltanschauung* were added to these or taken on board as and when necessary. In the end, fear of the Führer outweighed concern either for the cultural heritage or for the material basis of the much-invoked *Volksgemeinschaft*. General Röttiger put it as follows: 'People spoke of loyalty, honour etc. but what they really meant were personal cowardice and a shirking of responsibility'.[71] The words of General von Brauchitsch, commander-in-chief of the army, in a 1938 directive about officer education were, by and large, fulfilled: 'The officer corps should be second to none in the purity and genuineness of its National Socialist *Weltanschauung*. It is the standard-bearer which remains immovable even when all others fail.'[72]

To judge by one of his diary entries, Dönitz quite clearly placed loyalty to Hitler above 'the preservation of the substance of the German people'.[73] And in September 1944, in an addendum to an order of Hitler's, Field Marshal von Rundstedt, commander-in-chief in the West, informed his soldiers that the severity needed in 'the struggle for the survival or disappearance of the German people' should not be restricted by cultural values: 'it must be fought through'.[74] After the first major military defeats, the political and military leadership showed themselves very sensitive to any suspected loosening of the identity of the *Wehr-* and *Volksgemeinschaft* or any doubts about the unity of the party, the people and the Wehrmacht. Calls for resistance to such signs of weakness — some of the most forceful of which emanated from General Schmundt, chief of the Army Personnel Office — tended to be very much in the spirit of Goebbels and in particular of his 'articles of war for the German people'.[75] Article I of these stated: 'Anything may be possible in this war except one thing, that we shall ever capitulate . . . anyone who talks of this or even thinks it commits a base treason against his people's right to exist — and must be ejected in shame and dishonour from the community of German fighters and workers'.

In his order of 5 January 1944,[76] General Schmundt informed the army's officers: 'Any officer who does not recognise the crucial values of our *völkisch* and political life and does not wholeheartedly approved them has outlived his suitability as an officer'. A year later, Schmundt's successor, Burgdorf, went one step further when he made the paradoxical statement that an officer who 'allowed himself to be seized by doubt in quiet moments' was the equivalent of a traitor and would be held responsible for the 'disadvantageous result of a military engagement'.[77]

Appeals of this sort were an indication of how many spokes were getting in the wheels of the *Volksgemeinschaft*. There is no mention in such statements of other, far less tangible manifestations of weariness and creeping opposition. These can be traced only in some of the sentences of the military courts or in censored letters from the front such as that written by Private H.R. on 9 August 1944: 'We would like to shout out loud: Stop your swindling, you murderers. You have robbed us of the good times. Why doesn't he go, only he has no home to go to, no one would take him in or his so-called saviours of the people . . .'[78]

This silent opposition of an unknown number of soldiers throws doubt on the image of the *Volksgemeinschaft* as a thoroughly stable socio-political entity, as does research into the civilian mood of this period.[79] The overall picture, however, is one of the Wehrmacht continuing to function almost perfectly right to the end. Although in the Allied-occupied parts of the country, the population did not join the Wehrmacht in 'fanatical resistance' to the enemy, in 1946 the British occupation authorities still found that about 10 per cent of the population were outspoken Nazis and about 60 per cent were 'drifters': people who would have been ready to follow a 'strong leadership'.[80] The situation was similar towards the end of the war in the Western prisoner-of-war camps. Here hopes fed on the imminent introduction of miracle weapons and on the belief in a final great offensive. In Soviet POW camps, both because of the stereotypes so widespread among German officers and soldiers and because of the Soviet Union's own behaviour, considerable differences of opinion and different groupings arose among the German soldiers. It was the officers who were more prone to ideological arguments. While the ordinary soldiers, who for practical reasons or just out of resignation simply wanted to 'last out', were less worried about the connection between National Socialism and patriotism, there were sharp clashes between officers. In general, however, the opponents of the National 'Freies Deutschland' Committee fell into two camps: the one representing a mixture of fanatical National Socialism, exaggerated patriotism and loyalty to the 'Führer': and, in the other, a large number of conservatives. Many equated 'loyalty to the oath' with 'loyalty to the Führer', while others regarded the oath of loyalty (*Fahneneid*) as taboo, as a kind of unpolitical pledge for its own sake. A large section was suspicious of Soviet promises and considered the supporters of the National Committee and its slogan 'For Germany, Against Hitler' as fantasists.[81] Even at Nuremberg, Jodl and Rundstedt still saw the 20th of July plot on Hitler's life as an act of treachery, while in 1950 tank General Guderian, like others, including General Blumentritt, argued that in future only men 'willing to take the oath of loyalty should enter into consideration'.[82]

Such attitudes offer proof of what was suggested at the beginning: that despite the tensions arising out of 'organizational' special interests, the military and National Socialism forged an active solidarity with each other. One of the most important joint fields of operation was their practical and theoretical work in the service of the *Volksgemeinschaft*. Here enemy stereotypes, ambition, ideas of the political 'order' and military practice came together. In combination these 'values', based on historical precedents and deliberately reinforced in the 'Führer state' through political education, condemned active resistance to a marginal role — not only in the Wehrmacht but also in society at large.

Notes

1. L. Kettenacker, 'Sozialpsychologische Aspekte der Führerherrschaft', in *Der "Führerstaat": Mythos und Realität. Studien zur Struktur und Politik des Dritten Reiches,* G. Hirschfeld and L. Kettenacker (eds.) (Stuttgart 1981), 98-132.

2. Cf. R. Lepsius, *Extremer Nationalismus. Strukturbedingungen vor der nationalsozialistischen Machtergreifung* (Stuttgart 1966).

3. M. Broszat 'Soziale Motivation und Führerbindung des Nationalsozialismus', in *Nationalsozialistische Außenpolitik,* W. Michalka (ed.) (Darmstadt 1978), 99 (= Wege der Forschung, Bd. CCXCVII).

4. Note to the Bavarian War Ministry 31.7.1914, in W. Deist, *Militär und Innenpolitik im Weltkrieg 1914-1918,* Part I (Düsseldorf 1970) No. 78, 93.

5. K. Saul, *Der 'Deutsche Kriegerbund'. Zur innenpolitischen Funktion eines 'nationalen' Verbandes im kaiserlichen Deutschland,* in MGM 1970/1, 95-159 (95).

6. A. Westphal, *Das deutsche Kriegervereinswesen, seine Ziele und seine Bedeutung für den Staat* (Berlin 1903), and *Kriegervereine gegen Sozialdemokratie* (Berlin 1899).

7. M. Messerschmidt, 'Preußens Militär in seinem gesellschaftlichen Umfeld, in *Preußen im Rückblick* (Göttingen 1980), 43-88 (71) (= Geschichte und Gesellschaft, Sonderheft 6).

8. Cf. B. Thoss's treatment of this question, 'Menschenführung im Ersten Weltkrieg und im Reichsheer', in *Menschenführung im Heer* (Herford 1982), 113-138 (= Vorträge zur Militärgeschichte, Bd.3).

9. E. Ludendorff, *Die politischen Hintergründe des 9. November 1923. Die Rede General Ludendorffs vor dem Volksgericht in München 1924* (München n.d.), 2, and *Die überstaatlichen Mächte im letzten Jahre des Weltkrieges* (Leipzig 1927).

10. N. Reynolds, 'Der Fritsch-Brief vom 11. Dez. 1938', in *VZG* 1980, 358 ff (370).

11. W. Wette gives an outline of the political yardsticks of the right-wing groups in 'Ideologie, Propaganda und Innenpolitik als Voraussetzungen der Kriegspolitik des Dritten Reiches', in *Ursachen und Voraussetzungen der deutschen Kriegspolitik, Das Deutsche Reich und der Zweite Weltkrieg,* vol. 1 (Stuttgart 1979), 26-173.

12. Wette, 94 ff.

13. M. Geyer, 'Der zur Organisation erhobene Burgfrieden', in *Militär und Militarismus in der Weimarer Republik,* K.-J. Müller and E. Opitz (eds.) (Düsseldorf 1978), 15-100 (35).

14. Schultheß, *Europäischer Geschichtskalender,* U. Thürauf (ed.) vol. 74 (1933) (München 1934), 1.

15. Letter of 17.3.1933, BA-MA N 34/21; K.-J. Müller, General Ludwig Beck, Boppard 1980, No. 8, 339.

16. Th. Vogelsang, 'Neue Dokumente zur Geschichte der Reichswehr', in *VZG,* 1954, Doc. No. 8, 434 f.

17. For Krieck, see G. Müller, *Ernst Krieck und die nationalsozialistische Wissenschaftsreform* (Frankfurt a.M. 1978).

18. Krieck, *Nationalpolitische Erziehung (Leipzig 1932), 13.*

19. Cf. in more detail, M. Messerschmidt, *Die Wehrmacht im NS-Staat* (Hamburg 1969), 21 ff.

20. M. Domarus, *Hitler. Reden und Proklamationen 1932-1945,* 4 vols, (München 1965), vol. I, 2, 534. Speech of 15 September 1935 to the SA and SS and other formations.

21. H. Foertsch of the Wehrmacht office on 17 April 1934 at a discussion with officers: then the struggle is decided 'in our favour', BA-MA, W 01-5/156.

22. M. Messerschmidt, 'Bildung und Erziehung im "zivilen" und militärischen System des NS-Staates', in *Militärgeschichte,* ed. by the Militärgeschichtliches Forschungsamt (Stuttgart 1982), 212.

23. Thus General Adam, Head of the *Truppenamt* in a questionnaire to the *Wehrkreiskommandos* of 16 February 1931, BA-MA II H 227.

24. Cf. A. Schildt, *Militärdiktatur mit Massenbasis? Die Querfrontkonzeption der Reichswehrführung um General von Schleicher am Ende der Weimarer Republik* (Frankfurt a.M. 1981).

25. Report by Oberstleutnant Ott to the group and regional commanders on 15 December 1932, in *Vogelsang, Neue Dokumente,* 430.

26. Institut für Zeitgeschichte, F. 32/1-2.

27. Letter to Blomberg of 20 August 1934, Schultheß, 1934.

28. See Müller, Beck, Doc. 21-23, 412-414.

29. General Ludendorff, *Der totale Krieg* (München 1935).

30. Ibid., 120.

31. *Denkschrift über die Stellung und Befugnisse der Heeresführung im Kriege*, n.d., a transcript is dated 9.12.1935, BA-MA, N 28/2, Müller, Beck, Doc. No. 36, 466-469.

32. A manuscript of Beck's, 'Die Lehre vom totalen Krieg. Eine kritische Auseinandersetzung', BA-MA, N 28/5 (Nachlaß Beck); a lecture given to the 'Mittwochsgesellschaft' on 17 June 1942, summarized in Klaus Scholder (ed.), *Die Mittwochsgesellschaft. Protokolle aus dem geistigen Deutschland 1932 bis 1934* (Berlin 1982), 292 f.

33. E.g. *Der Reserveoffizier. Ein Handbuch für den Offizier und Offizieranwärter des Beurlaubtenstandes aller Waffen* (Berlin), which by 1941 was already in its fourteenth edition.

34. F. Altrichter, *Das Wesen der soldatischen Erziehung* (Oldenburg 1942), 17.

35. F.v. Cochenhausen, 'Wehrerziehung und Wehrwissenschaften', in *Die Wehrwissenschaften der Gegenwart*, F.v. Cochenhausen (ed.), (Berlin 1934), 9-16 (10).

36. M. Geyer, 'Stichwort "Militarismus" ', in *Geschichtliche Grundbegriffe. Historisches Lexikon zur politisch-sozialen Sprache in Deutschland*, O. Brunner, W. Conze and R. Koselleck (eds.), vol. 4 (Stuttgart 1978), 1-46 (42).

37. H. Picker, *Hitlers Tischgespräche im Führerhauptquartier 1941-1942* (Stuttgart 1965), 366 (21.5.1942).

38. W. Picht, *Die deutsche Volkshochschule der Zukunft. Eine Denkschrift* (Leipzig 1919), 7 ff.

39. A. Hitler, *Mein Kampf*, jubilee edition (München 1939), 420.

40. F.v. Cochenhausen, 'Wehrwissenschaften-Wehrpolitik-Wehrerziehung', in *Erziehung zum Wehrwillen. Pädagogisch-methodisches Handbuch für Erzieher* Sliska (ed.), (Stuttgart 1937), 17.

41. Reichswehr Ministry directive of 16.4.1935, in Messerschmidt and U.v. Gersdorff, *Offiziere im Bild von Dokumenten aus drei Jahrhunderten* (Stuttgart 1964), Doc. No. 101, pp. 260-262. General v.Fritsch, Chief of the Heeresleitung, expressed these thoughts less explicitly in a directive of 21 December 1934. He did, however, speak of the officer preserving 'the honour of his caste', ibid., Doc. No. 100, 259 f.

42. Ibid., Doc. No. 96, 254.

43. Cf. Messerschmidt, *Wehrmacht im NS-Staat*, 15 f.

44. BA-MA, II L 51/7. See also *Offiziere in Dokumenten*, Doc. No. 97, 255.

45. *MOV*, 1933, No. 17, 234 f.

46. Cf. Messerschmidt, *Wehrmacht im NS-Staat*, 43.

47. Draft of the Personnel Office received by the Home Department of the Wehrmacht Office on 13 February 1934, BA-MA, W 01-5/173.

48. BA-MA, III M 503/3, Reden und Ansprachen Konteradmiral Schuster, Bl.29-37.

49. Cf. M. Messerschmidt, 'Aspekte der Militärseelsorgepolitik in national-sozialistischer Zeit', in *MGM* 1/1968, 63-105.

50. Siegfried Sorge, *Der Marineoffizier als Führer und Erzieher* (Berlin 1937). For the book's effect within the navy, see E. Raeder, *Mein Leben. Bis zum*

Flottenabkommen mit England 1935 (Tübingen 1956), 241 f.

51. Directive concerning 'politische Erziehung und Unterricht' of 30 January 1936, BA-MA, II W 22.

52. Proceedings in BA-MA, H 35/30, Akte Reichswehrministerium — Abteilung Inland — Nationalpolitischer Lehrgang vom 15 Januar 1937 bis 23 Januar 1937. The speeches by the Party leaders were printed for the *Dienstgebrauch* as *Nationalpolitischer Lehrgang der Wehrmacht vom 15. bis 23. Januar 1937* (Berlin 1937).

53. Letter of Liebmann of 24 May 1938. Thereupon, the Home Department sent on the subjects referred to. Proceedings in BA-MA, H 35/31.

54. H. Dietz, 'Das Strafrecht der Wehrmacht im neuen Reich. Zur Neuordnung der Militärgerichtsbarkeit' in *Deutsches Recht* (*DR*), 1933, 163-172.

55. W. Hülle, 'Die Stellung des Militärrichters und seine Aufgaben im künftigen Verfahrensrecht', in *Zeitschrift für Wehrrecht* (*ZWR*) 1937/38, vol. 2, 3-17.

56. E. Schwinge, 'Der Schuldbegriff des Militärstrafrechts', in *ZWR* 1937/38, 443-448.

57. Quoted by Schwinge in his commentary on the *Militärstrafgesetzbuch* (Berlin 1944), 427.

58. Cf. in greater detail, M. Messerschmidt, 'Deutsche Militärgerichtsbarkeit im Zweiten Weltkrieg', in *Die Freiheit des Anderen*. Festschrift for Martin Hirsch (Baden-Baden 1981), 111-142.

59. R. Lehmann, 'Die Aufgaben des Rechtswahrers in der Wehrmacht', in *DR* 1939, 1265-1269.

60. Communication of the Oberkriegsgerichtsrat of Dienstaufsichtsbezirk 2 in Kassel of 28 September 1943, BA-Zentralnachweisstelle Kornelimünster, Sammlung Todesurteile in der Wehrmacht.

61. E.g. A. Hillgruber, 'Die "Endlösung" und das deutsche Ostimperium als Kernstück des rassenideologischen Programms des Nationalsozialismus', in Manfred Funke (ed.), *Hitler, Deutschland und die Mächte* (Düsseldorf 1976), 94-114; Chr. Streit, *Keine Kameraden* (Stuttgart 1978); H. Krausnick u. H.-H. Wilhelm, *Die Truppe des Weltanschauungskrieges* (Stuttgart 1981); J. Förster, 'Zur Rolle der Wehrmacht im Krieg gegen die Sowjetunion', in *Aus Politik und Zeitgeschichte. Beilage zur Wochenzeitung 'Das Parlament'*, B 45/80 v. 8 November 1980, 3-15.

62. BA-MA, H 42/1.

63. Draft of a speech of 15 February 1944, *IMT*, vol. XXXV, 640-D, 242 f.

64. Cf. note of General Röttiger, Chief of the Staff of Army Group C in Italy, of 28 September 1945, BA-MA, N 422/1.

65. BA-MA, III H 219, Akte Kommandeur 11. I.D./Höhere Artillerie Kommandeur 320, Bl. 105 f.

66. BA-MA, N 422/11, sheet 4.

67. R. Chr. Frhr. v. Gersdorff, *Soldat im Untergang* (Frankfurt 1979), 145 f. For Himmler's speech notes, IfZ, Mikrofilm MA 316.

68. E.v. Manstein, *Verlorene Siege* (Bonn 1955), 580.

69. BA-MA, N 63/118, Bl. 62.

70. See, for example, H. A. Turner jr., 'Faschismus und Anti-Modernismus' in *Nationalsozialistische Außenpolitik,* 148-174.

71. BA-MA, N 422/1, 10.

72. Directive of 18.12.1938. An extract appears in *Offiziere im Bild von*

Dokumenten, Doc. No. 109, 276.

73. Quoted by K. D. Erdmann from BA, R 62/11, Geschäftsführende Reichsregierung Dönitz, cf. Hansen, *Das Ende des Dritten Reiches. Die deutsche Kapitulation 1945* (Stuttgart 1966), 365.

74. D. Zboralski, 'Rundschreiben 255/44 der Parteikanzlei der NSDAP', in *ZMG,* 1965, 703 ff. This circular quotes a telex from Rundstedt to Bormann.

75. Published by the Zentralverlag der NSDAP, Franz Eher, München 1943.

76. BA-MA, H 37/222.

77. Directive of 2 January 1945, See Messerschmidt, *Wehrmacht im NS-Staat,* 439.

78. O. Buchbender and R. Sterz, *Das andere Gesicht des Krieges. Deutsche Feldpostbriefe 1939-1945* (München 1982), 147.

79. Cf. I. Kershaw, *Der Hitler Mythos. Volksmeinung und Propaganda im Dritten Reich* (Stuttgart 1980); M. Broszat, E. Fröhlich and F. Wiesemann (eds.), *Bayern in der NS-Zeit. Soziale Lage und politisches Verhalten der Bevölkerung im Spiegel vertraulicher Berichte* (München 1977), and M. Broszat and E. Fröhlich (eds.), *Bayern in der NS-Zeit II. Herrschaft und Gesellschaft im Konflikt,* (München 1979).

80. B. Marshall, 'German Attitudes to British Military Government 1945-1947', in *Journal of Contemporary History,* 15, 4 (October 1980), 655-681.

81. Cf. in much greater detail, K.-H. Frieser, *Die deutschen Kriegsgefangenen in der Sowjetunion und das Nationalkomitee 'Freies Deutschland'*, Phil. Diss. (Würzburg 1981), 178 ff.

82. On Jodl, Rundstedt, Guderian and the controversies of the 'forties and early 'fifties cf. G. Meyer, 'Zur Situation der deutschen militärischen Führungsschicht im Vorfeld des westdeutschen Verteidigungsbeitrages', in *Anfänge westdeutscher Sicherheitspolitik 1945-1956,* vol. 1: *Von der Kapitulation bis zum Pleven-Plan* (München 1982), 577-735 (662-669). The thoughts of a large number of generals after the war are to be found in G. Breit, *Das Staats- und Gesellschaftsbild deutscher Generale beider Weltkriege im Spiegel ihrer Memoiren* (Boppard 1973).

Manfred Messerschmidt
is Chief Historian at the
Militärgeschichtliches Forschungsamt,
Freiburg, and Secretary-General of the
German Commission for the History of the
Second World War. His publications
include *Die Wehrmacht im NS-Staat. Zeit
der Indoktrination* (Hamburg 1969), and
*Militär und Politik in der Bismarckzeit und
im Wilhelminischen Deutschland*
(Darmstadt 1975). He is currently working
on a contribution to the Handbook on the
History of Prussia, and on a book on the
German army since the eighteenth century.

Index Volume 18 Numbers 1-4 1983